THE COMPLETE
HORSE

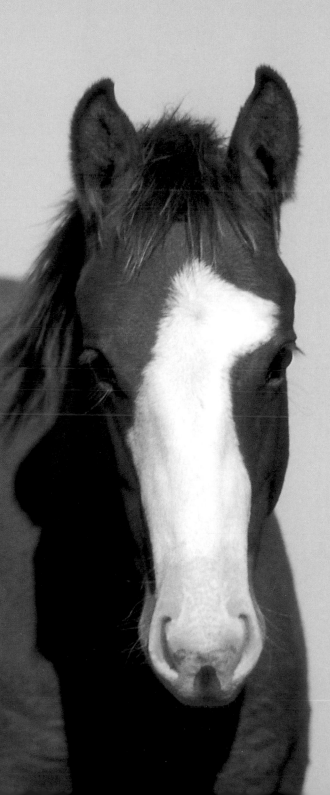

❧

**FOR MY MOTHER
AND TO THE MEMORY
OF MY FATHER —
A GENTLE MAN.**

❧

THIS IS A CARLTON BOOK

Text and design copyright © 1999
Carlton Books Limited

This edition published by
Carlton Books Limited 1999
20 St Anne's Court
Wardour Street
London
W1V 3AW

A CIP catalogue for this book is available
from the British Library

ISBN 1 85868 675 X

EXECUTIVE EDITOR: Sarah Larter
MANAGING ART EDITOR: Zoe Mercer
PICTURE RESEARCH: Catherine Costelloe
PRODUCTION: Sarah Schuman

Printed and bound in Dubai

JUDITH DRAPER

THE COMPLETE
HORSE

A COMPLETE GUIDE TO
RIDING, HORSE CARE AND
EQUESTRIAN SPORTS

CONTENTS

INTRODUCTION

What does Queen Elizabeth II have in common with world renowned tenors Luciano Pavarotti and Fracisco Araiza? Or the ruler of Dubai with a member of the Caribinieri? Or a newspaper tycoon with a farmer's daughter? Or the president of a motor manufacturing giant with a scrap metal merchant? Horses. The love of horses transcends all boundaries of class, age and wealth. It is a universal love that unites people of all races and creeds. We live in a time which has seen man conquer the seas and skies, land on the moon, flood the world with microchip technology, and delve into the mysteries of genetics, yet millions of people from every walk of life and all corners of the earth still find man's oldest means of transport infinitely fascinating and rewarding.

Paradoxically, it is the onward march of science and technology what has enabled so many people to turn what may have been a vague dream of owning a horse into a reality. Compared with other companion animals such as cats and dogs, the horse

is far more demanding of time and energy, and without the benefits that this technological age has brought, only the privileged few would have the leisure to indulge their passion.

So where does this passion for horses come from? Perhaps the love of horses is in our genes. Winston Churchill believed so. There is something in the body of the horse, he said, that is good for the spirit of the man. And why not? After all, for several thousand years, the horse was as indispensable to mankind as food and shelter. Hardly surprising then that it should take more than a few decades of mechanization to expunge horses from our psyche.

Whatever the explanation, the second half if the 20th century has seen an explosion in riding as a leisure activity and in equestrian sports as diverse as dressage, three-day eventing, show jumping and endurance riding. A whole new generation, prompted by a strange, deep-seated longing, has taken its first tentative steps on horseback and become hooked for life on all things equestrian.

Until a few decades ago, horse lore was handed down through the generations. Learning to ride was as natural as learning to walk. But then the chain was broken and nowadays the first connection most people have with horses or ponies is via their

local riding school. While the desire to be with horses is still there, all too often what was once an instinctive understanding of the equine species has to be learned from scratch.

Riding and owning a horse is a joy and a privilege – and a great responsibility. We owe it to the animals in our care not only to provide them with food and water, shelter and vetinary attention, but also to try and understand the world from their perspective.

If this book helps to enlighten, encourage and enthuse the rider, and more importantly, benefits the horse, it will have served its purpose.

WHAT IS A HORSE?

1

PART ONE

The scientific answer to that question would be: a solid-hoofed *perisso-dactyl quadruped*. For the human beings who for several thousand years depended upon him, often for their very lives, the answer would sound rather less technical but probably be a good deal more complex – and subjective.

The reason is simple: man owes the horse a debt he can never repay. It was the horse which enabled him to widen his horizons by providing him with the fastest, most efficient and most flexible means of transportation on earth prior to the invention of the internal combustion engine. The horse took him hunting, carried him into battle, enabled him to patrol the frontiers of great sprawling empires, gave him kudos and provided him with sport and recreation. The life of man has been entwined with that of the horse as with no other animal. Little wonder that the horse, largely redundant in the "developed" world as a means of transport, should nevertheless still be held in such esteem by so many people..

Today there are more than 150 distinct breeds and types of horse and pony, three of which are recognised as having had a profound influence upon many of the others: the Arabian, the Barb and the Andalusian. The Arabian is the oldest and purest of all the domesticated horse breeds. Horses of Arab type are depicted in ancient art dating from as far back as 2,000–3,000 BC. Living for centuries with the desert tribes, Arabian horses became superbly adapted to life in a hostile environment. They have the soundest of limbs and feet and tremendous powers of endurance. The Barb is a similarly tough, if rather less refined breed, whose homeland is the coastland region of North Africa – Algeria, Morocco and Tunisia – while from across the sea in Spain comes the elegant Andalusian.

The influence of the Arabian and Barb upon other horses stems from the time of the spread of Islam across North Africa and into Spain from the seventh and early eighth centuries AD. Both breeds, but particularly the Arabian, were used to improve native stock, and the Barb was instrumental in the development of the Andalusian, which when taken to the Americas by the 16th-century Conquistadores provided the foundation stock for a variety of new breeds.

When it comes to new breeds, however, there is nothing to compare with man's crowning achievement: the Thoroughbred. Descended from stallions imported into England chiefly from the Middle East during the late 17th and early 18th centuries, the Thoroughbred was successfully developed into the ultimate racing machine and was exported to all corners of the world. Thanks to his size, speed and stamina, he has been the major factor in the production of the modern sports horse. Today equestrianism is a huge, worldwide and fast-growing leisure industry. Thousands of years after he submitted to domestication, the solid-hoofed *perissodactyl quadruped* known as the horse is still a major factor in the life of mankind.

THE ORIGINS OF THE HORSE

With his willing-to-please nature, his "user-friendly" shape, his strength, his speed and his stamina, the horse might have been specifically designed for the service of mankind.

During a period of some five thousand years the horse has carried man on his back, served as his chief form of tractive power, ploughed the land and provided sport and recreation. No other animal is so perfectly designed to carry a saddle or to wear a draught collar. No other is blessed with the docility, courage, speed and capacity for hard work as the horse. Where did this paragon among animals come from? And what was his life like before humans learnt to tame and train him?

The study of fossil remains has allowed us to gain a fascinating insight into a number of aspects of the long evolutionary process that has given us the modern horse – a process which is believed to have taken at least 60 million years.

In terms of animal classification the horse, **equus caballus**, is a member of the family *equidae*, which is part of the order *perisso-dactyla*. All the animals in this order are descended from the *condylarthra*, a group of primitive mammals which were the ancestors of all present-day hoofed mammals.

The discovery of a small but unmistakably horse-like skeleton in North America during the nineteenth century provided scientists with a very clear idea of what the horse's ancestors of the paleocene epoch (65 to 54 million years ago) and eocene epoch (53 to 38 million years ago) looked like. *Eohippus*, or the dawn horse, as he is known, was about the size of a terrier-type dog.

With his small teeth, and feet equipped with both toes and pads – four toes on the front feet and three on the hind – he was well adapted to life as a brows-ing, forest-dwelling animal. To protect him against predators, it is likely that he had a dappled coat which would have blended well into his surroundings.

During the oligocene epoch (37 to 26 million years ago) *eohippus* was succeeded by two similar horse-like animals known as *mesohippus* and *merychippus*. They were bigger than *eohippus* with straighter backs (his was arched) and longer legs. One of the toes on their forefeet had disappeared, leaving them with just three on each foot. Their teeth, too, were undergoing changes, enabling them to eat a more varied range of plants.

However, it was the miocene epoch (25 to 7 million years ago) that brought the most significant evolutionary changes to the ancestors of *equus caballus*. This was the period when forests began to give way to great tracts of grassland. A grassland environment made the early horse-like animals much more vulnerable to predators than they had been in the shelter of the forests. Of necessity they began to develop longer legs to enable them to move swiftly over open ground. Their necks grew correspondingly longer so that they could graze comfortably at ground level.

The three-toed foot, with its dog-like pad, which had been so useful for crossing soft, wet ground, also began to change. Two toes of each foot gradually lost contact with the ground; the

ABOVE: *A Bronze-Age Danish model of the Dawn Horse.*

BELOW: *The evolution of the horse, from the left:* **eohippus,** **mesohippus, merychippus** *and* **pliohippus.**

Order Perissodactyla
ODD-TOED HOOFED MAMMALS

Sub-order Ceratomorpha
   Family tapiridae: Tapirs
   Family rhinocerotidae: Rhinoceroses

Sub-order Hippomorpha
   Family equidae: Horses, asses, zebras

RIGHT: *Przewalski's Horse, the only truly wild horse still in existence.*

BELOW: *Caspian ponies, the descendents of Horse Type 4.*

remaining single toe eventually became a hoof. The remains of the pad can be seen at the back of the modern horse's fetlock: it is the horny growth called the ergot.

As the animals adapted to their new environment, their teeth continued to change. In the forests they would have browsed on the leaves of low-growing shrubs; now they needed powerful incisors capable of tearing grass and a set of cheek teeth (molars) strong enough to grind it. As the teeth improved, so the skull and jaw had to become deeper in order to house them, and so the overall appearance of the animal changed. It was at this point in the horse family's history that things appear to have become more complex and are thus more difficult to trace. A number of sub-families are believed to have developed, though in time they mostly became extinct.

Just one, *pliohippus*, survived to provide the link to the modern horse, *equus caballus*. *Pliohippus*, which evolved about ten to five million years ago, was a true plains-living animal, well adapted to its changed environment. With a single hoof on each of its long legs and a large heart and lungs, it had the speed to outrun predators. This is the direct ancestor of our modern *equus caballus*, who only emerged in comparatively recent times – about one million years ago.

During the Ice Ages of the pleistocene epoch, *equus* is believed to have migrated over land bridges to Europe, Africa and Asia. The disappearance of these land bridges as the ice receded some 10,000 years ago prevented horse populations making the reverse journey. So it was that North America ended up without an equine population until very recent times. For reasons not yet divined, the native population died out and it was not until

European colonists arrived a few centuries ago that the horse was reintroduced to that continent.

The horses that thrived in other parts of the world developed into three distinct types as a result of their different environments. Two breeds, the Asiatic Wild Horse (Przewalski's horse), which was discovered living in the wild in Mongolia in 1881, and the less primitive looking Tarpan from eastern Europe are the progenitors of today's light horse breeds. The third breed was the slow-moving heavy horse known as *equus silvaticus*, which lived in northern Europe and is the basis for modern breeds of heavy horse.

By the time man began to domesticate the horse, four sub-species had evolved. Northwest Europe was home to Pony Type 1, which resembled the Exmoor pony. Northern Eurasia had the bigger, heavier Pony Type 2, akin to the modern Highland pony. Horse Type 3, a little taller still but far lighter in build and perfectly suited to hot climates, could be found in Central Asia. It probably resembled the Akhal-Teke, which has thrived for the last three thousand years in Turkmenistan. Horse Type 4, the smallest but most refined of the quartet, was found in western Asia, and was the forerunner of the Caspian pony.

Today there are more than one hundred and fifty different breeds and types of horses and ponies spread throughout the world – all of them descendants of the little animal known as *eohippus*.

THE HORSE AS NATURE INTENDED

Understanding the instinctive behaviour of the wild horse is crucial to our understanding of his domesticated relatives.

Although a minority of today's horses live a "natural" life on the few remaining grassland tracts large enough to support quantities of free-ranging animals, the truly wild horse no longer exists: all are, to some extent, managed by humans. However, despite their long association with man, all horses still possess, to a marked degree, the instincts of their wild ancestors. It is only by understanding how and why horses behave as they do that we can hope to enjoy a harmonious relationship with them. The primary consideration governing good horsemastership is that horses are sociable animals. Forcing them to live solitary lives is both cruel and, usually, counter-productive. When deprived of the company of other equine animals, horses and ponies may well befriend other species such as cows or sheep, donkeys or even human beings. But all too often if deprived of the company of other horses they end up developing behavioural problems, including "vices", which are distressing to both them and their owners (see pp.104–7).

Seeking to eradicate such behaviour through force or punishment simply confuses and distresses the horse even more. Of course, giving a horse or pony one or more equine companions is not necessarily the solution in every case, since it is impossible to predict which horses will become friends. Like humans, some may show animosity towards each other, while others may forge extremely close bonds. Horses who seriously dislike each other should not be forced to live in close proximity to one another. In the end one of them will probably end up being injured.

As well as being a herd animal, the horse is a nomadic grazer. In the wild he would spend as many as 20 hours a day grazing. Again, it is unfair and entirely unnatural to confine him in a stable for 23 hours a day, with meals at set intervals and little, other than an hour's exercise and his daily hay ration, to occupy his time. Careful management –

Within a herd horses form small family groups, like this stallion with "his" mares.

which includes giving him the company of other horses, adequate exercise and plenty of distractions – is essential to prevent stress. Ideally, every horse and pony should be turned out to grass for as long as possible each day. Despite the inevitable restrictions of a fenced paddock, he can then, for the most part, revert to behaving like a horse.

Another vital part of the horse's behavioural pattern is his instinct to run from danger, real or imagined. With his long legs, large heart and lungs, the horse is built for swift flight. Since he has few

physical defences against attack from predators, such as lions, the appearance of danger prompts him to take the safest course of action: to run away, fast.

Although he has been domesticated for thousands of years, the horse still reacts to frightening situations by attempting to flee. A piece of paper fluttering across his path, a bird flying out of a hedgerow, a lorry letting off its air-brakes nearby – any sudden cause of alarm can prompt his desire to flee as if the devil were at his heels. To punish

Horses are by nature herd animals.

him on such occasions, as some riders do, will only compound his initial fears.

The wise horseman concentrates on instilling confidence into the horse. Once you have gained the trust of a horse, he can be trained to do all manner of unnatural things, from tolerating noisy traffic or negotiating a course of brightly coloured fences, to carrying a man into battle or jumping through a hoop of fire.

Survival and Reproduction

In the wild, horses build up their fat reserves during times of plentiful food. During the winter months, when grazing is scarce and less nutritious, they draw on these reserves and lose condition. Much of their food intake is used to keep them warm.

In their wild state, mating and breeding follow the same pattern each year. The natural scheme of things ensures that foals are born in the late spring when the weather is mild and there is plenty of grazing for the mares on whose milk they depend. During the spring and summer, mares come into season for approximately five days every three weeks, and ovulate on the last but one day of their heat. Gestation takes around 11 months. Although stallions are fertile throughout the year they do not usually show a particular need for sex during the winter. Like mares, their sex drive increases as the days become longer during spring.

Because of the link between hormonal levels and daylight, it is possible for horse owners to bring the breeding season forward by keeping the domesticated horse in artificially-lit conditions during the winter months.

A stallion can detect the smell of a mare in-season, quite literally, a mile away. If he is attracted to her, his instinct is to begin courtship prior to mating. It is this instinct which can make domesticated stallions more difficult to control, especially for inexperienced handlers and riders, and which, in many countries, has led to the gelding of the majority of male horses used for riding.

However, if correctly managed, many stallions will combine stud duties with a career as, for example, a competition horse, with no problems. In recent years the demand for horses for specific sports such as show jumping, dressage or carriage driving has led to more and more stallions being kept entire. The majority take the switch from one activity to another in their stride. Show-jumping riders, for instance, often remark on how a stallion who competes for much of the year, but is also used for breeding, soon gets to know that when a certain horsebox arrives it will be taking him off to stud. On his return to his regular home he quickly resumes his role as a competition horse.

HORSE SENSE

Nature has endowed the horse with well-developed senses, an excellent memory and the ability to communicate both vocally and through easily understood body language.

Hearing

The horse's hearing is more sensitive than that of a human. His large, funnel-shaped ears are so mobile – they are controlled by 16 muscles – that he can pick up sounds from all directions. He can concentrate on something happening behind him by laying back both ears, or he can flick one ear back while the other remains pointed forward, thus staying alert to sounds all around.

Sight

Large eyes positioned at each side of a wide forehead provide the horse with a remarkably wide field of vision. It has been likened to a cinemascope screen, extending virtually all around his body. The only blind spots occur immediately behind him and a short way in front of his head.

He focuses by raising and lowering his head, or tilting it to one side, and also by rolling his eyes. Tradition has it that showing the whites of the eyes indicates bad temper in a horse, but often the whites appear simply because he is rolling his eyes back in an attempt to look at something behind him.

To focus on close objects the horse either has to keep his head low or to tilt it to the side. When he is prevented by his rider from moving his head in this way to focus on a strange object, the horse's usual reaction is to make a quick move to the side

– what we call "shying" or "spooking" – to get a better view. Punishing the horse for such a manoeuvre is misguided, since it teaches him he has good reason to fear the unfamiliar.

Smell

The horse's highly developed sense of smell plays an important part in his life. He can detect water from quite a long distance and also uses his nose when selecting food. The well-developed "homing instinct" of many horses (the independent little Iceland horse is a good example) is attributed to their ability to recognize a trail by smell.

Horses recognize one another by smell, too. Watch them put their noses together as they meet, often blowing down their nostrils. They can also detect the smell of other horses on our clothes. Smell is important in communication between the sexes. A stallion will smell the urine and vulva of an in-season mare and can differentiate between the droppings of a mare and those of another stallion. A mare recognizes her foal by smell and vice versa.

Touch

The horse's sense of touch varies from one part of its body to another. The neck, shoulders and withers are particularly sensitive areas, and so too is the muzzle, which is equipped with whiskers that have

a large supply of nerves to the brain. Little is known about their function in horses but they certainly serve to inform the horse how far his nose is from an object. It is a great pity that in some areas of equestrianism, such as showing, it has become the fashion to shave off equine whiskers for the sake of appearance. We cannot know what effect this has on the horse.

As well as using their noses, horses use their front feet to sound out an unfamiliar object on the ground. In addition, they use their sense of touch in communicating with their companions – watch them mutually grooming each other with their teeth, particularly on the sensitive withers and shoulders. Humans have cashed in on this sensitivity to touch by developing "aids" with which to communicate their wishes. The horse is not born knowing that when we squeeze with our legs we wish him to go forward, or that when we put pressure on the bit in his mouth we expect him to turn, stop or whatever. But his sensitivity to touch enables us to train him relatively easily to do our bidding.

Taste

The horse's sense of taste is less easy to assess. Horses certainly respond to certain foods. While they will spit out bitter-tasting plants, most seem to find sweet things palatable. Peppermint is a well-known favourite. Some horses will attempt to get

into your pockets if they expect to find a packet of mints there.

Memory

Horses have excellent memories, something which can be both a blessing and a hindrance to their human masters. If handled kindly and patiently, horses soon learn to carry out our wishes in response to certain vocal or physical prompts and will remember those commands indefinitely. This, of course, makes it possible for us to train them to do all sorts of things which would normally be outside their sphere of activity.

On the minus side is the ease with which they learn to associate certain things with certain places. Ask the horse to canter or gallop at the same spot a few times and he will soon expect to do so every time he reaches that spot. Perform the same dres-

sage test over and over again and he may start to anticipate movements at certain points in the arena. Equally pronounced is the horse's capacity for remembering bad experiences.

When an owner finds that their newly acquired horse has a behavioural problem of some kind, it is more than likely that he associates what he is being asked to do with something unpleasant in the past. The horse who is sweetness and light when groomed by a woman, but will not let a man into his

ABOVE: *Mutual grooming is both useful and pleasurable.*

LEFT: *Horses recognize each other by smell.*

FAR LEFT: *The horse has acute hearing, thanks to his large, mobile ears.*

stable, has probably been bullied or beaten, by a man. The horse who refuses to go into a horsebox or trailer has probably had such an unpleasant time during a previous journey that he never wants to travel again. The horse who can jump perfectly well but persistently refuses to do so, has probably been overjumped, jabbed in the mouth or otherwise mishandled so often that he is sick of the business.

Since the horse cannot speak our language he cannot explain exactly what has happened, But it

ABOVE: *Between stallions and mares body language is an important means of communication.*

LEFT: *Ears laid flat back indicate fear in this horse being threatened by a companion.*

should never be forgotten that "misbehaviour" in a horse is virtually always the result of ill-judged or unkind human behaviour toward him.

Horse Talk

Horses have a variety of noises in their "vocabulary". The quiet nicker, which so often greets an owner or groom as they appear with an eagerly awaited feed, is also used as a greeting between equine friends, a mare and her foal, or a stallion and a mare.

Horses use the much louder neigh to keep in touch with each other. If your only previous experience of hearing horses neigh is at the cinema, when they are in a terrifying situation or as they crash to the ground during a cavalry charge, forget it. Horses do not neigh in such situations, whatever film directors would have us believe.

Separate two devoted equine friends, however, and they will neigh to each other incessantly. Horses' neighs are as individual as human voices, so they easily recognize each other. Squeals are prompted by excitement, often of a sexual nature, while a mare not ready for mating may utter an angry scream at an importunate stallion. Less heard is the loud roar produced by fighting males. Snorts, generally speaking, indicate alarm, although some horses of an excitable disposition snort a lot in a playful way.

Horses can also be heard grunting and groaning, though not, it seems, as a means of communication with their fellows, rather in response to certain situations. A horse might grunt when making a big effort to jump a fence, when he is in pain or while trying to get to his feet after a fall – film directors, please note. A horse may also groan while getting up from a snooze, while swimming or while struggling to give birth.

Body Language

Horses also communicate through body language. In the wild, a look-out horse adopts an alert, tense posture to prepare the rest of the herd for flight from possible danger. An excited stallion tucks in his head, arches his neck and performs prancing movements with a high tail and general air of showing off. The relaxed, sleepy horse stands with lowered head, half-closed eyes, droopy lower lip and a resting hind foot.

Because horses naturally equate tension with danger and the need to flee, tense humans tend to have a bad effect on them. On the other hand, a laid-back, relaxed person will soon gain a horse's confidence and friendship.

The horse's ears are particularly expressive. You can detect from their position where the horse's attention is directed and also what mood he is in. In a relaxed, sleepy horse the ears droop. In an alert one they will be pointed in the direction of the object or noise which has caught his attention. In an angry or fearful horse they will lie flat. Ears that are merely turned back rather than laid back often indicate that the horse is concentrating on something behind him, though they can also indicate that the horse is afraid.

Tail movements are another indicator of the horse's mood. The excited horse holds his tail high, while the fearful one clamps it down between his legs. A lashing tail indicates irritation or anger.

Equine mouths and noses are extremely expressive, too. A tightening of the mouth may indicate one of a number of emotions ranging from anger to fear or confusion. A soft, floppy mouth usually denotes relaxation, but it is also seen in a horse in severe pain when it is accompanied by a dull, rather than a sleepy, eye and a generally withdrawn appearance. Flared nostrils can be a sign of excitement or fear. The mouthing movements commonly made by foals are interpreted as a sign of submission.

A horse in search of a titbit will make a "long nose" and wiggle it about as he tries to gain entry to a pocket. But he may make a long nose for a number of other reasons. Accompanied by a tight mouth, a long nose is a sign of tension or fear, whereas a long nose and slightly open mouth may precede a session of mutual grooming. Many horses respond to being groomed by a human by nipping their groom. Irritation may be the cause – they may be ticklish or sore or simply fed up – but usually it is because their natural response is to reciprocate. Some horses will simply hold their groom's shirt or sweater between their teeth while being brushed. Beware of an open mouth with bared teeth, though: it probably means that the horse is going to bite.

An excited horse showing typical "high-tail" action in his paddock.

WHY DO THEY DO THAT?

Studying how horses respond to situations tells us about their individual characteristics and helps us form a better relationship with them.

Horses often kick up their heels from sheer high spirits.

Pawing

Pawing with the forelegs is chiefly associated with two things: food and frustration. Horses will paw while grazing to reveal a tasty root, and will dig through snow to reach the grazing beneath. During a drought, free-ranging horses will paw at dried-up watering places in an attempt to unearth water. Stabled horses often paw the ground when their feed is late. Pawing is also often seen when an eager horse is restrained from doing what it wants. Stallions are prone to pawing, especially when prevented from getting to a mare they wish to cover. Opinions differ as to why horses tend to paw immediately before rolling, but it certainly serves as a timely warning to the rider, particularly if you are in the middle of a stream, in which case you should quickly urge the horse to move forward.

Striking Out

A quick upward and outward strike with a foreleg serves as a warning to another horse not to become over-familiar. As with pawing, it is stallions who tend to be the most free with their forelegs.

Biting

Because horses are by nature defensive rather than aggressive, it is unusual for them to go on the attack with their teeth. Biting is most often seen in stallions. Wild stallions will attempt to bite each other when fighting, aiming at their opponent's jugular – though really serious equine battles are not all that common. It is also usual for a stallion to take hold of a mare's shoulder or neck with his teeth when mating with her.

In the domesticated stallion biting is more likely to be the result of frustration at being confined. When other domesticated horses resort to biting there is usually a very good reason. A brood mare who threatens to bite an approaching human is acting protectively towards her foal. Horses who bite when having their girths or rugs adjusted may be suffering from back pain, or they could have particularly sensitive skin and be ticklish. Remember, too, that offering a titbit every time you approach a horse or pony may result in even the most well-mannered individual nipping at anyone who passes in the anticipation of being given food.

Kicking

In their natural herd environment horses use their hind legs both to defend themselves and to offer a defensive challenge to others. A sudden swing round of the hindquarters and a lifted hind leg warns that a kick may be in the offing. Kicking, often with one leg, also denotes annoyance – for instance when a horse is being pestered by insects. The hind legs are useful for removing flies from the abdomen, which is out of reach of the tail. But, remember that kicking at the abdomen may also indicate abdominal pain, which could signal a colic attack.

Stabled horses who kick may be bored or be expressing irritation at their neighbours. Housing incompatible horses side by side, for example, can trigger kicking. This type of behaviour can sometimes become habitual and continue even if the source of irritation is diagnosed and removed. Continuous kicking of the stable walls causes injuries to the hocks and back. Wall-kickers should be turned out to graze as much as possible. If they must be kept in, they need plenty of exercise and diversions.

Bucking

It is natural for horses to buck from sheer *joie de vivre*. A wild horse would also use this movement to try to throw a predator off – which, of course, explains why a young horse may buck once or twice when asked to carry a saddle for the first time. Once he realizes there is nothing to fear, the bucking usually stops.

In the correctly schooled, ridden horse bucking is rarely intended to dislodge the rider. Again, it is probably the result of high spirits, though it can denote some form of discomfort or, as when a rider has hit the horse with a whip, displeasure.

It is usually possible to feel a buck coming and to take evasive action. The requirement is to keep the horse's head up – to buck properly, rather than just kick up his heels, he needs to lower his head. If a horse is really intent on bucking off his rider he will do so by combining the upward thrust of his back and hindquarters with lowering his head and neck, dropping one shoulder – and perhaps twisting his whole body for good measure.

Head Nudging

Horses move their heads for a number of reasons. A gentle forward nudge is a common way of gaining attention; a more violent thrust is a form of threat. An angry horse may lunge forward with its whole body.

Head Jerking and Shaking

Jerking the head sharply backwards indicates disapproval or fear, and may be followed by rearing. A shake or toss of the head is a sign of irritation or frustration.

Rearing

Rearing is very much part of stallion behaviour. In the wild, stallions rear up when fighting or displaying, and colts can often be seen rearing in play. Because it increases a horse's height, rearing no doubt makes him appear more formidable to an opponent. In the ridden horse rearing is extremely dangerous. With the weight of a rider on his back – and the possibility of the rider being caught unawares and thrown off balance – there is the danger of the horse falling over backwards, injuring both himself and his rider.

Therefore, care must be taken when training the young horse – who may rear out of sheer high spirits – not to allow it to become a habit. The key to prevention is forward movement: if the horse is being made to go forward, he cannot rear. With a habitual rearer there is often a simple underlying cause. Perhaps he is afraid of something he knows he will encounter in the direction in which he is being asked to go. Or, and this is often the problem, perhaps the bit or bridle is hurting him or he is afraid of a painful jab in the mouth from rough hands. By removing the pain or fear and persuading the horse to move forward, rearing can usually be prevented.

Flehmen

The curious rolling back of the upper lip, known as Flehmen, has nothing to do with laughing. It is a response to certain smells and tastes. There is a common misconception that it is a purely sexual response, because a stallion will do it when smelling the urine of a mare.

In fact, it occurs among horses of both sexes and all ages. Above the horse's soft palate there is a highly specialized smelling device known as the vomeronasal or Jacobson's organ. To use this organ, the horse inhales deeply and curls up his lip in order to fully savour a smell or taste.

A horse showing Flehmen, the curious posture associated with his senses of smell and taste.

CONFORMATION

A well-proportioned animal is better balanced and more able to work than one who is formed.

The term "conformation" is used to describe a horse's shape. Although all horses and ponies have the same constituent parts – with the notable exception of the Arabian, who has fewer ribs and vertebrae than other breeds – conformation varies from breed to breed. What constitutes ideal conformation for one purpose does not necessarily apply for another, but certain guidelines should always be followed.

Bone

Horsemen talk of "good bone" or "plenty of bone". This refers to the measurement taken round the cannon bone just below the knee, and it governs the weight-carrying ability of the horse. It varies according to the breed or type of horse. Generally speaking, a heavyweight 16.2 hands high (hh) horse should have at least 9 in (23 cm) of bone. A lightweight riding horse of similar stature should have not less than 8 in (20 cm).

"No Foot, No Horse"

This age-old maxim still holds true. Although remedial farriery can improve poor foot conformation quite dramatically, the soundest horses start life with a good set of feet. Looked at from the side, the slope of both fore and hind feet should be a continuation of the slope of the pastern. Good forefeet are rounded in shape, good hind feet are more oval.

Both sets of feet should look like a matching pair. All four feet should point directly forwards. Large, flat feet are best avoided: they are often

Hindquarters should be muscular and strong: power here is essential as the quarters are the horse's "engine".

The croup should be the same height as the shoulders. A high croup throws more weight on to the forehand, adding to the strain on the forelegs.

A well-muscled, medium length back, rising slightly towards the croup. An over-long back tends to be weak, a short one can restrict the horse's action.

Loins should be short and well-muscled.

Hind legs should neither be tucked up under the horse nor stretched out behind him when he is standing still.

The riding horse should have a curved, fairly long neck (the top line convex, the lower line concave), without undue fleshiness around the throat. In the harness horse, who needs strength rather than speed, a shorter neck is acceptable.

The head should be in proportion to the body. A heavy, over-large head has a detrimental effect on the horse's balance and puts extra weight on his forehand, which already carries 60 per cent of his total weight. An under-sized head will have a similarly detrimental effect on his balance.

Withers should be well defined; if they are too high or poorly defined it may make saddle-fitting difficult.

Large, wide nostrils will make breathing easy.

The head should be well set, with good clearance between the lower jaw and the top bone of the neck (the atlas). This makes it easier for the horse to flex at the poll when asked to perform collected gaits.

Jaws should meet evenly at the front to enable the horse to graze efficiently.

A reasonably broad chest will ensure that the forelegs are not set so close together that they will brush against each other when in motion, causing injuries.

The body should be deep and reasonably broad. Depth through the girth – from the top of the withers to below the elbow – gives plenty of room for the lungs to expand

Forelegs should be straight and strong with large, flat knees, short cannon bones and medium length pasterns.

Shoulders should be well sloped, to enable the horse to take longer strides. Straight shoulders tend to produce jarring which can cause strains and injuries in the forelimbs, as well as giving a less comfortable ride. The shoulder should be muscular without being too heavy. A slightly straighter shoulder is acceptable in the harness horse, in whom strength is more important than extended paces.

prone to corns and bruised soles. Similarly, upright "boxy"-looking feet are not desirable, since they are prone to jarring.

The Genes Machine

Horses come in a wide variety of colours. Inherited genes control equine coat colouring. There are dominant genes – for example, bay is dominant to black, while grey is dominant to both black and bay. There are recessive genes – chestnut is recessive to all other colours.

Horses' eyes are generally dark, though some are blue. Where there is a congenital deficiency of colouring pigment, albinos occur, with pink skin and white hair.

Coats of Many Colours

BAY Reddish coat with black mane, tail and limbs.

BLACK All black coat but with occasional white markings on the legs and/or the head.

BRINDLE Brown or grey coat with streaks or patches of a darker colour.

BROWN Mixed black and brown hairs, with black limbs, mane and tail. Very dark brown horses may appear almost black.

CHESTNUT Can vary from a pale golden colour to a rich, red gold. The mane and tail may be darker or lighter than the coat. The darkest shades are known as liver chestnut.

CREAM All-over cream coat – also called cremello – with unpigmented skin.

DUN Light sandy-coloured coat with black mane and tail. Often there is a dark dorsal stripe, known as an eel-stripe, running from the neck to the tail. Dun can vary from yellow to "mouse". The skin is black. Some dun horses have stripes on their withers and legs. Known as zebra markings, they are probably the remains of a form of camouflage.

GREY Coat varies from almost white to very dark, known as iron grey. The skin is black. A grey coat flecked with brown is known as flea-bitten; a light grey coat with darker rings is called dappled.

PALOMINO A gold coat with white mane and tail (opposite).

PIEBALD Large, irregular patches of black and white.

ROAN A body colour that is interspersed with white hairs. Chestnut body colouring intermixed with white hair that has a pinkish-red tinge is known as strawberry roan. Black or brown body colouring with white hair gives a blue tinge and is known as blue roan.

SKEWBALD Large, irregular patches of white and any other colour except black.

SORREL A light-red chestnut.

SPOTTED Small, roughly circular patches of hair of a different colour from that of the main body colour and distributed over various areas of the body.

WHITE MARKINGS White markings occur on the horse's legs, face and occasionally on the body. They provide an invaluable means of differentiating between one horse and another and are always noted in detail on registration papers and veterinary certificates. A white facial marking may be described as a blaze, snip, star, stripe, interrupted stripe or white muzzle, depending on its size and location.

HOOF COLOURS Hoof horn varies from blue or black to white. Some hooves are marked with dark stripes.

Dapple grey

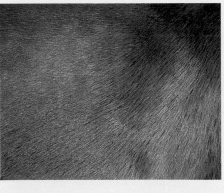

Chestnut

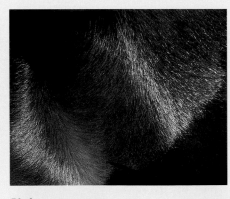

Black

Dun

Piebald

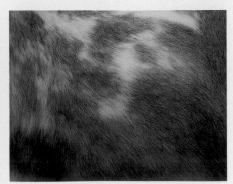

Skewbald

2

SO YOU WANT TO RIDE?

Riding is unlike any other sport. It is a partnership between two living creatures who have very different perceptions of the world and different powers of reasoning, who do not speak each other's language and one of whom is infinitely stronger, physically, than the other. Yet it is possible for the well schooled horse and rider to achieve the most remarkable harmony, as if they were one being, rather than two.

As well as being a healthy, enjoyable pastime, riding can also be immensely character building, especially for the young. The best riders have an inherent love of and respect for animals; but in addition to that, they must acquire the ability to "think horse" – to put themselves in the horse's place and see things from his perspective. Several thousand years of domestication have not eradicated the horse's basic instincts and only by learning to understand the horse's viewpoint will the rider progress to become a true horseman.

To ride successfully involves much more than learning to start, steer and stop. The human being needs to be patient and tactful, to have respect for his partner, to treat him at all times with fairness. Self-discipline is always a desirable virtue, but never more so that when dealing with animals, and especially when trying to forge a partnership with an animal as large and inherently nervous as the horse.

Size is the thing which puts so many people off horses – they find it scaring. For every person who rides there are several more who say they would like to, but are not brave enough. What they do not realize is that the horse is by nature a gentle, peace-loving creature, designed by nature to fly from danger, not to attack. Despite his size and bulk, riding well is not a question of strength. It is to do with balance, co-ordination, a feel for rhythm and general all-round physical fitness.

How else would a tiny, lightweight jockey control a strapping, super-fit Thoroughbred at racing pace, or a petite woman partner a powerful show jumper or three-day eventer? That is one of equestrian sport's greatest attractions: even in the most demanding of the competitive disciplines, sex is not an issue: men and women compete on level terms and both are equally successful.

Neither age nor physique should deter anyone from taking up riding. Certainly, learning to ride at a young age, when the body is at its most supple, is definitely an advantage. But plenty of people have their first riding lessons much later in life and still make good progress. A slim build and medium height may be the ideals, but they are certainly not essential. Look around at famous horsemen and women and you will see short, tall, thin and fat people all achieving international success.

Ultimately, what it all comes down to is understanding – the human being's understanding of the mind of another animal. When that is achieved, man and horse really do appear to be one. As the sporting author R.S. Surtees aptly put it: "There's no secret so close as that between a rider and his horse."

There is a lot more to riding a horse than simply staying in the saddle. Even if you are lucky enough to be blessed with natural talent, always remember that the most gifted horsemen and women – yes, even those competing at Olympic level – regularly seek help from an expert on the ground.

Learning to ride is not at all like learning to drive or to ride a bike. Your chosen means of transport has a brain and will of his own and will not necessarily respond in a predictable manner when you press what you think is the right button. If learning from an experienced instructor is best for any would-be horseman, it is absolutely essential for the good of the horse. It follows that the beginner needs to find a reputable establishment which has a supply of well-schooled horses.

Never forget rule number one: a novice rider cannot learn to ride with any degree of competence on a novice horse. If the horse does not fully understand what we expect of him, then a beginner in the saddle is certainly not going to be able to show him. The net result will be a confused, miserable animal and a human with no hope of acquiring the basics of good horsemanship. Choosing the right school and instructor, therefore, is of paramount importance if you are going to enjoy and benefit from your early experiences of riding.

In most countries where riding is popular that choice should not prove too difficult. Usually schools need to be licensed by their local authority (if in doubt, check this out). However, licensing tends to be more concerned with safety, essential insurance cover and the welfare of the animals. It does not guarantee an appropriate level of instruction or the provision of suitable horses.

The best way to set about finding a good school is to contact your national equestrian federation. In Britain, for example, there is no excuse for patronising one of those dubious "schools", where you are encouraged to hire an ill-fed, poorly prepared nag and ride off into the sunset, trusting to luck.

Reputable establishments apply for approval from one of two organizations – and often both – the British Horse Society (BHS) and the Association of British Riding Schools. They advertise the fact that their staff have attained teaching qualifications – the BHS administers a comprehen-

WHICH SCHOOL?

Everyone who aspires to the art of horsemanship needs help from a competent person on the ground.

sive examination structure in this field. And to help you select there are regularly updated publications listing schools, detailing their facilities and explaining what the teaching qualifications mean.

Other countries, including Australia, France, Denmark, Germany, Italy, the Netherlands, Norway, Sweden and Finland, also have internationally recognized riding instructor qualifications. Although things are more fragmented in the United States – with individual States "doing their own thing" – it should not prove too difficult, with perseverance, to find a school or "barn" where you can acquire good basic horsemanship skills.

Wherever you are based, before booking a course of lessons it makes sense to visit your select-

ABOVE: *A well-equipped indoor school makes riding lessons a pleasure whatever the weather.*

ABOVE, RIGHT: *A tidy, workmanlike yard with alert-looking horses – but the chewed door tops could indicate a dietary problem.*

ed school to see whether you like the look and feel of it. Ask to watch a lesson, so that you can see what will be involved. If possible, go in the company of an experienced rider who will be able to help you to make an informed judgement. Decide whether you find the atmosphere, the people and the surroundings congenial. Do the horses seem suitable for their level of riders? What about the

What to Look For

THE HALLMARKS OF A GOOD RIDING SCHOOL ARE:

- A clean, neat and tidy yard and stables.
- Contented, relaxed horses or ponies.
- Well turned out, helpful staff.
- A businesslike but friendly atmosphere.
- Properly equipped riders – no one should be allowed to ride unless they are wearing a hat, correctly secured with a chin harness, and safe footwear (see pp. 28–33)

What to Avoid

NEVER PATRONIZE STABLES THAT HAVE:

- Dirty, untidy premises.
- Unkempt staff.
- Scruffy and/or dejected-looking horses.
- Lack of professional supervision.
- People riding in any old clothes: baggy jeans, trainers or "wellies", and with no hard hat.

personality of the instructor? Is he or she – in Britain it will probably be a she as there are far more women instructors than men – articulate? Is she helpful? Most importantly, are people ENJOYING themselves – riding is after all meant to be FUN.

Booking Lessons

When booking your first lesson, be scrupulously honest about your previous riding experience. A good establishment will ask you a number of pertinent questions before they book you in. Expect to be asked your height and weight.

If they fail in this respect, you would be wise to look elsewhere. If you are a complete beginner, say

so. If you have ridden a little before, tell them, but never claim to be more accomplished than you really are: you will only have yourself to blame if you are "over-horsed".

Armed with all this information, the school can pair you up with a mount of the right size and temperament. Ask what items of clothing you will be expected to have. The beginner does not need a complete riding outfit, but safety and comfort are essential. Some schools keep a selection of spare hats for the benefit of first-timers, who may not want to go to the expense of buying their own until they decide to ride regularly. Check that the school can loan you a hat which complies with the latest safety standards and that they will help you fit it.

WHAT TO WEAR

The two criteria to bear in mind when choosing riding gear are safety and comfort.

Leg Wear

Close-fitting leg wear is essential as it prevents chafing of the insides of the legs. This is why ordinary trousers and jeans are not suitable. Some people do find that close-fitting jeans are fine when worn under full-length chaps, and this arrangement can be useful for everyday riding. However, full-length chaps are not ideal for school purposes, when the instructor needs a clear view of your legs in order to correct your position.

Jodhpurs, which originated in India, are excellent – and not too costly – for the beginner. They are also a blessing in very hot weather, when riding boots – to the knee – would be too hot. They are close fitting, reach down to the ankle and can be worn with specially designed, ankle-length jodhpur boots.

Riding boots are worn with breeches, which end just below the knee. Leather riding boots are the ultimate: they give protection to the whole of the lower leg without restricting movement. They are essential for many sports, but they are expensive. Properly designed rubber boots (as opposed to Wellingtons) are a good alternative for everyday use. They are much cheaper than leather, look quite smart and are easy to keep clean. On the minus side, they can become too hot in summer and too cold in winter. There are a variety of other knee-length boots which are also suitable for everyday wear. These include "field" boots (with laces at the ankle).

Jodhpurs and breeches should have "strappings" – patches of reinforcing material – at the knees. The strappings may be of the same material as the garment or simulated suede. The latter gives more protection and wears better.

Nowadays, there are also very good close-fitting riding trousers on the market. As with jodhpurs and breeches, they come in a variety of weights of cloth.

When buying legwear, you will find something for every occasion and every extreme of weather. Dark colours are practical for everyday riding, but for most

Hacking jackets, in suitably muted colours such as these, are both smart and practical.

There is no getting away from the fact that riding is a risk sport. No matter how well trained the horse and how accomplished the rider, sooner or later everyone falls off – even the professionals. More often than not it will only be your pride that is dented; however, there is no point in taking unnecessary risks.

There are two golden rules when it comes to safety: first, never get on a horse unless you are wearing a hat that fits properly, is made to a recommended standard and is fastened correctly with a chin harness. Top dressage riders and other competitive types may still wear unsecured top hats, but that is their business.

Second, never get on a horse unless you are wearing safe footwear. Wear boots or shoes with a smooth, not ridged, sole, and a clearly defined heel. A smooth sole allows your foot to come free of the stirrup iron quickly and easily in an emergency. The heel prevents your foot sliding right through the iron – if you fell off and that happened, you could be dragged by one leg: a horrible, potentially fatal, experience. Never ride in Wellington boots or other footwear, such as ordinary trainers, which is not designed for riding.

organized sporting occasions light colours are required – see the rules governing the various disciplines pp.162–187). If you are skinny, look for jodhpurs or breeches with a reinforced seat. No one wants to end up saddle sore. All legwear should fit snugly but not be so tight that it restricts movement. Bear in mind that over-tight breeches and jodhpurs look less than flattering on the larger figure.

Above the Waist

A shirt, with or without a sweatshirt (depending on the weather) is fine for informal riding. Provided they fit well – neither too tight, not too baggy – they will look neat and workmanlike and allow freedom of movement. Long-sleeved shirts are best as sleeves afford some protection in the event of a fall – and will also protect you from equine teeth.

However high the temperatures, avoid riding in a vest, collarless shirt or low-necked suntop, none of which offers protection, either from the abovementioned eventualities or from sunburn. In colder weather you can either choose from the wide range of casual riding jackets available or go for a traditional hacking jacket, which looks best worn over a shirt with a collar and tie. More formal riding jackets are only really necessary for organized events such as shows or hunting. In the latter case, when you might be in the saddle in horrible weather conditions for several hours, a good quality coat will keep you warm and dry.

Wet Weather Wear

There is a huge range of waterproof clothing available. Much depends on individual preference and the severity of the weather. You can choose from short, medium or full-length coats in anything from waxed cotton to the latest (expensive) "breathable" fabrics. Coats come with storm collars and cuffs, warm linings – detachable or otherwise – leg straps and, in some cases, an "apron" to cover the front of the saddle. Some are straight cut, some have drawstring waists. Whatever style you choose, always go for "quiet" materials: some horses become extremely spooky if you wear "noisy" clothes, which crackle with every movement. Who can blame them? You are, after all,

perched up on their backs, predator-like. And avoid baggy coats that will flap about on a windy day. These, again, may cause spooking. Make sure your long coat fits well – without being so tight that it restricts movement – and always fasten the leg straps to keep the skirt in place.

Underwear

Comfortable underwear is a must. Wear the very skimpy variety and you may well regret it. If you want to go the whole hog, you can buy items specially designed for riding. There are comfortably cut briefs for both sexes, as well as, for women, "minimum bounce" sports bras, which are a boon to the those with a fuller figure.

Keeping Warm

Many people find silk underwear a comfort in cold weather. Some follow the example of jockeys and wear a pair of tights under their breeches. If you suffer from chronically cold feet, you may need to invest in two pairs of boots, one half a size larger than your foot size to allow for an extra pair of thermal socks in winter. There is nothing worse than riding with freezing cold feet – that moment when you have to dismount can be purgatory.

ABOVE: *Riding gloves are made in materials for every occasion.*
ABOVE, TOP: *When choosing wet weather wear, always opt fo "quiet" garments such as these waxed jackets.*

Gloves

Gloves are not essential, but they are advisable for riding in wet or cold weather. For everyday wear string gloves are best as they are easy to wash. Leather gives a good feel on the reins, though it can prove slippery in very wet weather. Some gloves come with a non-slip surface, some are guaranteed waterproof, others have no fingers. It is a matter of choice – shop around until you find what suits you.

SAFETY FIRST

Riding is a risk sport, no matter how "bombproof" your horse, so always wear protective gear designed for the job.

A Hat is a Must

Falling from a great height, as riders often do – sometimes at considerable speed – is obviously a hazardous business. Yet countless riders the world over risk permanent injury by failing to protect their most vulnerable organ: the brain. In the United States it is estimated that only one in eight riders ever bothers to wear protective headgear. In Britain, where people have become much more safety conscious in recent years, it is still not compulsory for anyone over the age of 14 to wear a hard hat when they ride on the roads, in spite of the fact that there are an average of eight horse and rider-related accidents every day.

The majority of professionally organized competitive sports quite rightly insist on the wearing of proper headgear by everyone, regardless of age. No self-respecting riding school would accept less, and more and more people who ride their own horse, either schooling at home or out hacking, now appreciate that it makes good sense to protect their head.

Most riders cite comfort, or lack of it, as the reason for riding bare-headed. It is a selfish attitude. The chances are that it will not happen, but that does not alter the fact that it only takes one unfortunate accident to render you dependent on others for the rest of your life. Thanks to continued medical research into brain injuries, enormous improvements have been made over the last few years in protective headgear – and will no doubt continue to be made. Manufacturers are constantly

A correctly fitted hat to a recognized standard is essential. This is a "crash hat" fitted with a smart velvet cover.

striving to make hats which are both effective and comfortable to wear.

Standards to Go By

Hat standards are being improved all the time, but currently riders should choose a hat, either a jockey skull ("crash hat") or riding hat (with a soft peak), which conforms to one of the following:

EN 1384:1997

This is the European standard. It may be prefixed by other initials, depending on which country is testing the hat – eg, BS EN indicates that the hat has been tested in Britain.

PAS 015:1994

This is the British Standards Institute's enhanced EN 1384 which, though it predates the BS EN 1384, is

designed to provide improved protection to the crown and intermediate areas. It tends to be bulkier than the European standard hat.

ASTM F 1163

This is the American standard. American hats may have larger ventilation slots than their European counterparts. There is continued, heated debate about the advisability of ventilation slots. One school of thought propounds the view that there is the danger of injury through penetration by foreign objects. There are as yet no conclusive statistics. People who ride in hot countries or for long periods, for example, 100-mile (160 km) endurance riders, understandably value the heat reducing properties of the ventilated hat.

Hat Tips

- **Buy your own hat and have it professionally fitted. Borrowed hats are unlikely to fit as well as one chosen for your particular head.**
- **Always buy the most advanced standard hat available. If in doubt, check with your national federation. Be aware that even when new standards are introduced, retailers may continue to sell the previous standard hats for a while.**
- **Never ride without a hat.**
- **Always fasten the chin harness.**
- **Avoid chincups. They can cause jaw injuries.**
- **Never wear a hat with a rigid peak. They can cause neck injuries.**
- **Always wear a hat when leading a young or unpredictable horse.**
- **Replace your hat once it has been subjected to an impact – it may have saved your head once, but it might not do so twice.**

Body protectors are being improved all the time.
They are now lighter and more comfortable than the early ones.

Body Protectors

The success of modern body protectors is reflected in the fact that they have virtually eliminated the incidence of broken ribs in falls sustained by steeplechase jockeys – usually caused by blows from the hooves of passing horses. Although they cannot prevent serious injury in some circumstances, they are a must for everyone who rides at speed, particularly over fixed fences, and anyone who may be considered vulnerable – such as an older rider with more brittle bones.

Protectors come in different "classes", giving different degrees of protection, and may have detachable – or sometimes integral –shoulder protectors. You will find that the body protector and the shoulder protectors are given different standards. This is because the shoulder is stronger than the ribcage and different criteria apply. Correct fitting is vital – appropriate instructions provided by the manufacturer should accompany each garment. Choose the level of protection which best suits your risk level. If in doubt, consult your national federation.

On your Marks

As well as the standards, two other marks may be found in hats and on body protectors in Europe: the CE Mark and the Kitemark.

The CE Mark ensures that an item meets the basic safety requirements as laid down by the European Committee (it is illegal to make any Personal Protective Equipment or PPE which does not carry the CE Mark). Under European law all safety protection equipment falls under one of the European Directives on PPE. The Directive is not a standard, it is a set of requirements – manufacturers state that their equipment meets the requirements laid down for their particular Directive (hats and body protectors come under separate Directives). But there is no batch testing and some goods do sometimes fall below the required standard and have to be recalled.

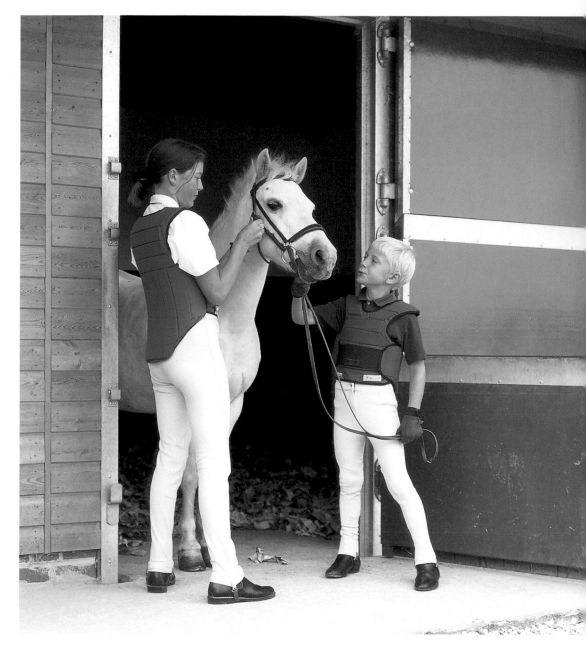

Does Your Body Protector Cover You?

- A body protector should cover the entire circumference of the torso.
- At the front, the bottom edge should be not less than 25 mm (1 inch) below the rib cage.
- At the back, the bottom edge should be not less than 15 cm (⅗ in) below the level of the top of the pelvis (the iliac crest) on an average adult.
- Laterally, the protector should reach the level of the pelvis.
- The top of the back of the protector should just reach the level of the seventh cervical vertebra, which is the prominent bone at the base of the neck.
- The front of the protector should reach to the top of the sternum, the breast bone.
- Together the body protector and shoulder protectors should cover the collarbone.
- Arm inlets should be of minimum dimensions and roughly circular in shape.

OPPOSITE: *A yellow Day-Glo tabard and armbands make this rider instantly visible to other road users.*

The Kitemark is the registered trademark of the British Standards Institute and can only be affixed to products which have passed the required tests. Look for the Kitemark on both hats and body protectors.

Get the Right Fit

Since your life may depend on it, your hat must fit correctly. It must fit snugly so that it will not move in the event of a fall. It should be worn straight and well down over the forehead – a riding hat worn on the back of the head is useless. The chin harness, an integral part of the hat, should be adjusted so that it is comfortably tight. A loose harness will not do its job. Excess lengths of strap should be trimmed off.

When shopping for a hat or body protector in Britain, there is no need to trust to luck when it comes to fit: look for a retailer displaying a BETA (British Equestrian Trade Association) certificate, indicating that staff have been awarded a BETA certificate in Safety (hat and body protector fitting) or in Hat Fitting. BETA trained staff will help you through the intricacies of fitting your

first hat and body protector. Heads come in a variety of shapes, and a make of hat which fits one head might be totally wrong for another. Be prepared to shop around.

Be Seen to be Safe

Riding on the roads can be a nightmare, but for many people some roadwork is unavoidable. It is your responsibility to make sure that you can be seen by other road users, especially from behind. Always wear specially designed, high visibility items. Day-glo yellow fitted with retro-reflective strips, which appear dull grey in daylight but are in fact brilliantly reflective, is currently the best high-visibility material available.

FOR THE RIDER: Tabard (or Sam Browne belt). Hat cover. Arm bands. Leg bands. Clip-on light (attach to the boots, back of collar and/or tabard).
FOR THE HORSE: Leg bands or brushing boots – because of the horse's continuous leg movements, these are the best warning of all to other road users. Exercise sheet with clip-on light. Slip-on strips on the bridle.

LEFT: *A selection of high visibility items for horse and rider. Leg bands for the horse are particularly useful – the horse's continuous leg movements make them instantly visible to motorists.*

> ## Gearing Up
> ### FOR SAFETY
>
> - **Coats and jackets should always be worn fastened, both in the saddle and on the ground. A loose, flapping garment can spook a horse.**
> - **Tie pins should be fastened horizontally, or at an angle, never vertically.**
> - **A hunting tie (also known as a cravat or "stock") can help support the neck in a fall. In an emergency it can be used as a bandage.**
> - **Long hair should be tied back or, better still, worn in a hairnet or plaited and put up into a bun. Loose hair can spook a horse and can also become entangled in "foreign objects" such as tree branches.**
> - **Never wear ear-rings, nose studs or other jewellery when riding – they can cause serious injury.**
> - **Choose elastic-sided jodhpur boots – the strap-fastening ones are more likely to become caught up.**
> - **Never wear boots or shoes which have been repaired with half- soles – if you fall, and the sole begins to part company with the upper, your foot could become jammed in the stirrup iron.**
> - **Always use the correct size of stirrup irons – there should be about 1 cm (½ in) clearance either side of your boot. Too big, and your foot could slip right through; too small, and your foot could become trapped.**

3
PART THREE

IN THE
SADDLE

For the majority of people the most disturbing aspect of getting on to a horse for the first time is how far away the ground seems. Yes, it certainly is a long way down, but have no fear – it is a sensation which quickly fades into insignificance once you start grappling with the technicalities of actually riding!

When learning to ride you will find that great importance is attached to acquiring the correct "seat". You will be surprised at how many things you can do wrong in the seemingly simple process of keeping the horse between you and the ground. This is because sitting on a horse involves a lot more than merely putting a leg on each side of a saddle. One of the endless fascinations of riding is finding how much better it feels, and how much better the horse goes, when you do things the right way.

To understand the importance of a good seat you need, as always, to consider life from the horse's perspective. Remember what it is like to carry a heavy rucksack or to give a child a piggyback? To make the job as easy as possible your burden needs to be carefully positioned so that it impedes neither your balance nor your movement. A rucksack fitted too low, nestling in the small of your back instead of well up on your shoulders, becomes an awkward encumbrance. So, too, does a child in the same position, or one who flops to one side. Walking is difficult enough, but try running and you will quickly realize just how vital it is to position your burden in the right place.

Exactly the same applies to the horse when you sit on his back. Carrying a heavy weight is not natural for him either. It is hard enough work on its own, particularly at fast paces or when jumping. But if his burden – you – sits too far back or too far forward, or bounces about in the saddle like an old sack of potatoes, then his life will become doubly arduous. He will find it very difficult to keep his balance and that in turn will put undue strain on his body.

One of the commonest faults committed by the beginner rider – in addition to looking down to see where the ground is – is to become tense. Tension is anathema to effective riding, so take every opportunity to practise exercises which help you to relax. A good instructor will incorporate mounted exercises during your lessons. But unmounted ones are equally helpful. General physical fitness is a great benefit to any rider. The more relaxed, fit and supple you are overall, and the more in control of what the various bits of your body are doing, the better you will ride.

If it all sounds daunting at first, and you develop aches in muscles you didn't even know you possessed, don't be discouraged. These will pass, and in the fullness of time you will find yourself sitting tall in the saddle and beginning to appreciate the joys of riding. Suddenly the ground will not seem so far away after all.

HOW TO HANDLE A HORSE

By nature the horse is a nervous animal. So before you mount up for the first time, consider how to win his confidence and stay safe in his company.

Since the horse will quickly pick up your mood, both from your tone of voice and your body movements, always be calm when making your approach – no rushing, or sudden movements. Never creep up on him from behind – remember that he cannot see clearly right behind him and his instinct is to defend himself when taken by surprise.

Approach the horse from his left side towards his shoulder. Always speak to him quietly so that he knows you are coming. Stroke his lower neck and shoulder with your hand. Whatever you do, avoid swift, jerky movements; do not wave your arms about and never shout.

Leading a Horse

When leading a horse from the ground, position yourself alongside his nearside (left) shoulder. If he has been correctly schooled he will obey the voice command to "walk on". There is no point in walking ahead of a reluctant horse and trying to pull him along – most horses refuse to walk on if you stand right in front of them and, anyway, are considerably stronger than you.

A horse who refuses to "walk on" can be encouraged vocally by an assistant positioned a short distance behind and to the side. An experienced handler encourages a reluctant horse to lead properly by carrying a long schooling whip in his left hand, moving it behind him and tapping the horse's flank with it as he says "walk on".

The safest way to lead a horse is in a bridle, with the reins over his head. Horses are normally led from their left side – though a well-schooled horse will lead equally well from the right, or offside. Hold both reins in your right hand a short distance below the bit rings and with one finger dividing them. Take the buckle end in your left hand.

If you are leading the horse on a rope, for example when catching him from the field or turning him out again, hold the rope in the same way.

If you have to turn the horse, always turn him away from you: that is, with you walking around him. This keeps his hocks under him, which in turn keeps him balanced and more under control. If you allow him to walk around you, you will have far less control and he might inadvertently tread on your feet.

When you want him to stop, ask him to "Whoa" and apply light pressure on the bit via the reins – use a smooth action, not an abrupt jerk, which will hurt his mouth and cause him to resist.

The Power of Voice

Horses are immensely sensitive to the tone of your voice. They quickly learn to recognize an often repeated word, as well as the voice of a person whom they see on a regular basis. Never approach a horse without first speaking to him in a calm and kind tone. Always speak to him when handling him and before you move. The human voice can calm a nervous horse and encourage a lazy one. On the rare occasions when a horse needs scolding, a growling tone of voice is often all that is required to remind him of his manners.

Footwork

Even if you never possess your own horse, you must learn how to pick up a horse's foot because there will be times when his hooves need cleaning out and his shoes checked. For safety's sake, always follow the routine outlined here.

OPPOSITE: *Always approach a horse from his left side, towards his shoulder (Note: trainers are not ideal footwear for working with horses.)*

RIGHT: *To lead a horse, hold the rope or lead rein close to his head and walk beside him, not in front of him*

Safety Tips

- When leading a horse through a doorway or gateway, make sure you keep him straight. Knocking himself against a doorframe or gate post can cause serious hip injuries.
- When leading a horse, never wrap the spare end of the lead rope around your hand. If the horse takes fright, you could be dragged.
- When leading a nervous horse, or even a quiet one, in an unfamiliar situation, always wear gloves as they will protect your hands from rope burns should the horse jump away from you.
- When leading a horse on a headcollar, never hook your fingers through the metal "D" rings.
- Never wear sandals or other flimsy footwear when handling a horse. An iron-shod hoof can cause serious injury to a human foot.
- When handling horses on the ground try, whenever possible, to walk round in front of them. If you must go round the rear end, be sure that you tell the horse what you are doing: speak to him first, put a hand on his quarters or on his tail, and walk close to him. The closer you are to the horse's rear end, the less likely you are to be hurt if he does kick out. Be calm and positive. If you creep nervously about, he will pick up your fears.
- Never sit down or kneel on the ground when handling a horse's feet. If something startled him and he jumped sideways, you would be unable to get out of his way quickly.

TO PICK UP THE NEARSIDE FOREFOOT

First speak to the horse. Place your hand on his neck and turn to face his hindquarters. Run your left hand down his shoulder, down the back of his forearm, past his knee and down the back of his tendons. When you reach the fetlock joint say "Up" and squeeze slightly. When he raises his hoof, support it at the toe end with your fingers. Reverse the process for the offside forefoot.

TO PICK UP THE NEARSIDE HINDFOOT

First speak to the horse. Stand alongside his hip, facing his tail. Place your left hand on his quarters and run it down the back of his leg until you reach his hock joint, then move your hand to the front of his leg and carry on running it down on the inside front of the cannon bone. When you reach the fetlock joint, squeeze and say "up". When the horse raises his hoof, slide your hand down to hold the hoof from the inside. Reverse the process for the offside hindfoot.

Avoid unbalancing the horse by lifting the foot too high or pulling it too far back. Never leave your hand behind the horse's leg – if he kicked out he could break your arm.

> A horse that is reluctant to pick up a forefoot can be encouraged to do so if you lean slightly against his shoulder, thus pushing his weight on to the other foreleg.

MOUNTING AND DISMOUNTING

It may seem a long way up – or down – but there is no need for mounting – or dismounting – to be an undignified scramble.

Y ou can get on to a horse in one of four ways: by means of a "leg-up", using the stirrup from the ground, using a mounting block or vaulting on.

Although using the stirrup from the ground is not the best method for the horse's back or the saddle, it is essential that you know it because there will be times when you have to mount from the ground without assistance. Traditionally, riders mount from the nearside (left), but it is useful, and equally correct, to be able to do so from the offside (right).

Leg-up

A competent assistant can help you into the saddle quickly and with the minimum disturbance to horse and saddle. Face the horse, holding the reins and saddle as for mounting with the stirrup, and bend your left leg at the knee. The assistant should hold your left leg with their left hand under the knee and their right hand under the ankle. As you get ready to spring, the assistant lifts your leg, mainly from the knee. Syncronize your movements by counting to three. Once you are high enough, gently swing your leg over the horse and lower yourself into the saddle, at which point the assistant releases your leg.

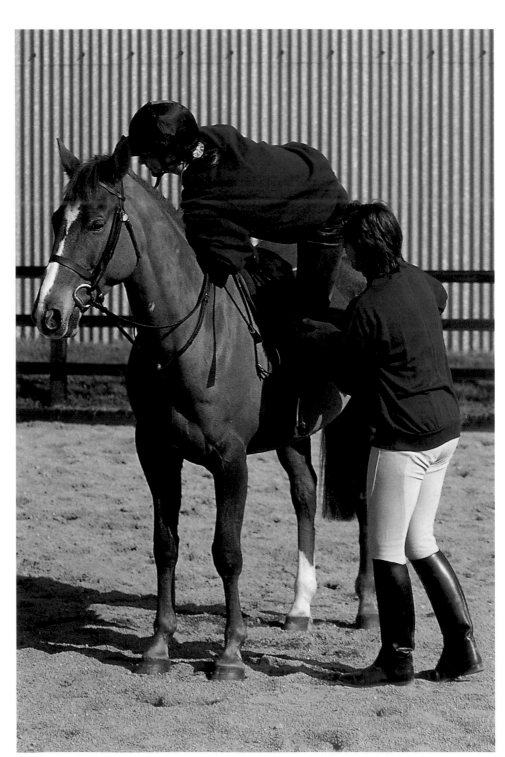

How to give a rider a leg-up.

Mounting with the Stirrup

Hold the reins in your left hand with the left rein between your third and fourth fingers and the right rein lying across the palm of your hand. Place your hand in front of the withers. Both reins should be in light contact with the horse's mouth, with the right rein slightly shorter than the left.

With your back to the horse's head, take the stirrup iron in your right hand and turn it toward you clockwise. Put your left foot in the stirrup iron. Pivot round to face the horse, placing your left knee against the saddle and pointing your toe down to avoid digging the horse in the side. With your right hand take hold of the far side of the saddle, either at the waist or the front arch. If possible, avoid catching hold of the cantle (back) of the saddle.

Spring off the ground, transferring your weight on to your left foot and leaning forward with your upper body.

Swing your right leg over the horse's back, taking care not to hit his quarters – if you startle him and he moves suddenly, you might be thrown off balance. At the same time move your right hand forward to the pommel for support.

Gently lower your seat into the saddle. Never land on the horse's back with a thump. Put your right foot in the offside stirrup iron. At first you may have to look down and turn the stirrup leather with your right hand in order to do this correctly, however, in time you will acquire the knack of feeling for the stirrup iron with your toe.

Finally, take the reins in both hands.

Using a Mounting Block

Mounting from a block, either a purpose-built one or some other solid structure about 2 ft (60 cm) high, is highly recommended, since it puts the least strain on the horse's back and the saddle. Simply lead the horse so that he is standing close to the block and use the same method as for mounting with the stirrup from the ground.

Vaulting On

If you are strong and agile enough, vaulting on is a good alternative to the mounting block. Place your left hand on the horse's withers, your right hand on the front of the saddle, and spring up, straightening your arms as you do so before swinging your right leg over the horse's back and lowering yourself into the saddle. Being able to vault on is particularly use-ful when riding very fit, fidgety horses, such as racehorses, when mounting with the stirrup would be difficult and potentially dangerous. However, you need to be strong and fit.

Mounting from a block puts less strain on the saddle tree and the horse's back than mounting from the ground.

Tips for Mounting and Dismounting

- **To adjust your stirrup leathers to roughly the correct length before you mount, face the saddle, place the knuckles of your right hand against the stirrup-bar of the saddle and adjust the leather until the bottom of the stirrup iron reaches your armpit. Check that both leathers are the same length by looking at them from in front of the horse.**
- **To adjust your left stirrup leather once you are mounted take the reins in your right hand, take the spare end of the leather in your left hand, with your thumb on top of the buckle. Disengage the tongue of the buckle and move it up or down to the required hole. When you have finished, ensure that the buckle is**

close to the stirrup-bar by pulling down on the inside of the leather. Keep your foot in the iron all the time. To adjust your right stirrup leather proceed as above using the other hand.
- **To tighten the girth when mounted take the reins in one hand, move your leg forward and up, keeping your foot in the stirrup. Raise the saddle flap with your free hand and adjust the buckles as necessary, making sure that the tension on both is the same. The girth buckles should be at the same height on both sides of the saddle. Ensure that the buckle guards, which prevent the buckles from damaging the saddle flap, are lying flat before lowering the flap.**

- **If you regularly mount using the left stirrup, this leather will eventually stretch and wear out. Make a habit of switching over the left and right stirrup leathers from time to time.**
- **Don't dismount by swinging one leg over the horse's withers. It could lead to a nasty accident if the horse moved suddenly.**
- **Don't dismount by keeping one foot in the stirrup iron unless there is a very good reason, such as a physical disability. In that case, never dismount unless there is someone to hold the horse's head. If the horse moved suddenly while you were still dismounting, you could have a fall and even be dragged by the horse.**

Dismounting

The usual way to dismount is from the left side although, as with mounting, it is useful to be able to do so from the offside, too. You may occasionally find yourself having to dismount in an awkward situation – say on a narrow path – where it is simply not possible to use the nearside.

To dismount from the near side, take the reins in your left hand; place this hand on the horse's neck and place your right hand on the pommel of the saddle. Take BOTH feet out of the stirrup irons. Lean forward and swing your right leg over the horse's back, taking care not to hit him. Land on both feet, bending your knees to absorb the impact.

To dismount from the offside, take the reins in your right hand, place this hand on the horse's neck and place your left hand on the pommel of the saddle. Take BOTH feet out of the stirrup irons. Lean forward and swing your left leg over the horse's back. Although you may see people doing it, it is not considered safe to dismount by leaving one foot in the stirrup until you have swung your other leg over the horse's back. The one exception is Western riding, where the design of the saddle makes it difficult to dismount in any other way. It is safest to have both feet free of the stirrups before you start your descent. Then if the horse made a sudden movement you would be less likely to fall with your foot caught in the stirrup.

THE RIDER'S SEAT

To ride effectively you need a balanced, supple and independent seat – that is, you must be able to apply the leg and rein aids independently of the movements of your upper body. Above all, you should never have to rely on the reins – and, therefore, the horse's mouth – to retain your balance. When you first learn to ride you will be taught the basic dressage seat, used for slow work on the flat. Later, when you learn to jump, you will adopt the forward or light seat. Should you eventually take up race-riding, you will need the jockey seat, which is like the forward seat but with even shorter stirrups and a more forward position. There are also different seats for different styles of saddle, for example the Western seat and the side-saddle seat.

If at first you don't succeed – don't despair! The experts, who make the correct seat look so easy, have been practising for years. Remember, every human being is a different shape and size and while some lucky people naturally have the long, lean look that seems "made" for riding, others may have short legs, fat hips or feet that stick out. There are also obvious differences between the sexes; men usually have flatter thighs than women, which gives them an advantage right from the start. If you don't have a natural seat immediately, don't give up – practice makes perfect, and there have been some very successful riders with less than ideal physiques.

Holding the Reins

The reins – one in each hand – should pass between your little finger and third finger, across the palm of your hand and lie over the top of your index finger, between the finger and your thumb. Your thumbs should be uppermost. Held in this way, the reins will not slip through your fingers.

How well you ride depends upon the way you sit in the saddle – the rider's seat is the basis of all good horsemanship.

The correct way to hold the reins. These "plaited" reins allow for more grip than plain ones.

The spare end of the reins should hang down beside the horse's withers and shoulder.

Contact

The weight you feel in your hands when you take up the reins is known as the contact. It should be constant: neither too heavy, nor too light. Because the horse's head and neck move as the rest of his body moves your hands and arms should try and match his movements. To maintain correct contact you must have supple wrists, elbows and shoulders.

Learning on the Lunge

One of the best ways of acquiring a balanced, independent seat is to ride on the lunge. This involves the horse moving in circles around the lunger, who controls the diameter of the circles by means of a long lunge-rein attached to a special noseband. A horse that has been taught to lunge will be used to circling at a regular pace and will obey the trainer's commands. Relieved of the necessity of controlling the horse, the novice pupil can thus concentrate solely on their position in the saddle.

With a good instructor to continually correct your mistakes, it is possible to make quick progress on the lunge. Lunge work can be done at walk, trot or canter and even over poles on the ground and small fences. It should always be practised on both reins, that is, on clockwise and anti-clockwise circles.

Riding without stirrups will help to develop a deep seat and there are a number of exercises which you can try, to help you to become more supple. These include shoulder-shrugging, lower back exercises, arm bending and stretching, leg swinging, ankle and leg rolling and bending down to touch your inside toe with your inside hand. Each exercise should be clearly explained by the instructor and practised first at the halt. Riding on the lunge is tiring, so do not try to achieve too much in one go.

The Basic Seat

- Sit in the deepest part of the saddle, with your weight evenly distributed on both seatbones and your muscles relaxed.

- Keep your hips square with those of the horse.

- Aim to keeep your upper body upright but relaxed; it should not be stiff.

- Keep your head erect; look straight ahead between the horse's ears.

- Avoid sticking your chin out or pulling it in too much: either extreme will affect the suppleness of your body.

- Place your thighs as close as possible to the saddle; turn them inwards slightly from the hips so that your knees lie comfortably against the saddle.

- Rest your calves against the horse's sides.

- Relaxed your leg muscles – there should be no tension or gripping, that will tend to lever you up out of the deepest part of the saddle.

- Your heels should be the lowest part of your feet, with your feet parallel to the horse's sides and the balls of your feet resting on the stirrup irons.

- Allow your arms to hang down freely from the shoulders and lie lightly against your body. Avoid clamping them against your sides, or turning your elbows out.

- Bend your forearms slightly inwards.

Seen from the side, (as in the diagram, left) a perpendicular line dropped from the ear to the ground should pass through the point of the shoulder, the elbow, the hip and the heel. It should be possible to draw a straight line from the elbow, down the forearm and hand, and along the rein to the horse's bit

THE HORSE'S PACES

All horses have four basic paces or gaits: the walk, the trot, the canter and the gallop.

The Walk

The walk is a four-time pace, that is, there are four beats to each stride. All four beats should be equally spaced. When riding at walk, you should be able to count a regular one-two-three-four, one-two-three-four. There is a great deal of truth in the old adage that the horse who walks well also gal-

lops well. The walk may seem a boring pace to ride, but it tells you a great deal about the horse. If he takes long strides and looks purposeful, he will almost certainly be athletic at the faster paces.

The walk steps should be regular and rhythmic. An uneven walk is a serious fault and indicates poor schooling. As a result the horse tenses up and is unable to use his muscles correctly.

TYPES OF WALK

MEDIUM WALK: the first pace experienced by the novice. The horse moves forward purposefully, with the rider maintaining a soft rein contact. The horse should over-track, that is, his hindfeet should step in front of the hoof prints made by his forefeet.

FREE WALK: the horse is given freedom from rein contact so that he can lower and stretch his head and neck. He should over-track. Free walk is used to allow the horse to rest and relax after a period of concentrated work.

COLLECTED WALK: the horse is asked to take as short steps as possible without slowing down. The walk must remain active. The hindfeet do not overtrack, but are set down no farther forward that the prints of the forefeet. The collected walk is used in the more advanced training of the horse and rider.

EXTENDED WALK: rather like the free walk but the rider retains light rein contact. The horse should stretch out, taking ground-covering strides but without any suggestion of hurrying. The extended walk is used in the more advanced training of the horse and rider.

The Trot

The trot is a two-time pace. The horse moves his legs in diagonal pairs: the off hind and near fore are raised together, followed by the near hind and the off fore, and so on. There is a moment of suspension as the horse springs from one diagonal to the other when all four feet are off the ground together. The footfalls should be even and regular; when riding at trot you should be able to count a rhythmic one-two, one-two, one-two. The horse should flex his hocks and bring them well under his body.

TYPES OF TROT

WORKING TROT: the horse takes regular, active but moderate length steps. His hindfeet should be set down roughly in the prints of his forefeet. This is the trot used in basic training.

MEDIUM TROT: the horse takes longer steps than in working trot but he should not speed up. His neck lengthens slightly and his hindfeet are set down in front of the prints of his forefeet.

COLLECTED TROT: by engaging his hindquarters more – that is, bringing them further underneath his body – the horse takes shorter, higher steps. His hindfeet are set down no further forward than the prints of his forefeet. The horse's outline changes: his head becomes higher and his body appears to be shorter and more upright. Despite the shorter steps, activity and impulsion should be maintained and the horse should not slow down.

EXTENDED TROT: the horse shows as much forward thrust as possible, moving with ground-covering strides and a lengthened outline. The hindfeet should be set down well in front of the prints of the forefeet.

The Canter

The canter is a three-time pace with a moment of suspension when all four feet are off the ground. The canter should be relaxed and the strides even and regular. The horse is said to lead with one or other of its forelegs, though, in fact, the pace begins from the hindlegs. When the horse is cantering on the near fore the sequence of footfalls is: off hind, near hind and off fore together, near fore. The moment of suspension comes after the near fore leaves the ground and before the off hind touches down again. When the horse is leading with his off fore, the sequence of footfalls is: near hind, off hind and near fore together, off fore followed by a moment of suspension.

TYPES OF CANTER

WORKING CANTER: a regular, active pace which should give you the feeling that you are riding uphill. The horse should cover approximately his own length with each stride. This is the canter used in basic training.

MEDIUM CANTER: the horse's strides are more springy and ground covering than in working canter and his outline more extended, but his rhythm

should not change. You should still have that uphill feeling.

COLLECTED CANTER: the horse takes shorter higher steps. Increased engagement of his hindquarters results in his neck becoming more raised and arched. Collected canter is used in more advanced training.

EXTENDED CANTER: the horse takes long strides, covering as much ground as possible without losing rhythm. His outline should lengthen. He should remain calm and light to ride.

The Gallop

The gallop is a four-time pace. With the near foreleg leading, the sequence of footfalls is: off hind, near hind, off fore, near fore, followed by a moment of suspension. With the off foreleg leading, the sequence is: near hind, off hind, near fore, off fore, followed by a moment of suspension. The horse's stride lengthens and quickens, though he should still maintain a regular rhythm. His outline lengthens considerably. As his strides become longer, so his back becomes lower.

Which Gait?

THE TÖLT (pronounced, terlt): a rapid four-time "running" movement in which the sequence of footfalls is near hind, near fore, off hind, off fore. The horse carries his head fairly high. The Iceland horse is a prime example of a breed which excels at the tölt, achieving tremendous speed even over rough ground. The tölt is surprisingly comfortable for the rider.

THE PACE: a two-time gait in which the horse moves his legs in lateral pairs, that is near hind and near fore together, followed by off hind and off fore together, with a moment of suspension in between. Some breeds, such as the American Standardbred, have a natural tendency to pace.

OPPOSITE: *Walk*.

FROM THE TOP: *Trot, canter, gallop.*

The gait can be encouraged by the use of special harness. Pacing Standardbred harness racehorses achieve speeds approaching those of galloping Thoroughbreds.

RIDING: THE BASIC TECHNIQUES

There is more to riding than simply sitting on a horse. The accomplished rider looks as if he is part of his horse.

At walk the rider must allow the hands to follow the horse's head and neck movements.

The Walk

You sit in exactly the same position at walk as you do at halt, except that you must allow your body to move slightly with the movement of the horse. Sit up tall, relax, and allow your hip joints and back to "go with the horse".

When you have your first lesson an assistant should lead the horse to begin with so that you can concentrate on your position and not have to worry about the brakes and steering. Once you have found your balance and become accustomed to the feel of the horse's movement, you can take up the reins. To hold your hands in the right place, imagine that you are reading a book – but avoid looking down, because this will affect your balance. Keep your head up and look ahead, between the horse's ears.

Remember that your shoulder and elbow joints should be "elastic" and move fluently, allowing your hands to follow the natural movements of the horse's head and neck. Your hands should never move up and down, only forward and back. Try to imagine that the horse is "taking" your hands with the reins. Allow them to follow him as if your elbows were on springs.

The Trot

There are two ways to ride at trot: rising or sitting. The novice rider begins by learning the rising trot, which is by far the easiest to master. When you first trot you will find the horse's movements much more bouncy than at walk – some horses are bouncier than others. Although it may seem difficult at first, raising and lowering your upper body in harmony with the horse's movements is an almost natural response – and it certainly takes out the bumpiness.

The aim is to rise out of the saddle slightly as one diagonal pair of legs touches the ground, and sink lightly back into the saddle as the other diagonal touches down. Rising in the saddle is rather like getting up out of a chair: you need to incline your body slightly forward from the hips in order to stay in balance. From sitting on your seat bones you switch to balancing, via your knees, on your feet. You must avoid tipping too far forward and also take care not to round your back. When your seat returns to the saddle it must do so softly – there should be no thumping down on to the poor horse's back. Your lower leg position remains the same as at halt: there should be a steady contact with the horse's sides.

As always, your hands should maintain a soft contact with the reins. You will find that there is less taking of the rein by the horse at trot than at walk because his head tends to move less.

Changing Diagonal

If your seat is in the saddle when the horse's near foreleg and off hindleg hit the ground, you are said to be riding on the left diagonal. You are riding on the right diagonal if your seat returns to the saddle when the off foreleg and near hindleg touch down. It is important to change the diagonal regularly so that the horse's muscles and legs on each side do an equal amount of work. Continually riding on one diagonal puts undue strain on one pair of legs and leads to over-development of one set of back muscles. To "change the diagonal", as it is known, you usually sit in the saddle (though you can stay with your seat out of it instead) for an extra beat before resuming rising trot. If you find this difficult to begin with, sit for several beats (you must count an even number, otherwise you will end up back on the same diagonal). To know which diagonal you are on, you may find it necessary, to begin with, to glance down to check which foreleg is hitting the ground as you return to the saddle. With practice you will be able to feel the diagonal. Feeling what the horse's body is doing beneath you is a major part of good horsemanship.

The Sitting Trot

The sitting trot, in which your seat remains in constant contact with the saddle, is more difficult to master than rising trot and must be learnt in easy stages. Most beginners find it hard because they become too tense and attempt to hold themselves in the saddle with their knees and thighs, or even with their lower legs. The art, as always, is to relax, but no one can pretend that it is easy to maintain the necessary elasticity of the pelvis, hip joints and thighs

and the "soft" lower back. You will find it easier to master if you can ride a horse with a smooth trotting action rather than a very energetic one.

The Canter

The canter is a smoother pace than the trot and therefore easier for the novice rider to master.

Your body should remain upright. There must be no "collapsing' at the waist or rounding of your back. You should go with the horse's movement from your hips, at the same time keeping your upper body as still as possible. Your seat should remain in the saddle – there should be no bouncing up and down. Bouncing in the saddle, a common fault, is the result of stiffening of the hips. If the horse is leading with his near foreleg, your left hip should be slightly in front of your right one and vice versa if the horse is leading with his off fore. Note, however, that your outside shoulder – that is the one opposite to the leading foreleg – should not get "left behind". As with the walk, you must maintain a steady contact with the reins, your hands and elbows following the movement of the horse's head.

One of the most common mistakes in canter is to stiffen the leg muscles and try to grip with the lower legs. If you do, you will start bouncing in the saddle. Concentrate on staying relaxed. Allow your legs to lie softly against the horse's sides.

TOP: *An experienced rider showing a perfect leg position at trot.*

ABOVE: *The correct relaxed, upright position at canter. Note the steady contact with the reins.*

Trotting Tips

- **In the beginning try mentally counting "one-two, one-two", or saying "up-down, up-down" as you attempt to synchronize your movements with those of the horse.**
- **Have someone lead the horse at first and use a neck-strap (fitted round the horse's lower neck) so that you can catch hold of it if you lose your balance.**
- **Never try to pull yourself out of the saddle when rising to the trot: let the horse's movement "push" you up.**
- **Keep your feet directly underneath you – swinging your lower leg backwards or forwards will adversely affect your balance.**

Stopping a Galloping Horse

If you have difficulty stopping a galloping horse, try shortening one rein and bracing that hand against his neck. With the other hand make a series of firm but short checks: check-release, check-release, check-release. One long, dead pull on the reins of a hard-pulling horse will get you nowhere – he will outpull you every time.

Galloping

The faster the horse goes, the further forward his centre of gravity. To stay in balance with him, the rider must adopt a more forward position. At a gallop your upper body should be inclined forward and your seat lifted out of the saddle. You will need to shorten your stirrup leathers to achieve the correct position. Your lower leg should remain directly under you, in the same position as for the other paces. Your hands should be on either side of the horse's neck and you should maintain a steady contact with his mouth. Good balance is the key to riding at the gallop. You should feel as if your weight is pulling down via your lower leg into your heel. You must not use the reins to help you and there must be no bumping up and down in the saddle.

The Halt

To perform a good halt is not as straightfoward as it might seem. Yes, you can simply haul on the reins and the horse may well stop, if only to escape the discomfort. But this type of halt is about as artistic as an emergency stop in a car. In all probability the horse will skew to one side or the other. To halt correctly – that is, with the horse in balance, standing squarely, perfectly still and attentive to you – requires the same combination of leg and rein aids used in other downward transitions. To obtain halt, you should drive the horse forward with your legs and weight into a non-yielding hand. This must be a momentary action only and when the horse obeys, you must yield with your hands immediately. If the horse steps backwards after halting, it will probably be because you have failed to yield the reins quickly enough. The more experienced rider prepares the horse for the halt by first performing one or more half-halts to shift his weight back. Eventually it is possible, on a correctly schooled horse, to halt directly from trot and even from canter. These movements are often required in dressage tests.

Common Seat Mistakes

THE FORK SEAT

If you sit with too much weight on your thighs and groin, it is known as the fork seat. Your weight comes off your seat bones, your lower legs move back and your back will probably be hollowed. Sitting in this way you will find it impossible to go with the movement of the horse and you will bounce up and down when cantering. It will also be difficult for you to hold your hands in the correct position. The fork seat is often the result of riding with stirrups that are too long; or it may be caused by riding on a saddle on which the deepest point is too far forward.

THE CHAIR SEAT

The chair seat is usually caused by riding with the stirrups too short, which forces you to sit too far back toward the cantle instead of in the deepest part of the saddle. It may also be the result of habitually riding in a jumping saddle, which is designed to be ridden in the forward seat and not for doing flatwork. You will find it difficult to go with the movement of the horse and to use your hands independently. Your lower leg will be too far forward and you will tend to sit hunched up, with your head forward instead of erect.

Exercise Time

Mounted exercises can be fun and are a great way of improving your balance, strengthing your muscles, improving your co-ordination and helping you to relax in the saddle. They can be done during a group lesson or on the lunge. Here are some of the most popular ones:

ANKLE ROLLING

Without stirrups, roll your toes inwards towards the horse in a big circle.

LEG SWINGING

Without stirrups, swing your lower legs forward and backward alternately – as if you were walking. Avoid kicking the horse.

HEAD ROLLING

Rotate your head in a circle, first one way then the other.

SHOULDER ROLLING

Shrug your shoulders and roll them backwards.

ARM CIRCLING

Hold the reins in one hand. Allow your other arm to hang down by your side, then raise it forward, up and back in a large circle.

TOE TOUCHING

Hold the reins in one hand. Bend down and touch your toe with the other hand.

To improve your co-ordination, try doing two of the exercises at the same time, for example, ankle rolling and arm circling.

Agility Exercises

There are some good exercises designed to improve the rider's agility, but as they are performed without reins or stirrups they should only be attempted on a very quiet horse, with an assistant to hold his head.

HALF DISMOUNT

Raise your right leg and bring it over the horse's neck so that your foot is alongside his shoulder – stay facing forward. With your left hand on the front of the saddle and your right hand on the back, roll on to your stomach, sliding your right leg underneath your left leg as you do so. Straighten your arms to take your weight and then swing your right leg over the horse and so end up back in the saddle. Repeat the exercise the other way round, starting with taking your left leg over the horse's neck.

ROUND THE WORLD

Raise your right leg and bring it over the horse's neck until you are sitting at right angles to the horse. Swing your left leg over the horse's hindquarters

OPPOSITE: *The correct forward position at the gallop. This rider would be safer wearing boots with smooth soles.*

ABOVE, TOP: *Toe-touching is an excellent suppling exercise. Practise on both sides!*

ABOVE: *Arm swinging is another useful exercise to perform while mounted, provided the horse or pony is quiet.*

and sit facing his tail. Swing your right leg over his quarters until you are sitting at right angles to the horse on the off side. Finally, raise your left leg and bring it over the horse's neck to end up back in the saddle, facing forward. To perform this in the opposite direction, take your left leg over the horse's neck, sit at right angles to the horse on his off side, swing your right leg over his quarters and so on.

Some people are "naturals" when it comes to learning to ride, making swift progress with never a backward glance. Others take much longer to master each new step. Sometimes it is one particular skill which proves a stumbling block. It may be the rising trot, or the forward jumping seat, or you might have some positional fault which you find hard to overcome. Additionally, it does not help that many horses and ponies have gaps in their education which make it impossible for the novice rider to communicate with them successfully.

It is intensely disheartening to feel that you are not making progress. This is why it is essential for the beginner to choose a good riding school with well-schooled horses and qualified instructors who will quickly spot the underlying cause of your problems and help you to sort them out.

The Rising Trot

Mastering the rising trot is child's play to some people, purgatory to others. It is a common mistake for beginners to rise much too far out of the saddle, so that one moment they are literally standing up in their stirrups, and the next they are banging down heavily on to the poor horse's back.

If you have this problem, first make sure that it is not the horse who is causing your difficulties. Some horses do have a very bouncy movement at the trot which can throw the beginner too high out of the saddle with each stride. Those with less than perfect forelimbs and straight shoulders may give you a particularly uncomfortable, jarring ride, causing you to bounce about.

There is also the problem of horses being naturally one-sided, which can make trotting on one diagonal infinitely more uncomfortable than trotting on the other. This is why it is so important to work horses regularly on their stiff side to help supple them up and make them a more comfortable ride. If you find that you are all over the place at rising trot, ask to ride a really well-schooled horse with smooth paces and you may find that the problem is solved at once. If you can once get the feel of the movement on a comfortable horse, you will never look back.

If you continue to have problems, remember to

PROBLEM SOLVING

Learning to ride involves so many different skills there are bound to be times when you find things difficult. Don't despair, there is always a solution!

count "one-two one-two" in rhythm with the horse's feet and above all try to relax. Stiffening up and hunching your shoulders is a natural response to feeling insecure, but it will make you bounce about even more. The more relaxed you are and the closer and quieter your legs lie against the horse's sides, the easier it will be for you to get into the rhythm of the movement. Make sure that your stirrups are the right length – neither too long, nor too short.

A good position at rising trot. Note the straight line from the rider's elbow, through the hand and rein to the horse's mouth.

When you ride the rising trot correctly, it should feel as if it is the movement of the horse which is raising your seat slightly out of the saddle, not you consciously hauling yourself upwards. Incline your body forward slightly without tipping forward and try to go with the movement. Avoid rounding your back. Keep your head up and look ahead.

Sitting Trot

Like the rising trot, the sitting trot is easier to master on a smooth, well-schooled horse. Check that your stirrups are not too short. Count in time to the trot and try to concentrate on allowing each of your seatbones to move forward slightly as each corresponding hindleg comes under the horse. Trotting without stirrups will help you to get the feel of the horse's movement.

Bouncing at Canter

The rocking movement of the canter should be comfortable to sit to, but many novice riders find it difficult to keep their seat in the saddle and end up bouncing about. Stiffness in the hips and back is the main cause. Concentrate on sitting tall, but relaxed, in the saddle and try to move with the horse's movement. Imagine that you are sitting on a rocking horse and let your hips and back absorb the movement. It will feel as though you are swinging backwards and forwards, but when you ride at canter correctly, your shoulders will actually remain still. Remember to take deep breaths to help you to relax. Avoid leaning forward or gripping with your knees and lower legs. Lessons on the lunge will help you to develop a deep, secure seat.

Common Problems

LOOKING DOWN

Because your head is so heavy, how you carry it has a great bearing on both your balance and that of the horse. Unfortunately for some people looking down at the horse or at the ground seems to be second nature. It is a habit which must be eradicated, as it causes all sorts of other problems and prevents you riding well.

TOP: *Looking down and tipping too far forward at trot cause the lower leg to swing back.*

CENTRE: *At canter the rider must absorb the horse's movement through their hips and back rather than through the knee.*

BOTTOM: *Poor position at trot: the rider is leaning forward and gripping with her legs.*

Looking down tends to make you move your shoulders forward, which in turn affects the position of your hands. If your shoulders come forward you will tend to slouch, and slouching leads to gripping upwards with your legs.

If you habitually look down – even if you are not aware of it, your instructor will tell you – every now and again take a moment to consciously focus straight ahead at the horizon. Note when you do, how you immediately feel taller in the saddle, how your legs feel more relaxed, and how much more in balance you are with the horse.

Looking ahead should make you feel more alert, more in command, less introspective. Looking down can be a difficult habit to cure, but it is important that you do cure it, so persevere!

GRIPPING WITH YOUR LEGS

When you feel insecure in the saddle it is a natural reaction to clamp your knees against it in an effort to keep your balance. But in fact, gripping tightly makes you less secure because you will tense up, your legs will tend to come up instead of hanging softly on either side of the horse, and you will end up sitting perched on top of the saddle rather than sitting deeply in it. The best way to cure this particular problem is to ride without stirrups, preferably on the lunge.

ROUNDING YOUR BACK

Riding with a rounded back is neither attractive nor effective. You will, in all probability, end up gripping with your knees and perching on top of the saddle, and you will be unable to use your legs and arms correctly. If you know that you tend to slouch, concentrate on sitting tall in the saddle, with you head up and your eyes looking straight ahead. You should feel the difference immediately and with your weight in better balance, the horse should go more sweetly for you. Make sure your posture is good when you are not riding, too.

COLLAPSING YOUR HIPS
OR SHOULDERS

Riding lop-sidedly, with one hip or shoulder "collapsed", is a common fault and although you may not be aware that you are doing it, it will be

Avoid rounding your back: it makes it impossible for you to sit in the right position.

quickly spotted by anyone on the ground. It is a habit that must be broken because it puts an uneven weight distribution on the horse for which he will have to compensate. It also puts strain on other parts of your anatomy and on the saddle. Lessons on the lunge will help to correct the problem as will practising good posture when you are off a horse.

Remember that collapsing one hip is not the same as putting more weight on one seatbone.

HEAVY HANDS

Arguably the greatest gift any horseman can have is good hands. Hands which maintain a light, yielding contact with the horse's mouth enable the rider to convey the rein aids with subtlety – there should never be any pulling back on the reins. Correctly positioned, your knuckles should be vertical to the ground and at a height which enables you to maintain a straight line from your elbow, down your forearm and down the reins to the horse' mouth. Your thumbs should be slightly bent and should press down lightly on the reins. Your fingers should be closed.

HANDS FACING DOWNWARDS

If you ride with the backs of your hands uppermost, it is impossible to give subtle rein aids by using your wrists. You will have to use the whole of your arm, and probably move your body as well.

STIFF WRISTS

Any stiffening of your wrists makes it impossible for your hands to maintain an elastic contact with the horse's mouth.

WRISTS TURNED INWARDS

Riding with your wrists turned inwards produces a hard, unyielding contact with the horse's mouth.

FINGERS NOT CLOSED
ON THE REINS

If you fail to close your fingers on the reins and allow your third finger to be pulled forward, your reins will become longer and longer and you may end up having to move your hands back towards

LEFT: *Incorrect hand position: downward-facing hands make it impossible for the rider to give subtle rein aids.*

ABOVE, TOP: *The wrong way to hold the reins!*

ABOVE, BOTTOM: *Stiff, inward-turned wrists prevent an elastic contact with the horse's mouth.*

your stomach to maintain the correct contact or to apply the aids.

CROSSING YOUR REINS

Crossing one hand over the other is a bad fault since it constricts the horse's neck and may make him tilt his head. Holding your hands in this way leads to incorrect action of the bit and will confuse the horse.

WRONG LENGTH OF REIN

Riding with your reins too long or too short makes it impossible to give the rein aids correctly and will seriously affect your position in the saddle.

STIFFNESS

Stiffness of any kind will make it difficult for you to ride well and will cause your horse to stiffen up, too, as he tries to compensate for the discomfort of carrying a tense rider. You may need to do appropriate suppling exercises off the horse before you ride and once in the saddle you must remember to breath correctly and try to relax.

Stiffening up because you are nervous – or downright frightened – is a different matter. Horses are highly intuitive and will quickly sense if you are scared. Depending on their character, they may respond either by becoming jittery themselves or by taking advantage of you. If you are determined

that you want to ride, in spite of certain nervous reservations, it is imperative to recognize your limitations from the outside and to find a sympathetic instructor. Private lessons will help, and be prepared to discuss your problems with the instructor. They will be in a better position to help if they understand what is troubling you. A steady "schoolmaster" horse who is willing but quiet and unflappable is the best mount for the nervous rider.

If your nervousness stems from having had an accident – say a fall while jumping – never be afraid to ask your instructor if you can to go back to basics in order to restore your dented confidence.

The horse, like any other domesticated animal, has to be "educated" before he can understand what we want him to do. Our various means of communication are known as the aids, and during training the horse is taught to respond to two distinct types. They are known as the natural aids and the auxiliary aids. To ride effectively you need to learn how to apply all of these aids.

It is essential for the novice rider to learn on a horse who has been well schooled, one who will come up with the correct response when you make the correct request. It seems complicated at first, but it is an eminently simple and effective way of conversing with the horse once you know how. Our task is made simpler thanks to the horse's sensitivity to touch. When an experienced horseman rides a well-schooled horse, the aids are often so subtle that it is impossible for the observer to detect them.

THE NATURAL AIDS

A series of centuries-old, tried and tested "messages" enable the rider to communicate his wishes to the horse. They are called the aids.

The Natural Aids

THE LEGS

Put simply, the legs are used to drive the horse forward and to control sideways movement. At all paces your legs should lie softly against the horse's sides, enabling you to keep in constant communication with him. You must have a balanced, secure seat if you are to have complete control over your lower leg movements, hence the importance of getting the seat right first.

To ask the horse to walk on from halt, you

The lower leg is used on or behind the girth to control forward or sideways movement.

simply nudge him gently slightly behind the girth with the inside of your leg, just above the ankle. Use both legs simultaneously. When the horse responds, stop using your legs – never keep your legs clamped to the horse's sides.

To go into trot, use the same aid just a fraction more strongly. Do not resort to kicking. The readiness with which a horse responds to the aids depends on how effectively you apply them, and also of course on his level of training. And you have to make allowance sometimes for his mood. A fit horse who is raring to gallop across country may not feel much like concentrating on the finer points of a dressage test and it can sometimes be hard work to get his full attention. A horse who has spent years carrying inept beginners in a riding school may be less than responsive.

To apply the aids for canter, you must first go into sitting trot. If you are working in the school on, say, the right rein (that is, you are travelling in a clockwise direction), you will want the horse to canter with his off foreleg leading. To do this, use your inside (right) leg ON the girth and your outside (left) leg BEHIND the girth. You must at the same time apply the correct hand aids.

To ask the horse to strike off on his near foreleg, use your inside (left) leg ON the girth and your outside (right) leg BEHIND the girth.

THE REINS

Normally the hands follow the movement of the horse's head and neck. It is by ceasing this action that you indicate to the horse that you wish him to slow down or halt. The reins are also used to help control direction. The rein aids should be applied by squeezing your fingers, never by a backward pull, and they should be applied briefly. Always keep a steady contact, briefly increase it, then immediately decrease it again.

The rein aids should never be used on their own, but always in conjunction with the leg aids. To ask the horse to canter on, say, the right leg, you use

Remember ...

The weight and leg aids are the most important aids. When riding a correctly schooled horse the rein aids are used the least.

The terms "inside" and "outside", as in "inside leg" or "outside rein", always refer to the inside and outside of the bend of the horse. For example, if the horse is circling to the right, your right leg is your inside leg, your left leg is your outside leg.

the right rein to flex the horse to the right. At the same time, the left rein is used to regulate the amount of flexion and to control the speed, and the leg aids are given as above. As soon as the horse strikes off into canter, your hands, particularly the inside (right) one, should yield slightly. The rein aids are reversed for cantering on the left leg.

THE BODY OR WEIGHT

The weight aids are essentially forward-driving aids. The horse feels the influence of your seat at every stride and you can influence him in three distinct ways through your body: by increasing the weight on both seat bones; by increasing the weight on one seat bone; by easing the weight on the seat bones.

The weight aids have tremendous influence on the horse (particularly at the top level of dressage),

but, because they are more subtle and less noticeable than the other aids, it can be more difficult for a trainer on the ground to assess how well or otherwise you are using them.

Increasing the weight on both seat bones increases the activity of the horse's hindlegs. It encourages the horse to step further under his body with his hindlegs, thus putting more of his weight on to them. It is used in the halt and in transitions (changes from one pace to another). To increase the weight, you should stretch your body upwards and tighten your back and buttock muscles. This muscle tightening should be momentary, not continuous. If necessary, it can be repeated for several strides.

Increasing the weight on one seat bone is used as an adjunct to the leg and rein aids in movements

Cantering on the left lead. The rider's inside hand flexes the horse to the left.

where the horse is flexed or bent. A well-schooled horse interprets this as a request to turn. When increasing the weight on, say, the left seat bone, your left hip will be lowered slightly (but you must not lean over or "collapse" your hip) and there will be more weight on your left stirrup. Your body must remain upright.

Easing the weight on the seat bones does not mean raising your seat out of the saddle. It involves putting more of your weight on to your thighs and stirrups, with only a slight forward incline of your body. The experienced rider will ride like this when loosening up a horse or to ease the weight on a young horse's back during training.

THE AUXILIARY AIDS

To reinforce the natural aids, the competent rider makes use of the schooling whip and spurs, as well as the voice.

The Voice

Of all the aids the voice is the one most often used. We speak to horses from the day they are born: in the field, in the stable, during a quiet hack in the countryside, when we are training them and while competing (though not in competitive dressage, where audible use of the voice is not permitted). Horses are particularly receptive to voice tone and they soon learn to obey important commands such as "w-a-l-k", "t-r-o-t" or "move over". They instinctively know the difference between a friendly voice and an unkind one. Used correctly, the voice gives the horse confidence. It is indispensible when training the young horse.

The correct way to carry a schooling whip. It is used behind the rider's lower leg to reinforce the leg aids.

The Whip

The whip is used primarily to reinforce the leg aids. Only rarely should it be used to correct a deliberate disobedience and even then the rider must be very sure that it IS the horse – and not himself – who is at fault. Never use your whip in impatience or anger.

There are two main types of riding whip, the long dressage whip and the short stick used in other activities such as jumping. The long dressage whip should never be used to punish a horse as it would have a cutting effect. The short stick used for jumping should have a broad piece of leather at the end which, when used as a means of correction (perhaps if the horse refuses) will sting but not harm the horse. In racing, special cushioned whips are being used more and more to protect the horses.

You should learn to carry a whip as soon as you can handle the reins confidently, but until you are really proficient in the saddle it is best to use a short one so that there is no possibility of your hitting the horse by mistake. With a short stick, if you do need to use it behind your lower leg to reinforce your leg aids, you should hold the reins in one hand and use the stick in the other. If you try to use the stick while still holding the reins, you may give the horse a painful jab in the mouth.

On the rare occasion that you have just cause to reprimand the horse for naughtiness, you must do so instantly, otherwise he will not associate the punishment with the crime.

When you are more experienced you should carry a dressage whip for work on the flat. This is long enough to enable you to touch the horse just behind your lower leg without the necessity of taking your hand off the rein. There should be no disturbance to the horse's mouth and care must be taken not to flick the horse on the flank or high up behind the saddle. Such a move is unlikely to have the desired effect. It will simply make him tense up.

The schooling whip, like the leg aids, should be used in time with the horse's movement. Any length of whip can be used to tap the horse down the shoulder as a means of controlling sideways movement. The well-trained horse will respect the whip, but not be frightened of it. If you come across a horse who is evidently scared when he sees you carrying a whip, then you can be sure that

he has had an unpleasant experience. It will take time and patience to regain his confidence.

Holding a Whip

The whip should be held between your thumb and index finger and should lie across your palm and rest across your thigh. For safety, always hold your whip close to its top. If the whip pokes up above your hand, it could cause injury should your horse suddenly spook. Choose a whip with a knob at the top - they are easier to hold. And get into the habit of riding with it in either hand.

Changing your Whip Hand

Practise changing your whip from one hand to the other so that in an emergency you can do it quickly and efficiently without scaring the horse. With a short stick, hold your reins in the same hand as your stick, then take hold of the top of the stick with your free hand, pull it through your other hand, pass it over the horse's withers and take up the reins in two hands again. A dressage whip may be too long to be pulled through neatly in this manner. In that case, you should rotate it in an arc over your hands from one side to another. To change it from your left hand to your

Spurs enable the experienced horseman to use the leg aids with more finesse. They should <u>never</u> be used by the novice rider.

right, for example, first hold both reins and the whip in your left hand. Pass your right hand over your left hand and take hold of the whip, immediately below your left hand, using your thumb and index finger (your right thumb must be next to the little finger of your left hand). Then release the whip from your left hand and rotate it up and over the horse's withers.

Spurs

Spurs are used to reinforce the leg aids. They enable the accomplished rider to apply the leg aids with rather more finesse. They are made of metal and must be carefully fitted so as not to cause injury. Rowels (spiked wheels) should not be used. The shanks of the spurs must be smooth. They should face directly to the rear and should have a downward curve. Very long spurs should not be worn.

In most competitive sports the rules specify a maximum permitted length of about 1¼ in (3cm). Excessive use of the spurs is penalized. Spurs should only be worn by a rider who has acquired a truly independent seat and legs. They are, therefore, not suitable for the novice.

TRANSITIONS

Transitions are rather like changing gear in a car: the aim is to execute each one as smoothly as possible.

The half-halt is a subtle but invaluable means of preparing the horse to do something different.

Transition Tips

To begin with you will find it easier to do canter transitions on a circle or when approaching a corner of the school. This increases the engagement of the horse's inside hindleg and so makes him balance himself more efficiently.

To see how a horse shifts his weight back on to his hindquarters, try recording a steeplechase on video. Look for a riderless horse who continues to jump alongside his rivals. Watch in slow motion and see how he shifts his weight back in the stride just before he takes off. Horses know instinctively all about the half-halt!

A change of pace is called a transition. There are upward transitions – such as a change from trot to canter – and downward transitions – such as a change from trot to walk. There are also transitions within the paces. For example, when you change from collected trot to extended trot, that is an upward transition.

Transitions are rather like changing gear in a car: the aim is to execute each one as smoothly as possible, so that one movement flows into the next with no jerky movements, no loss of balance, rhythm or tempo.

The key to good transitions is preparation. Before making an upward transition, you must ensure that the horse is going forward with plenty of impulsion so that when you implement the aids for the next pace, the horse's forward impulsion continues. Downward transitions are more difficult to execute well than upward. You must first ensure that the horse's hindlegs are well underneath him, otherwise he will fall out of balance when you ask him to change pace.

Although the temptation is to haul on the reins, the rein aids should in fact be used sparingly: it is primarily the action of the seat and legs which control transitions.

Performing Good Upward Transitions

- Never ask for an upward transition until you are satisfied that the horse is moving forward actively, is in balance, and is listening to you.
- For halt to walk: nudge the horse forward with both your legs in the region of the girth.
- For walk to trot: nudge the horse forward with both legs, using a slightly stronger aid than for halt to walk. At the same time shorten your reins slightly.
- Never fix your hands – allow them to follow the horse's movement.
- Never "drop the reins" – allow them to hang in loops, with no contact with the horse's mouth.
- Never "nag" at him with your legs. If he does not respond quickly to your leg aids, it is better to reinforce them with a light tap of your whip behind your leg. Constantly nagging with your legs will eventually deaden his responses.

TROT TO CANTER (ON THE RIGHT LEG)

- Make sure that the horse is trotting actively and in good balance before asking for canter.
- Place more weight on your inside (right) seatbone.
- Push the horse forward with your inside leg on the girth.
- Flex the horse slightly to the right by "asking" him

with your right rein; you should to be able just to see his right eye.

- Use your outside (left) rein to control the amount of flexion.
- Use your outside (left) leg behind the girth to control the direction of the horse's left hindleg.
- Immediately the horse strikes off into canter, yield slightly with your hands. Reverse the leg/rein aids to strike off on the left lead.

Performing Good Downward Transitions

TROT TO WALK

- For trot to walk, close your legs against the horse's sides and ride forward from your seat without allowing the horse to change his rhythm.
- Keep your hands quiet to "receive" the energy produced by your leg and seat aids.
- For a brief moment, take a stronger contact with the reins. Yield with your hands immediately the horse walks.
- If the horse does not respond at once, do not resort to pulling on the reins. Simply start again, repeating the whole sequence of aids. Fixing your hands will merely cause the horse to stiffen his back and adopt a shufflling, jogging gait.

CANTER TO TROT

- Make sure the canter is energetic.
- When you feel that the horse is really well balanced, relax your seat muscles and squeeze slightly with the reins.
- Keep your body relaxed and supple and ready to take up the rhythm of the trot immediately.
- Always squeeze and yield with your reins — never take a dead pull.

The Half-Halt

The half-halt is an invaluable preparatory aid used to warn the horse that you are about to ask him to do something different. In fact, the name is rather misleading for it is not so much a stopping action as a split-second gathering together of power. It can be compared with that momentary stillness seen when a human is about to throw a ball or lift a heavy weight, as they gather their strength and steady their balance before channelling all their efforts into the throw or the lift.

In the horse's case it involves asking him to transfer more of his weight on to his hindquarters by bending his hindleg joints. With his weight thus adjusted and his outline rounder and less elongated,

ABOVE, LEFT: *Medium trot. To make upward and downward transitions within a pace requires the same preparation as for changing from one pace to another.*

ABOVE, RIGHT: *The transition from trot to canter, with the right leg leading.*

he is better able to change pace or speed smoothly and without losing his balance.

The aids for the half-halt are the same as those for downward transitions. You use both legs and your seat to send the horse forwards, at the same time "containing" his forward movement with the reins. You will feel the extra weight in your hands, which should momentarily stop following his head movement. The well-trained horse will respond immediately by shifting his weight back.

With practice, you will learn to recognize this response — your reply must be to yield your hands instantly. The half-halt is used when preparing for a transition from one pace to another and when asking the horse to shorten or lengthen his stride within a pace. Repeated half-halts are also a good way of calming an excitable horse. Because it is — or should be — such a subtle movement, it is wellnigh impossible for the beginner to master it on an unschooled horse.

TURNS AND CIRCLES

Like human athletes, horses need to do regular exercises to become and stay supple and fit.

Strange as it may seem to the uninitiated, pulling on one rein is not the way to make a horse turn in that direction. The horse will bend his neck if you pull hard enough because he cannot avoid it, but his legs, and therefore his body, will in all probability continue going forward.

To ride a turn successfully you need to use rein and leg aids in unison. When you are more proficient you will be able to influence the horse by using your weight as well. To understand how to ride turns and circles effectively you need to understand the terms "bend" and "flexion".

When a horse turns correctly he appears to be bent uniformly throughout the whole length of his spine. In reality, it is impossible for the horse to bend his body to the same extent in every part from his ears to his tail, because of the different degrees of flexibility in the different groups of vertebrae. The horse's neck is reasonably flexible, his tail more so, but his body is capable of much less lateral movement. Indeed, the five sacral vertebrae

Ridden correctly, the horse bends round the rider's inside leg when taking a corner.

– beneath the loins, in the region of the croup – are fused firmly together, making lateral movement virtually impossible in that region. When turning, if the horse is to remain in balance, you must avoid asking him for too much bend in the neck. You must exploit what flexibility he has in his body, prevent his hindquarters from swinging out to the side, and ask him to flex his neck.

The horse is "flexed" when his head is turned sideways from the poll – the joint between his head and neck. He can be flexed without being bent – but he cannot bend without flexion. Flexion is an important element of the horse's training, making him soft and flexible through his poll. It helps to make him more obedient to the sideways-acting element of the rein aids.

To Obtain Flexion

Sit with your weight evenly on both seatbones. Keeping a constant contact on the reins, yield with

---

Perfect Circles

To ride an accurate circle – rather than an egg – imagine you are riding a diamond shape but heading for the next "point" before you reach the previous one.

*Circle at canter: the rider's outside hand controls the pace, and
the outside leg controls the hindquarters.*

the outside one and shorten the inside one by the
same amount. Avoid over-pulling with the inside
rein. When the horse is correctly flexed you
should just be able to see his inside eye and nostril.
His crest – the top line of his neck – will "flip over"
to the side on which he is flexed. If you overdo
your aids, the horse's weight will shift on to his
outside shoulder and he will lose rhythm.

To Obtain Bend

Flex the horse in the direction you wish to go. Use
your inside leg on the girth and your outside leg
behind the girth, to prevent his hindquarters from
swinging out to the side. Put a little more weight
on to your inside seatbone.

Corners and Circles

Like humans, horses tend to be "one-sided". With
horses, one-sidedness manifests itself as stiffness on
one side of the body. Working the horse on circles
and elements of circles will help to make his stiff
side supple by building up the muscles until they are
as well-developed as the muscles on his other side.
When schooling, always work the horse on his
"good" side first.

To learn how to ride circles correctly, begin by
practising turns at the corners of the school. Start
in walk to get the feel of applying the aids, then
progress to trot and finally to canter. Keep your
shoulders parallel to the horse's shoulders – your
outside shoulder should not swing back. Although
your weight should be a little more on your inside
seatbone, you must not lean inwards.

Ridden correctly, the horse will bend "round
your inside leg" and will maintain the same pace as
during the approach to the corner. The well-trained

horse can be ridden deeply into the corner – in
other words, if he were being ridden on a circle, it
would be a small one. However, the novice rider
should not attempt such tight turns to begin with.
Once you can ride corners competently you can try
large complete circles, no smaller than 20 m (66 ft)
in diameter.

Begin at a good active rising trot before
attempting canter. Remember that the horse
should bend round your inside leg and that his
pace should not slacken. Your inside hand governs
flexion and direction, your outside hand controls
the pace. Your inside leg is on the girth, creating
impulsion, your outside leg is behind the girth, control the hindquarters.

Serpentines

Start at one end of the school and ride three equal-
sized loops, finishing at the other end. Because this
makes the horse bend to each side alternately it is
an excellent schooling exercise. Practise it first at
walk, and then at trot. When you want to change
direction, allow him to go straight for a stride or
two before applying the aids to turn the other way.
When your horse is really supple he can be asked
to do more than three loops, which will make the
turns tighter. The horse can either be straight – that
is parallel to the ends of the school – when he
crosses the central line, or you can make the loops
pear-shaped.

ADVANCED MOVEMENTS

As you become more proficient in the saddle, you can try these more complicated exercises.

Counter-Canter

The horse is said to be performing counter-canter when he turns or circles with the "wrong" foreleg leading. For example, if he is leading with his left foreleg but circling to the right, that is counter-canter. The horse can be taught to do this on request, though not before he has learned to canter on a specific leg and is well balanced and able to achieve some collection. Counter-canter is a useful exercise since it increases the horse's suppleness, balance and obedience to the aids. The movement is required in some dressage tests.

PERFORMING COUNTER-CANTER TO THE RIGHT

- Cantering on the left leg, ensure that the horse is in balance and has some degree of collection.
- As you go along the long side of the school, ride a "loop" away from the wall and back again.
- As you loop back towards the wall (that is, to the right), ensure that the horse stays on the "wrong" (left) lead by keeping your inside (left) leg on his girth, your outside leg behind the girth and your weight on your inside seatbone.
- Keep the horse bent in the direction of his leading (left) leg.
- Ride shallow loops to begin with, then deeper ones.
- When you can ride loops successfully and without the horse falling out of balance, try a large circle.
- Reverse the process for counter-canter to the left (that is, with the right leg leading).

Remember...

In counter-canter, the "inside" refers to the side of the leading leg, even though the horse is travelling in the opposite direction.

The Rein-Back

Being able to "reverse" efficiently can be extremely useful, but it is not the easiest movement to perform on a horse. To rein back well the horse must be supple and have good balance. He should move backwards in a straight line, with clearly defined steps, moving his near hind and off forelegs together, and his off hind and near forelegs together (ie, in diagonal pairs). He should pick his feet up cleanly from the ground and take equal length strides. There should be no shuffling or sudden rushing backwards. The horse should remain calm. He should not raise his head, or hollow his back. He should be listening to you and ready to move forward again the instant you ask him.

Before attempting the rein-back, ensure that the horse is standing straight and squarely.

- With your legs, ask the horse to move forward but keep a feel on the reins rather than yielding them.

- Remain upright in the saddle.
- Keep your hips and back supple.
- As soon as the horse responds by starting to move backward, lessen the feel on the reins, without dropping the contact.
- As soon as the horse has performed the desired number of steps, ask him to move forward.

Turn on the Forehand

As the name suggests, this involves the horse moving his hindquarters around his forehand (his front end). One hindleg crosses in front of the other as he turns his quarters away from the direction in which he is flexed, pivoting round his inside foreleg. He makes a half-circle (ie, he turns through 180 degrees). It is an exercise which encourages the horse to move away from your leg. It also helps teach the rider to use the aids independently and to stay in balance when the horse takes lateral steps.

LEFT: Shoulder-in. The horse's forelegs come off the track, his hindlegs remain on it.

TURN ON THE FOREHAND TO THE LEFT

- Start from a good, square halt.
- Ask the horse to flex slightly to the right.
- Keep a steady contact with the outside (left) rein, otherwise the horse may start to walk in a circle.
- By applying your right leg just behind the girth, ask the horse to step sideways and round with his hindlegs. Put a little more weight on to your right seatbone.
- If the horse's response is rather sluggish, reinforce your right leg aid with little taps of your whip.
- Use your outside (left) rein to prevent the horse from moving forwards.
- Use your outside (left) leg to "support" the horse, to control the speed of the movement and to regulate the number of steps.
- When the horse has completed a half turn, ride him actively forward.

Shoulder-In

Shoulder-in is a lateral movement in which the horse is bent slightly and evenly from his nose to his tail round the rider's inside leg. His shoulders come off the track (that is, the normal path taken by both fore- and hind legs) while his hind legs remain on it. Thus, his outside shoulder is in front of his inside hindleg and he is looking away from the direction in which he is travelling. The shoulder-in should be performed at an angle of approximately 30 degrees to the side of the school.

In this movement the horse's inside foreleg crosses in front of his outside foreleg, while his inside hindleg is placed well under his body, in front of his outside hindleg and towards his outside foreleg.

Shoulder-in is an invaluable exercise for both horse and rider. It makes the horse supple, helps to straighten him and develops collection. It teaches the rider to control the horse's shoulders, which in turn makes riding in straight lines, and on circles and elements of circles, far easier.

RIGHT: A good rein-back, showing the horse's legs moving in diagonal pairs.

- Starting in walk, as you turn into the long side of the school, guide his shoulders off the track: keep the contact with your outside rein to guide his shoulders off the track and limit the bend in his neck, and use your inside leg to keep the horse going actively forward.
- Have a light, elastic contact with your inside rein to maintain the bend.
- Avoid pulling with the inside rein – this will simply encourage the horse to bend his neck, not perform shoulder-in.
- Use your outside leg, as necessary, behind the girth to control any sideways swing of the quarters.
- Put slightly more weight on to your inside seatbone.
- Keep your head and shoulders in line with those of the horse.

When you have mastered the art of bringing the horse's forehand off the track, you can progress to shoulder-in at trot.

THE ULTIMATE GOALS

You don't have to compete in the dressage arena to appreciate that an educated horse provides the best ride.

All horses, whatever their role, benefit from dressage. It is a word which evokes different responses from different riders: many are alarmed at the prospect, others merely bored, according to their disposition. Yet all it means is "training" (from the French, *dresser*).

What they fail to realize is that the point of training is to produce an obedient horse – one who understands what his rider wants him to do and is able, willing and – most importantly – happy to oblige. What better, therefore, than dressage?

Dressage involves developing the horse's mental aptitude and natural athletic ability so that he can perform the tasks we ask of him without mental stress or physical injury. It can be a lengthy process; it takes infinite tact and patience and is only to be undertaken by the experienced horse person. But the ultimate goal is well worth achieving, because it produces a horse with the following admirable qualities:

Balance

The first thing the horse has to do when asked to carry a rider is to adjust his balance to cope with this unexpected burden. Remember that it is unnatural for a horse to carry a weight on his back. It takes time for him to get used to it and the inept rider, unable to remain balanced, makes the task all the more difficult. Remember also that the horse's forehand is his heaviest part (think how heavy his head and neck must be). Adding a rider just behind his withers adds to the burden.

The aim of flatwork is to encourage the horse to shift some of this weight onto his powerful hindquarters by "engaging" them – that is, by ensuring his hindlegs are underneath him. Put simply, this makes him a more comfortable, agile and safer ride. Only when moving in the fast paces and jumping, when the horse's centre of gravity moves further forward, is it necessary for the rider to sit further forward.

Rhythm

To give a good ride, the horse needs to have regular, rhythmic paces. Balance is a prerequisite of

rhythm: only when the horse is balanced can he maintain regular steps at each pace, through transitions from one pace to another, and when negotiating turns.

Contact

Contact is a term used to describe the soft connection which the rider should have with the horse's mouth via the reins and the bit. Remember that contact should never be sought by pulling back with the hands: it should be the result of a forward thrust from the hindlegs, produced by the rider's leg and seat aids and "received" by the hands.

Once the horse has been trained to go forward into his bridle in this way he is said to be "on the bit". The energy generated by the hindlegs is "received" by the rider's hands through the reins and the schooled horse will relax his jaw and flex at the poll. His head will be vertical to the ground. It is not possible to put a horse on the bit by using the reins alone – the horse must be going forward with impulsion.

Impulsion

Impulsion comes from the horse's hindquarters. The horse is said to have impulsion when he "engages" his hindlegs and thrusts himself forward with energetic steps into his rider's soft, containing hands. He can only have impulsion if his back is supple and springy. Remember that impulsion is controlled energy, not speed. The horse cannot have impulsion while walking, a pace which does not have a moment of suspension.

Straightness

Only when the horse is moving straight can his weight be evenly distributed. But like left- and right-handedness in humans, it is natural for horses to be born favouring one side or the other. As a result the trainer must constantly work to improve the horse's straightness. The straighter the horse, the better able he is to push forward from his hindlegs; the more even is the wear on his limbs; the more even is the contact and the better he will achieve collection.

Suppleness

Like any athlete, the horse needs to be supple in order to perform well. There should be no tension in his muscles or his joints – nor in his mind.

Collection

The horse achieves collection by increasing the bend in his hock and stifle joints and bringing his hindlegs underneath his body with each step. This shifts his weight off his forehand onto his hindquarters. The horse adopts a more "uphill" outline – his quarters are lower, his neck is raised and he takes shorter, higher steps. These shortened steps should not lack energy.

At trot and canter he should still move forward with impulsion. When correctly "collected" the horse becomes extremely light in the hand and easy to manoeuvre. At its most marked, collection enables the horse to perform the piaffe – that is, to trot on the spot, without moving forward. This gathering together of controlled energy enables him to spring forward instantly into a fast pace if required.

ABOVE, TOP: *The horse is said to have impulsion when he thrusts himself forward with energetic steps.*

ABOVE: *Balance and rhythm enable the horse to negotiate turns.*

OPPOSITE: *You can put your flatwork to the test by entering dressage competitions.*

4
PART FOUR

GETTING AIRBORNE

Jumping has come a long way since the days when members of the seventeenth-century Swedish cavalry were advised, on arriving at an obstacle, to grab the mane, close their eyes and shout "hey". The more scientific approach advocated today enables man and horse to tackle fences with rather more finesse — and no doubt more safety.

Not that equine jumping prowess is restricted to modern competitive sports. Many daring leaps — some, one has to say, not entirely successful and other almost certainly apocryphal — have been recorded down the ages. In Lincolnshire a mare called Bayard, urged on by her rider and an attendant witch, is said to have jumped a distance of 300 ft (90 metres) in four great bounds — after which she expired; while to escape pursuit by the Roundheads, one Major Thomas Smallman once jumped his horse from the 800 ft (244 metres) high crest of the limestone escarpment in Shropshire known as Wenlock Edge. The pair landed in a tree. The unfortunate horse was killed though the major survived.

Closer to the present day, a hunter ridden by the 5th Earl of Lonsdale (1857–1944) was reputed to have cleared, in one leap, an obstacle comprising a set of rails, a ditch and a second set of rails, the distance from take off to landing measuring 32 ft (9.85 metres).

Yet, just as humans are not born knowing how to sit on a horse, so horses generally speaking are not born knowing how to jump — at least not to jump the large obstacles or ones arranged in a complicated sequence which feature in sports such as show jumping and horse trials. They normally prefer to go round rather than over impediments in their way — which is natural enough since they are built for speed.

Like humans, though, most horses seem to get a "buzz" from jumping once they have acquired the necessary technique. Some will even jump unprompted, perhaps to reach a friend in another paddock, or to get to the other side of a gate which lies between them, their stable and the feed store. Some actually seem to delight in their athletic ability. Many racehorses will complete an entire circuit, or more, of a course after falling or unseating their jockey. Staying with "the herd" is of course a strong incentive, but frequently horses will ignore inviting opportunities to go around the fences, choosing instead to jump every one — usually in better balance than when encumbered by a human burden.

So the answer to the much asked question, "Do horses actually enjoy jumping?" seems more often than not to be yes. Particularly when partnered by a competent rider who is neither nervous nor over-bold and who will not jab the horse in the mouth or throw him off balance by sitting in a faulty position. In jumping, balance and an independent seat are everything. If the horse is willing to have a go, it is the rider's responsibility to give him every chance to succeed. Hence the necessity for jumping lessons — and plenty of them.

Although all horses will, if necessary, jump little ditches and other impediments that they find in their way, nature has designed them primarily for galloping: left to their own devices the majority will skirt round obstacles rather than go over them. However, teaching a horse to jump is not a difficult process and once they have learnt how, the majority seem to get a buzz from it. Before you start learning how to ride a horse over fences take some time to study the physical process of jumping from the horse's standpoint. You will then understand why the correct jumping seat is so crucial.

As the horse approaches a fence he gathers himself together ready for take-off. The last stride before he springs upwards is shorter than the strides during the approach. The horse's forehand – his front legs, shoulders, withers, neck and head – are the heaviest part of his body, so he must shift his weight back on to his hindquarters in order to lift off in front. Immediately before take-off he stretches his neck and lowers his head slightly, sizing up the fence.

The horse appears to measure his take-off from the lowest point of the obstacle, so a fence with a solid groundline – such as a wall – or one with a pole close to or actually on the ground and slightly in front

HOW HORSES JUMP

Jumping is one of the most exciting aspects of riding – there are few things to equal the thrill of soaring over a fence in total harmony with your horse.

of the fence, will be easier for him to judge than a plank set 1 metre (3 ft) above the ground. Having assessed the fence, the horse's head and neck come up and he thrusts himself upwards and forwards. At this point a horse who has been well schooled will quickly fold up his forelegs – the better he can do this, the less height he needs in order to clear it

and the more he conserves his energy.

Watch top show jumpers in action and you will see how they "snap up" their forelegs. Indeed, some do so to such an extent that they have to be fitted with special leather guards to prevent them from injuring the underside of their bodies with the jumping studs fitted to their shoes.

As the horse reaches the highest point of the jump, he begins to lower his head and neck. His hindquarters rise level with his forehand. A good jumper raises his hindlegs at the stifle and flexes his hocks to avoid knocking the obstacle behind. The rounder the horse's outline over a fence, the easier it is for him to jump it cleanly.

If he jumps with his head high and his back flat, instead of rounded, he will have to jump higher to clear the fence. A poor jumping style like this takes much more effort and often leads to mistakes. Usually the horse's forefeet touch down on the landing side one after the other in quick succession. If the jump has not been fluent and well balanced, the horse may land steeply with both feet together. This has a detrimental effect on his limbs because of the extra jarring it causes. Once his hindlegs have touched down the horse bunches himself together again ready to go into the next canter stride.

How a Horse Learns to Jump

A horse is taught to jump by first being walked over a pole on the ground. When he will walk over this confidently and without losing balance the trainer asks him to trot over it. Gradually more poles are added, parallel to the first and with the distance between them carefully measured out to suit the horse's stride. Eventually the horse will be trotting competently over a "grid" of half a dozen poles.

All jumping training is based on trotting poles, which improve the horse's co-ordination and encourage him to lower his head and neck and round his back. As he does so, his balance will improve. He will also learn to raise his legs higher than he needs to when being schooled on the flat. As well as being used in a straight line, trotting poles can also be placed on a curve and the horse lunged over them, either with or without a rider. Lunging over trotting poles without a rider is particularly useful when training a young horse to jump because it puts less strain on his back and limbs.

Once the horse is confident and proficient over trotting poles he can be asked to jump a small fence consisting of two crossed poles. To ensure that he approaches it in balance it is positioned after a line of trotting poles. The fence should be no higher than about 15 in (38 cm). The distance between the final trotting pole and the fence must be carefully measured to enable the horse to land over the pole and then pop over the fence comfortably and without putting in a stride. For the average horse 9 ft (2.7 m) is about right. Crossed-poles are ideal "nursery" obstacles, because they encourage the horse to stay on a straight course and aim for the centre of the fence.

In time, the trainer will ask the horse to jump small single fences in different parts of the school. To begin with, to help the horse to take off at the right point, a trotting pole is placed before the fence.

Gridwork

When the horse is able to jump single fences in balance and without rushing, he can be introduced to gridwork. A grid is a series of small fences placed so that the horse has to bounce them – that is land over one and take off at the next with no stride between – or to take just one stride between. For example, a grid of five little obstacles might be set as follows: bounce-stride-bounce-stride, or bounce-bounce-stride-bounce. The spacings between them must never be too wide, but should match the horse's stride.

Gridwork develops the horse's technique, agility and suppleness, preparing him for jumping different types of fence and, eventually, a whole course.

Effective jumping style: note how the horse lowers and stretches his head and neck.

THE JUMPING SEAT

Jumping calls for perfect balance and the ability to "go with" the horse's movements in each phase of the jump.

At faster paces and when jumping, the horse's centre of gravity moves further forward. To give him the best chance of staying balanced and clearing the obstacle, the weight on his back needs to be correspondingly further forward. This means that the rider must adopt the jumping or forward seat.

Put simply, it involves inclining your body forward from the hips to take the weight off the horse's back. The first step is to shorten your stirrups. When learning to jump you will not be riding over anything very big, so to begin with you can ride in the same general purpose saddle that you use for everyday riding and you need only shorten your leathers two or three holes. The bigger the fences and the faster your speed – for instance when riding across country – the shorter you will need to ride. To jump at all seriously, you must have a saddle specifically designed for jumping.

The Five Stages of Jumping

APPROACH

Your lower legs must be directly underneath you and close against the horse's sides. Your seatbones should be slightly out of the saddle and your upper body inclined slightly forwards. Feel your weight as it is channelled through your knees on to the balls of your feet. Allow your hands to follow the horse's movement as he stretches his neck and lowers his head in preparation for take-off.

TAKE-OFF

When the horse's head and neck come up and he brings his hindlegs underneath him, take your weight out of the saddle to give him free use of his back. When his shoulders have come up, lean further forward, bending from your hips. Allow your hands to follow his head movement.

FLIGHT

Once the horse is airborne, sit still with your seatbones just out of the saddle and your lower leg under you and close to the girth.

LANDING

When the horse's forehand begins to descend, straighten your body gradually, still keeping your weight out of the saddle.

GETAWAY

As the horse's hindfeet touch down and he gathers himself together ready to take the first canter stride, return to your take-off position – seatbones slightly out of the saddle, leaning slightly forward. Be ready to drive the horse forward with your legs and, if necessary, your seat.

Remember ...

- When riding on the flat your shoulders should be on the same verticle line as your hips. When jumping they should be in advance of your hips, otherwise your will be "left behind".
- Instead of your weight being on your seatbones, when jumping it is transferred down through your thighs and knees more on to the balls of your feet.
- To take your weight off your seatbones you must "fold" your body – not stand up in your stirrups.

OPPOSITE AND ABOVE: *The rider's weight should be out of the saddle during take-off. During flight and landing the seat should remain just out of the saddle. The rider's lower leg should be positioned under him. Here it has moved too far forward and the rider's back is rounded. As a result his weight has come on to the horse's back during the landing.*

Adopting the Basic Jumping Position

- Shorten your stirrups by a couple of holes.
- Bend your body forward from the hips.
- Keep your back straight; it should be neither hollow nor convex.
- You should feel your weight more on your thighs, knees and stirrups rather than on your seatbones.
- Keep your knees close to the saddle.
- Place your lower legs against the horse's sides, close to the girth.
- Keep the straight line from your elbow through your hand to the horse's bit.
- Keep your head up and look directly forward.
- Practise the forward seat in trot and canter. Until you can maintain your balance at both paces you should not start jumping.

Things to Avoid ...

THE FOLLOWING FAULTS
HAVE AN ADVERSE EFFECT ON
THE HORSE'S BALANCE:

- Leaning too far forward during the approach.
- Losing rein contact during the approach.
- Taking off before the horse by leaning too far forward too soon.
- Getting left behind at take-off – if you do, you MUST let your hands and arms follow the horse's head movement to avoid jabbing him in the mouth.
- Swinging your lower leg back.
- Pushing your lower leg forward.
- Raising your heel above the level of your toe.
- Leaning to one side or the other at any stage of the jump.
- Looking down at any stage of the jump.
- Thumping down into the saddle on landing.
- Turning to look back at the fence.

YOUR FIRST JUMP

Some people find jumping the most exhilarating aspect of riding, others never overcome their nervousness. The secret is to get the basics right – then anyone should be able to enjoy it.

There is no better way of developing balance in the forward seat than riding over poles on the ground. To begin with, place individual poles at various points around your schooling area and walk your horse over them. Remember to keep your body inclined slightly forward, with your shoulders in advance of your hips, and allow your hands to follow the horse's head and neck as he stretches forward over the poles. When you can do this without losing your balance, try riding over the poles at rising trot.

Next make a grid of three poles, placed about 1.4 m (4ft 6 in) apart. Remember that you must adjust the distance between the poles to suit your horse or pony's stride. Having an assistant on the ground is invaluable.

Walk over the grid a number of times, maintaining the forward position, and when you feel confident attempt it at rising trot. Remember the straight line from your elbow, through your hand, to the horse's mouth, and remember to keep the correct position of your lower leg, that is, close against the horse's girth, with no swinging back of your lower leg. As you become more proficient you can add more poles until you have a six-pole grid, over which you can trot back and forth in perfect balance.

Next, raise the poles off the ground by putting bricks or blocks under the ends so that the poles are about 15–23 cm (6–9 in) above the ground. Alternatively you can use specially designed obstacles known as cavalletti. When trotting over the raised poles the horse will bend his knees and hocks more. This is a great exercise for improving your balance.

Crossed Poles

Just as the cross-pole fence is the horse's introduction to jumping, so it is used to give riders their first sensation of actually leaving the ground. Because it directs the horse towards the centre of fence, thereby encouraging him to jump straight, the cross-pole fence enables you to concentrate on your position in the saddle rather than worrying too much about the horse's approach.

Set a cross-pole fence, about 38 cm (15 in) high, at the end of your line of trotting poles or cavalletti. It will need to be about 3 m (9 ft) beyond the last pole, depending on the length of the horse's stride.

Wise Precautions

- Do your early jumping practice on a calm, well-schooled horse under the eye of a professional instructor.
- When you practise jumping at home, always have someone on hand to help adjust the poles or fences, and to help in case of an accident.
- In the early stages, fit your horse with a neck strap. The cardinal sin when jumping is to jab the horse in the mouth. If you do get left behind or otherwise unbalanced, you can catch hold of the neck strap for security rather than hanging on to the reins.

This little cross-pole fence, with a pole on the ground to act as a groundline, makes a perfect first jump.

ABOVE: *Riding over a grid of poles at trot is the basis for all jumping.*

RIGHT: *When you can maintain your forward position over trotting poles, try adding a small cross-pole fence.*

Ride the grid at rising trot and concentrate on maintaining your forward position, with your arms and hands following the horse's head and neck movements, as he pops over the little fence. When you can negotiate the grid and cross-poles confidently and without losing balance, place another cross-pole fence about 5.5–6 m (18–21 ft) beyond the first one. This will enable the horse to put in a canter stride between the two fences. This is your introduction to jumping from canter.

Remember that as the horse lands over these little cross-pole fences he will probably go into canter. Impulsion in the getaway after a jump is most important, so allow him to take a few canter strides before bringing him back to trot in order to repeat the exercise.

GRIDWORK

Riding over grids of small fences is an invaluable suppling and balancing exercise for both rider and horse.

When you have mastered riding in the forward seat down a line of trotting poles followed by a couple of cross-pole fences, you can start to do slightly more advanced gymnastic jumping exercises. This involves gridwork, that is, a series of small fences of different types, placed in a straight line following half a dozen trotting poles. Gridwork is an invaluable way of developing the rider's balance and security in the saddle. A well-built grid encourages the horse to jump fluently, which enables you to concentrate on your position.

A key aspect of jumping is to not attempt too much too soon. If you concentrate on getting your gridwork right, you should have no difficulty when you progress to jumping individual fences and, eventually, small courses.

Straight Grids

To start with, construct a grid of three small fences. Make the first one a simple cross-pole and set it at a distance of about 3 m (10 ft) from your last trotting pole. Then build a little vertical fence about 5.5–6m (18–21ft) from the cross-pole. Finally, construct a small spread fence (with the second rail higher than the first, to make it as easy as possible for the horse) at a distance of about 10–10.6 m (33–35 ft) beyond the vertical fence.

This grid will enable the horse to trot over the poles, pop over the cross-poles, take one canter stride, jump the vertical fence, take two canter strides and jump the spread fence. There is no need to be alarmed about going into those two little jumps at the faster speed of canter – the canter is actually a more comfortable pace at

which to approach a fence. The little spread fence will require the horse to make slightly more effort than the two previous ones and you will soon begin to get the feel of what it is like to jump bigger fences.

When you are thoroughly confident tackling this grid, add one or two more fences to the line, with one or two non-jumping canter strides between, as above. To ring the changes, you can introduce a "bounce" – that is, a distance which is too short for the horse to take a stride. He will land over the first fence and then immediately take off at the next. You can place the bounce at the beginning of the grid – in which case the distance between the two bounce fences should be in the region of 2.7 m (9 ft), or you can introduce it further along the grid. Since the horse will be cantering by this time, you will need to increase the bounce distance to about 3.6 m (12 ft). Whenever you do gridwork keep the fences small. 46–60 cm (18–24 in) high is quite sufficient.

As your balance improves, you will begin to find that riding grids is fun. When you reach that stage try doing the same thing without reins – preferably under the supervision of your instructor. If you can do it without losing your balance, you really are making progress.

A more advanced exercise is the bounce grid. To start with build three small fences with a distance of around 3 m (10 ft) between each. Practise riding down the grid at a controlled canter. Gradually add more obstacles, again 3 m (10 ft) apart, until you have a six-fence bounce grid.

When you are really proficient you should be able to ride this type of grid with neither reins nor stirrups – but it is not advisable to try this at home, at least not

ABOVE: *Introducing a small spread fence into your grids will help you to get the feel of jumping slightly larger obstacles.*

ABOVE, OPPOSITE: *Gridwork enables you to get used to jumping from canter, but still in a very controlled way.*

in the early stages. Do it in the safety of a riding school, under the expert eye of your instructor.

Jumping on Circles

Jumping on circles is another great suppling exercise, but as it is more tiring for the horse than jumping in straight lines, it should not be overdone. Remember that horses are nearly always stiffer on one side than the other – always work him first on his more supple side.

Begin by using poles on the ground. Set three poles in a fan shape on a 20 m circle, about 1.2 m (4 ft) apart on the inside of the circle and about 1.5–1.8 (5–6 ft) apart on the outside. Again the exact distances will depend on the horse's individual stride and at first you may need expert advice to get it right.

Begin by walking over the poles. Aim at the

centre of each and approach them from either direction. Then ride over them at a good active trot. Gradually increase the number of poles until you have a six-pole fan grid. As with the straight grid, when you are competent riding over the fan grid at trot, you can raise the poles slightly off the ground by putting bricks or blocks under the ends.

The next step is to ride over the grid at trot but allow the horse to go into canter as he comes over the last pole. If you have him well balanced, with his hindlegs well under him, he should automatically go into canter on the correct lead – that is, if you are circling to the left, he will lead with his near foreleg. This is the first stage in learning how to indicate to the horse which leg you wish him to canter on when he lands over a fence. It is an important skill when you begin to jump courses that have changes of direction.

Tricks of the Trade

- To prevent your horse becoming bored with gridwork, vary the fences: introduce little brush fences and a wall, rather than always building with poles.

- To avoid frightening the horse if he makes a mistake, always build fences which will fall down easily if he hits them.

- Always finish your jumping practice on a good note, when you and the horse have done something, however small, really well.

SINGLE FENCES

Jumping individual fences may look easier than gridwork but it is more difficult to do well. Take the experts' advice and begin by using placing poles.

Approaching a fence via a line of trotting poles is far easier than jumping it in isolation. Why? Because correctly positioned trotting poles ensure that the horse reaches the fence at exactly the right point of take-off, something the novice rider is unlikely to accomplish.

When jumping individual fences always try to aim for the centre of the obstacle. Avoid jumping close to the wing, except while saving time in a jump-off. This rider's heel has come up and her lower leg has swung back.

When you first start to jump individual fences, therefore, it is best to go through an intermediary stage and use placing poles. A placing pole is a pole positioned on – or slightly raised above – the ground a short distance in front of a fence. It is placed at exactly the right distance from the fence to ensure that the horse continues to reach the obstacle at the right take-off spot. This enables you to concentrate on your position in the saddle rather than worrying about what sort of jump the horse is going to make.

Jumping Single Fences

1. Build a small obstacle no more than 75 cm (2 ft 6 in) high. Place a pole on the ground 2.7 m (9 ft) in front of it. Ride towards the centre of the pole at an active trot. As the horse lands over the pole he will be perfectly placed to take off at the fence. Allow him to canter away from the fence, then go back to trot before trying it again.

2. Move the placing pole back so that it is 5.5 m (18 ft) in front of the fence. Try approaching in canter. The horse will be able to take one canter stride between the pole and the fence.

When you start to feel more ambitious it is better to build small spread fences than to keep making verticals higher – at this point 1 m (3 ft) is plenty big enough. The aim at this juncture is not to see how high your horse can jump but how well you can ride over a fence. Spread fences encourage horses to jump in a correct, rounded outline and this will help you to perfect your jumping style far more effectively than if you start putting your horse at 1.2 m (4 ft) verticals.

3. Move the placing pole back to a distance of 13.7 m (45 ft) from the fence to give the horse three canter strides between the pole and the fence. To prevent any possibility of the horse rushing at the fence, which he may well try to do in the hands of a novice rider, continue to ride at the placing pole at a good active trot, then allow him to canter to the fence and away from it on landing.

4. Remove the placing poles. Approach the single fences at trot. Most horses are perfectly capable of jumping small obstacles – up to about 1 m (3 ft) high – out of trot. When you are happy with a trot approach, ride at the fences from a steady, controlled canter. Ensure that it is steady and controlled, not a sprint from 90 m (100 yards) away.

Avoid Boredom

In order to avoid boring your horse out of his mind and possibly encouraging him to become careless through lack of concentration, build several little fences in different places and jump them at random rather than continually jumping the same one.

A correctly positioned placing pole ensures that the horse arrives at the fence at exactly the right take-off distance.

Practice Fences

You do not need huge amounts of expensive equipment to practise over at home, but what you do have must be safe, with as much variety as possible to keep the horse alert. Basic requirements include:

- A supply of poles, at least 10 cm (4 in) in diameter and at least 3–3.6 m (10–12 ft) long.
- Supports for the poles. Purpose-built wing-stands are best, being strong and stable. Alternatively, you can use specially-designed stacking blocks, or oil drums, provided they are rust-free and strong.
- Adjustable metal or plastic cups, which fit to wing-stands and support the poles.
- Filler materials – such as brush fences, wooden panels or small walls – to make fences look more solid.

Safe Fences

- Avoid building flimsy-looking fences. Horses will not respect them and are quite likely to jump through, rather than over them.
- Never use flimsy pieces of wood or rusty metal to construct practice fences. They can cause serious injury if the horse makes a mistake.
- If you use straw bales as fillers, ensure that they are tightly packed, otherwise the horse could catch his foot in the twine should he make a mistake.
- If you use oil drums placed end to end as a filler, prevent them from rolling by knocking wooden wedges into the ground on either side.
- To save your horse's legs from wear and tear, set up your practice jumps on well-drained, flat, stone-free ground, and never practise jumping when the ground is either very muddy or very hard.

Do it Yourself

Paint your poles, supports and fillers in a variety of bright colours and patterns to get your horse used to unusual fences. Then, if you decide to go in for jumping competitions, he will not be taken by surprise by unfamiliar fences.

If you are a DIY enthusiast, or know someone who is, cut costs by making your own practice fences. Simply copy the professional ones. Make sure that all rough edges are removed from poles and supports.

CHANGES OF DIRECTION

Making smooth changes of direction, with no loss of balance or impulsion, is an integral part of jumping a course of fences.

Part of the skill of jumping a course is to be able to maintain a steady rhythm, so that your horse approaches each fence in balance and with plenty of impulsion. In competitive riding, changes of direction are incorporated by course designers as part of the technical tests of the course. If a fence is placed a few strides after a corner, how well you jump the fence will in large measure be determined by how well you negotiated the corner. Therefore, if you want to progress to jumping courses of fences, you will need to learn how to change direction competently.

Serious jumping riders must learn how to perform flying changes – that is, they must teach their horse to change promptly from one canter lead to the other on request. However, for the beginner, it is sufficient to slow down to trot for a few strides before striking off on the new canter lead.

Simple Changes of Direction

Place four small fences on a large figure of eight. Each fence should have a placing pole 5.5 m (18 ft) before it. Ride to the first placing pole at a trot. Allow the horse to canter for a few strides after landing over the fence.

Go back into trot to approach the second placing pole and negotiate the second fence in the same way as the first.

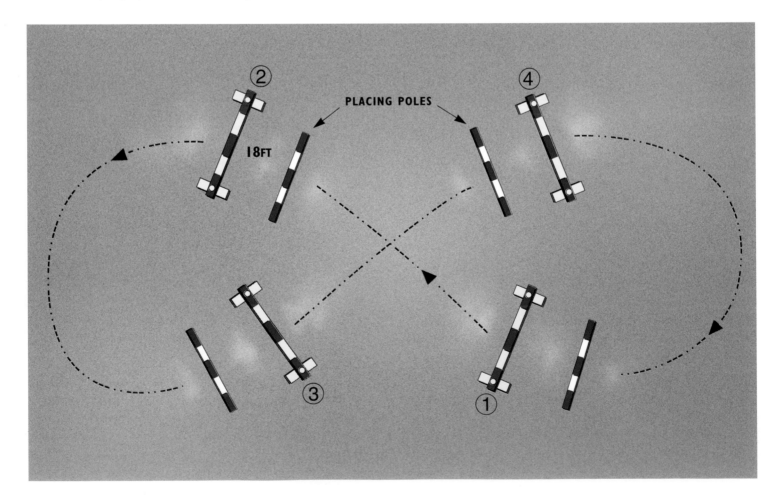

② 18FT PLACING POLES ④ ③ ①

Once you are back in trot after jumping the second fence, make a wide turn to approach the third placing pole.

Jump fences three and four in the same way as one and two. Move one or more of the placing poles further from the fence(s) to allow the horse to take three canter strides between pole and fence, and repeat the exercise.

- Remove the placing poles from in front of fences two and four, ensuring that the two fences are a measured number of strides from fences one and three. If you are riding a horse allow 3.6 m (12 ft) per canter stride; for a pony allow 2.7 m (9 ft).
- Trot to the placing pole in front of the first fence.
- Canter from fence one to two.
- Come back to trot to turn to fence three and approach the placing pole at trot.
- Finish the exercise in canter.
- Finally, remove all the placing poles and jump

all four fences from a steady canter, slowing down to trot for a moment or two after jumping fence two in order to strike off on the correct leg and again after fence four in order to repeat the exercise.

Landing on the Correct Canter Lead

If you watch the experts in action, you will see that their horses invariably land over a fence on the correct canter lead for the next turn, making it unnecessary to change leg on the flat. It is an invaluable skill to have, especially in a jump-off against the clock, and it is not particularly difficult to learn.

Build a small cross-pole fence in the middle of your schooling area and parallel to the long sides. At trot, approach the fence from a circle on your horse's more supple side.

As the horse is going over the fence, give the aids for canter on the same rein. For example, if

A cross-pole fence is ideal for practising changes of direction. In time you will find that your horse or pony invariably lands on the correct leading leg.

your horse is stiff on his offside, start by circling to the left and giving the aids for canter left as he is airborne, ie, use your left hand to turn his head slightly inwards, your left leg on the girth and your right leg behind the girth. As he lands you should find that he is cantering with his near foreleg leading.

If he is stiff on his nearside, start by circling to the right and giving the aids for canter right as he is airborne, i.e., use your right hand to turn his head slightly inward, your right leg on the girth and your left leg behind the girth. He should land cantering with his off foreleg leading.

Then, practise circling and jumping the fence in the same way but on the other rein. Finally, try riding a figure of eight at canter, jumping the fence where your two circles meet. Eventually, that the horse will change leg in the air every time.

If you plan to do any competitive jumping, you will first need some practice at riding over a complete course. Even if you have no desire to compete, there is a great deal of satisfaction to be gained from successfully negotiating a number of moderately-sized obstacles of different types, with one or two changes of rein along the way. When you can do this well it will mean that you are on the way to mastering the technique of keeping your horse well balanced and full of impulsion, and have learnt how to adjust his stride between fences.

Remember that it is the way the horse travels on the flat between his fences that most influences the way in which he actually jumps them.

If your riding school has the right facilities, you can practise jumping a course there, under the watchful eye of your instructor. If you have sufficient equipment of your own – for example, enough to build eight or 10 small fences – you can practise at home, too.

Building a Simple Course

- Make the first fence an easy one: an ascending spread – that is, one where the second rail is higher than the first – is the best. It should have a good groundline. This is the easiest type of fence for the horse and will give him confidence at the outset.
- Include a variety of different types of fence.
- Include a simple combination.
- Incorporate changes of direction – but avoid sharp turns.

Types of Fence

VERTICALS

Vertical or upright fences – that is, those in which all the poles or planks are in the same vertical plane – look simple enough but are in fact the most difficult for a horse to jump well. The reason for this is that the horse judges his take-off point from the ground line – the bottom of the fence – and he is more likely to take off too close to the obstacle and hit the top of it with his front legs.

When jumping a vertical, the horse will descend more steeply than when jumping a spread fence. This

JUMPING A COURSE

Drawing on your combined skills of flatwork and jumping you should be able to tackle a simple course of show jumps.

will affect his getaway stride after landing, making it somewhat shorter than when he lands over a spread.

SPREADS

Any fence made up of more than one vertical element is a spread. As its name suggests, a triple bar – also known as a staircase fence, because of its shape – comprises three elements, each one higher than the one before.

This is one of the easiest types of fence to jump because its shape is much the same as the arc described by the horse when he is in the air. Unlike verticals, you can and should take off quite close to a triple bar because the horse is unlikely to hit the low first rail and he needs to get in deep if he is to clear the width of the obstacle. He will land less steeply than when jumping an upright, and his getaway stride will be longer. Fences with two vertical elements – known in the show jumping world as oxers – are more difficult to jump than triple bars. Ascending spreads, where the front pole is lower than the back one, are easier than parallels, where both top poles are the same height. Both types of fence should be approached with plenty of impulsion, but beware of allowing the horse to increase his speed. If you do, his weight will come more on to his forehand and he may well hit the fence. Judging the right spot for take-off at big spread fences calls for considerable skill – take off too close and the horse will hit the front element with his forelegs; take off too far away and he will find it difficult to clear the back rail.

Distances in Combinations

Taking the average length of stride for a horse to be 3.6 m (12 ft), "true" distances in moderate-sized combinations would be:

- For a double of verticals with one non-jumping stride between: 7.3 m (24 ft). This is assuming that the horse lands some 1.8 m (6 ft) beyond the first fence and takes off the same distance from the second.

- For a double of a spread fence followed by an upright with one non-jumping stride between: 7.5 m (24 ft 6 in). This allows for the horse landing slightly further out over the spread fence than he would over a vertical.

- For a double of a vertical followed by a spread, or two spreads, with one non-jumping stride between: 7.15 m (23 ft 6 in).

An ascending spread fence like this one is easier to jump than a true parallel. This international rider has a sympathetic rein contact, though by looking down and leaning to one side he could unbalance the horse.

To jump a triple bar succesfully the horse needs to take off quite close to the first element.

COMBINATIONS

If fences are placed so close together that there is only room for the horse to take one or two strides between them, they are known as combinations. A two-fence combination is known as a double, three fences is a treble. The courses for novice jumping competitions will include simple doubles, so you need to know how to ride them.

At novice level, combinations should have "true" distances. That is the distance between the first fence and the second – and the second and the third in the case of a treble – should be carefully measured to allow for one or two average-length strides. At the top levels of show jumping, course builders provide horse and rider with difficult tests by shortening or lengthening the distances in combinations, which introduces a much more technical element into the competition. But at the lower levels the distances must be kept simple if horse and rider are not to lose confidence.

Walking the Course

However modest the size of the fences, you should always walk a course before you try to jump it. Not only does it help fix the route in your memory, it also enables you to stride out the distances between the fences so that you know in advance how many strides your particular horse will be able to take between each obstacle. When the fences are very small most horses who have been taught to jump correctly will be able to get out of trouble if they arrive too close or too far off a particular fence. But when the fences start to go up in height it becomes crucial to arrive at each one at the optimum take-off point.

Before you walk a course for the first time, measure your own stride. If you can make it 90 cm (3 ft) so much the better, because then it will be easy to work out distances quickly in your head. To measure the distance between two elements of a double, first stand with your back against the landing side of the first fence, then take even-length strides right up to the next fence. If the distance is a "true" one and your horse has a particularly short stride, you will have to be prepared to ask him to lengthen his stride after landing over the first fence otherwise he will have to reach for the second. If he is a very long-striding horse you must try not to let him jump in too far over the first fence and then, after landing, you must shorten his stride. Jumping in too far over the first part of a combination is a common cause of horses knocking down, or even refusing or running-out at the second. Such mistakes are not their fault – they cannot be expected to jump cleanly if the take-off point is wrong.

Shortening and Lengthening the Stride

When you come to jump a course of fences, and in particular combinations, you will soon realize how important it is to be able to lengthen and shorten your horse's stride at will – and how invaluable all that flatwork is, particularly the upward and downward transitions within a pace, in this case the canter.

Remember that horses usually shorten their stride when asked to go away from home, so if you are competing at a show, be prepared for this to happen when you turn away from the collecting ring. Conversely, they are inclined to want to "motor on" going towards home. The state of the ground also affects length of stride: a horse may shorten his stride by as much as 30 cm (1 ft) on muddy going and also when jumping uphill. Jumping in the cramped confines of an indoor school will also cause horses to shorten, whereas when jumping on good going, or downhill, or in a spacious outdoor arena, they may well lengthen their stride by up to 30 cm (1 ft). Bear these points in mind when building practice courses at home.

International riders assessing a course. The course walk is an important aspect of show jumping – whatever the size of the fences.

5

HORSES ARE
NOT MACHINES

If there is one golden rule of riding it is that the horse's welfare must always come first. Any instructor worth their salt will instill in the beginner right from the outset the importance of consideration for the horse. Ignorance of this basic precept can lead to only one thing – abuse. During man's long association with this generous, kind-natured animal, misuse through ignorance has been all too common. Make sure that you don't add to the catalogue of crime.

The best way to gain an understanding of horses and horsemanship is to take lessons from a qualified trainer. Professional instruction not only ensures the rider's safety, it also safeguards the horse's welfare. For most people taking their first faltering lessons in the saddle, staying aboard and sorting out the brakes and steering are problems enough, without worrying about what effect they may be having on the unfortunate and long-suffering horse.

This is why control of the horse or pony should, in the earliest stages, be taken out of their inevitably clumsy hands. Grinding the gears a few times when you are learning to drive will only hurt your pride, but jabbing a horse in the mouth because you cannot keep your balance causes pain to another living creature. It is not the horse's fault if he eventually becomes sour and resentful.

A common problem is when the rider, having mastered the basics on a good "schoolmaster" horse and acquired more confidence, then believes that they can ride anything. What so many people forget is that the horse is not a machine, programmed to carry out certain functions at the flick of a switch or the push of a button. Horses can only respond if they know what it is that is required of them, and to know that they must first be taught by knowledgeable, sympathetic trainers. The late Pegotty Henriques, a gifted and wise trainer and dressage judge, expressed it perfectly when she wrote: "Never forget that however severely you punish your horse for not obeying you, he cannot be expected to understand a lesson that he has not been taught." Sadly, all too many horses are reprimanded for being "disobedient" or "stubborn" when the problem stems from lack of correct education.

Problems of communication will also arise if the horse is in discomfort or is distracted from his work for some reason. Never forget that this is a living creature you are dealing with. He is not an automaton – he has a mind and feelings of his own and should be treated with understanding and consideration. Also, like people horses are individuals. An approach which works for one may not work for another. Learning to achieve the best with so many different characters is one of the enduring fascinations of working with horses. Bring patience and understanding to your horse and he will reward you in like kind.

Again, Pegotty Henriques put it in a nutshell: "The rider who always blames the horse is seldom right."

UNPREDICTABLE BEHAVIOUR

Always remember that horses have not been programmed to behave in the way we want — and they have certainly never read the instruction books!

This horse is napping (refusing to go in the required direction). He may be frightened, though it is often due to a faulty education.

There will be times when you are riding when you give all the correct aids but the horse still does not do what you want. Before you start accusing him of being stubborn or naughty, pause to ask yourself, "Does he really understand?"

Most horses are amenable creatures. They readily do what we ask provided (a) the question has been asked clearly, and (b) they have been taught the right answer. What you might be tempted to interpret as misbehaviour or lack of co-operation will be, almost every time, either rider error or a lack of good basic education.

While some horses will become utterly obedient, others may, occasionally, be governed by their deep-seated instincts. For instance, a normally well-behaved stallion may forget his manners if he suddenly finds himself in the vicinity of an in-season mare, and any horse may revert to his "flight" instinct if he has a sudden fright. Remember, too, that the fitter a horse becomes, and the more feed he is given, the more likely he is to become boisterous because of all his pent-up energy.

Never forget, then, that horses have minds and feelings of their own. Try to discover the reason behind their behaviour. Be kind, be firm, but never be quick to mete out punishment — it is rarely deserved.

Shying

Shying is something that every rider should know how to deal with, because most horses will shy at something from time to time. It may be something about which they have a particular hang-up, probably because they remember being frightened in the past, or they may simply be taken unawares by an unfamiliar object or a sudden movement.

When shying, the horse leaps to one side, away from the scary object, his natural instinct being to run away from it. Shying is particularly dangerous when you are riding on the road, when the horse may shy into the path of an oncoming vehicle.

HOW TO COPE WITH SHYING

- To control a shy to the right, use your right rein to turn the horse's head in the direction of the movement. This "blocks" his shoulder. Use your right leg to control the swing of his hindquarters.
- To control a shy to the left, use your left rein and left leg. Avoid turning the horse's head towards the frightening object — he will assume that you want him to approach nearer and will be even more "spooked".
- Be observant: anticipate problems and take precautionary action.
- Try to help a horse overcome his fears by accustoming him to whatever it is that scares him: repeatedly walk him past it, preferably in the company of another steadier horse, to show him that there is nothing to be frightened of.

Jogging

Riding a horse who refuses to walk but continually jogs along can be a wearing experience. It usually stems from a combination of excitement and lack of correct schooling. If the problem is only intermittent, it may be possible to cope with it by using frequent half-halts and quietening the horse with your voice. Always praise him when he does go back into walk. Hauling on the reins will do no good — he will probably simply go on jogging on the spot. You must continue to use your legs to drive him forward into your hands.

It may take quite a lot of patient re-schooling to get a confirmed jogger out of the habit. To re-educate such a horse involves plenty of flatwork at walk, encouraging him to relax and lengthen his stride. His work regime should be kept as varied as possible so that he does not become bored.

Refusing to Stand Still

Fidgeting when you are trying to mount, and moving forward the instant your seat touches the saddle, may have one of a number of underlying causes. Both problems can indicate that the horse has a sore back, or that the saddle is uncomfortable. Perhaps he has been ridden by someone who has habitually banged down heavily into the saddle when mounting so that he anticipates the discomfort, or perhaps he has been poked in the ribs by an inept rider's toe once too often. Some high-spirited horses, particularly if they are stabled and in peak fitness, find it hard to contain their excitement at the prospect of exercise. Or it can simply be that the horse's education was too rushed and that he was never taught to stand still in the first place.

Re-schooling the horse involves incorporating some mounting and dismounting sessions into his daily routine. You will need an assistant to hold the horse's head. They should stand in front of and slightly to the side of the horse, with their hands on the bit rings or the cheek pieces of the bridle. They should not hold the horse's head too firmly as he might panic and pull away. It may help to have the horse facing a

RIGHT: Many horses and ponies pull when they are excited, but pulling can also be the result of pain in the mouth.

wall or fence. To begin with use a mounting block, and mount as quickly and smoothly as possible. A verbal command to "stand" from the assistant may help. Praise the horse when he obeys, quickly check your girth, and then move quietly forwards.

Practise a few times on a daily basis. In time you should be able to dispense with the mounting block and, eventually, with the services of your assistant.

Pulling

Horses often pull when they are excited, especially if they are surrounded by other horses. But pulling can also be a horse's reaction to pain, so his mouth, teeth, bit and bridle need to be carefully scrutinized and any problems dealt with.

To cope with a horse who pulls through excitement, resist the urge to haul back on the reins. Remember, he is stronger than you. Instead, use repeated half-halts, resisting with your hands, then yielding, then resisting, then yielding, until he begins to listen to you. There is a big difference between a horse who pulls and a horse who runs away, so try to stay calm and relaxed. The more you tense up, the more he is likely to pull.

Lots of flatwork – especially transitions and half-halts – may eventually cure the problem. The horse needs to get his hocks well under him and his weight off his forehand.

ABOVE: Horses who constantly fidget may be in discomfort or they may never have been taught to stand still.

Bolting

Being on board a runaway horse is a terrifying experience, but fortunately bolting is relatively rare. Occasionally you do come across a habitual bolter – if you value your safety, have nothing to do with such an animal – but usually a horse or pony who suddenly takes off as if the devil were at his heels is either frightened or in pain.

It is easy to say don't panic. Not quite so easy to stay calm if you are the one in the saddle. You must, however, try to keep a clear head.

Eventually all runaways will stop through exhaustion. However, it may not be possible to stay with them to that point. If the situation

Stopping a Bolter

If you are in an open space, immediately try to turn the horse to one side or the other. If you can get him going in a large circle, you should be able gradually to reduce the size of the circle and thus slow him down.

Fix one hand against the base of his neck and repeatedly use a give and take action with the other rein. If you can do this in time with his strides, so much the better. Avoid the temptation to lean back and use a dead pull on both reins – he will outpull you every time.

If he normally responds to voice aids, for instance when being lunged, try telling him to "Whoa" in the same tone of voice. Otherwise talk to him in a calm voice (if you can!) and try to avoid gripping hard with your legs, which will only encourage him to go faster.

If you are lucky enough to have access to a ploughed field or one with high-growing vegetation, ride into it, as this will almost certainly have a braking effect.

If you have the courage, try giving him his head completely. Sometimes this seems to convince a runaway that there is in fact nothing to run away from and he will check his speed.

Managing a Buck

If you feel a buck coming and know you cannot prevent it, bridge your reins by passing the spare end of one rein through your other hand (under the thumb). If you should be thrown off balance, provided you keep your hands down, the "bridge" will help to prevent you being thrown so far forwards that you hit the deck. In extremis there is no reason why you should not grab hold of the horse's mane!

becomes life threatening – if you are approaching a busy main road or the edge of a quarry or a low hanging branch of a tree – you may have no option but to bail out. All you can do is select a piece of soft ground and curl up and roll on landing.

Bucking

All horses and ponies kick and buck for pleasure, particularly when they are turned out to grass after being stabled or when something exciting happens and they go for a "jolly" round their paddock. Many will give a little buck when they are being ridden

It is not difficult to sit on a horse who kicks up his heels like this. He needs to lower his head to buck properly.

from sheer *joie de vivre*. There is usually no harm in bucking and the temptation to do a rodeo act quickly passes. If you can keep the horse's head up and drive him forward strongly with your legs it is often possible to prevent him from bucking. However, if a horse bucks habitually, there may be a more serious underlying cause such as pain in his back – or elsewhere – or an ill-fitting saddle or other item of tack.

Perhaps he is having too much energy-giving

feed for the amount of work he is doing, or perhaps he is fed up with having an unbalanced rider bouncing about on his back. The cause must be traced and eliminated.

Water Shyness

Horses tend by nature to be suspicious of water, and who can blame them? They cannot know how deep it is, what the footing is like, or what dangers lurk in or around it.

A horse who has not been taught at an early age that there is nothing to fear from getting his feet wet should be taken back to basics. Ride him out in the company of a steady horse who will splash through anything, and practise going through large puddles – avoid small ones to begin with because he might try to dodge round or jump over them. Use firm leg aids, be patient and in time he will realize there is nothing to fear and will follow his companion. You will probably find it easier to start with if you choose a warm day. Asking the horse to leave his stable and walk straight through icy water on a cold winter's morning will only confirm his suspicions that getting wet is something to be avoided. Remember to praise him when he does well.

Progress in time to crossing streams and shallow pools or rivers, pausing in the water to let him sniff it, have a drink and generally relax. Where you know the footing to be level and safe, ask him to trot and eventually to canter through, to accustom him to the water splashing up around his legs and body.

To get him used to the idea of jumping into and out of water, which you will have to do if you want to compete in cross-country events, place a small log on the bank on the exit side. When he is confident jumping out over that, try asking him to jump over it into the water. Keep the obstacle very small and use firm leg aids without bustling him or giving him any cause for alarm.

Horses are naturally very wary of water but with patience, the rider can teach them to overcome their suspicions.

Horses refuse to jump for a number of reasons. It is up to the rider to look for the underlying cause.

JUMPING PROBLEMS

Most of the difficulties experienced with jumping can be cured by getting back to basics – get your flatwork and gridwork right, and the rest will follow.

Rushing

A sudden increase in speed as soon as he sees a fence in front of him is usually an indication that a horse lacks confidence. It is not, as a rule, a sign of eagerness to jump, though it may be in the case of an excitable animal.

Rushing is often the product of a rushed education so the cure is to go back to basics and do plenty of flatwork and gridwork, particularly at trot, to encourage the horse to go in a nice balanced, rhythmic way. A horse who is confirmed in this habit should stop jumping completely for a while and only be re-introduced to it via trotting poles and gymnastic exercises.

When he is jumping bounce- and one-stride grids calmly, he can be asked to jump a few individual fences – not a course – but he should be circled between each one and, if necessary, taken back to walk before being aimed at the next. It will also help if you put a placing pole in front of each obstacle. Only when he will jump single fences calmly and at a steady pace should he go back to jumping complete courses.

Refusing and Running Out

There are many reasons why a horse stops at a fence or ducks out to the side. He may lack the confidence to tackle a particular obstacle; something may be hurting him; he may be "trying it on"; he may simply have been jumped so much that he is sick and tired of it, or of course, there may be something amiss with your riding.

First analyse the problem and find the underlying cause. Then you can set about curing it.

TOO MUCH JUMPING

Overjumping is a common cause of refusals. Many people become so "hooked" on jumping, particularly when they first learn how, that they blunt their horse's enthusiasm. Avoid doing jumping practice every single day. When you do jump, keep the fences varied and avoid putting them in the same place every time. Always try to introduce variety into the horse's work and always stop jumping while he is still enjoying himself.

THE HORSE IS IN PAIN

If a horse who normally jumps well suddenly begins to refuse or run out, be suspicious: he is probably hurting. Get your farrier to look at his feet, your vet to check his limbs, back and mouth, and make sure that his tack fits correctly.

LACK OF CONFIDENCE

A lack of confidence may be the result of poor basic schooling or it could be induced by poor riding. Ask yourself whether the horse is really ready to jump the size of fences you are putting him at – overfacing a horse is the quickest way to lose his confidence.

Book some jumping lessons with a good instructor to make sure that you are riding correctly. You may be riding him at his fences too fast, with insufficient impulsion; or you may be "hooking back" and unbalancing him, or dropping the contact during the last few strides of the approach. Is your weight too far forward, making it difficult for him to take off, and are you steering a straight course to your fences? Has the horse been asked to jump on difficult ground conditions and had his confidence undermined by slipping, or jarring his legs? Have you been using the correct jumping studs in his shoes (see pp. 154–5)?

Back to Basics

To restore his confidence, do plenty of flatwork and go back to trotting poles and grids and very small fences. Make sure the fences have good groundlines and use placing poles. Make sure you ride to the centre of each fence, with a dead straight approach, and keep a steady contact with his mouth. Never ask him to jump a fence which scares you – any nervousness on your part will quickly be picked up by him and give him further cause for concern.

If he keeps stopping at one particular type of fence, try getting someone with a more experienced, really reliable jumper to give you a lead a few times, to show him that there is nothing to be scared of.

Always remember to fit him with the correct type of studs for the ground conditions. Slipping, either on take-off or landing, can quickly undermine a horse's confidence.

Jumping to One Side

Many horses show a tendency to jump to one side. Stiffness and/or pain in his back are the most likely causes. If the vet can find no physical problem, then suppling exercises should be undertaken. Riding circles and serpentines – first on his "good" side then, when he is thoroughly warmed up, on his stiffer side – will help. Jumping small fences on a circle will be beneficial, too.

Jumping Flat

Asking a horse to jump at too fast a pace or to stand too far off his fences encourages him to flatten in the air. He will then have a greater tendency to hit the fences. Flatwork, trotting poles and grids – using fairly short distances – should be used to help the horse to develop a more rounded outline, and to bring his hindlegs more underneath

him. When he starts jumping again, a placing pole should be used before each fence. To encourage him to jump with a rounded outline the poles can be moved a little closer to the fences than normal for his stride.

Disobedience

Occasionally a horse may refuse or run out from sheer naughtiness or stubbornness. Many horses will take advantage of an ineffective or indecisive rider in this way. If you are really sure that there is no other reason for such disobedience, it is in order to reprimand the horse – but punishment

Run-outs might be caused by lack of confidence or pain. (Note: never ride with your jacket flappng like this young rider).

must be meted out immediately so that he knows why he is being punished. This means you have to move very quickly to give him a slap with the whip while he is still facing the fence. Never do it when you are circling him away from the obstacle to have another try at it.

The unfairest thing of all is to do what some competition riders do – wait until you have left the arena and then punish him. By then he will have forgotten what his "crime" was, and will become confused and resentful.

6
PART SIX

A HORSE
OF YOUR OWN

A horse of one's own: wouldn't that be something to die for? No more of those fleeting visits to the local riding school; no more wishing that you had a horse of your own choosing available to you, personally, all day every day. To be able to ride whenever you want, to groom him, to take him to shows, to get to know every quirk of his character. What could be more enjoyable?

Well, yes, owning a horse is, or should be, a joy. As with any domesticated animal, if you are prepared to give of yourself, you will find endless rewards: friendship, understanding, loyalty, fun. Be warned, though. Owning a horse is a skilled and time-consuming business. You cannot discard him like a bike or a pair of skates when you have had your fun. The horse is a big animal, his needs are complex and his flesh heir to a bewildering array of ills. The days, weeks and months will suddenly seem a great deal shorter as your life begins to revolve around his requirements. As for the hole in your pocket, once those feed merchant's, farrier's and vet's bills start coming in …

Horse ownership is both a privilege and a responsibility. There are so many aspects to be considered that it should not be rushed into lightly. The chances are that if you have only been riding for a short time you will only have a rudimentary idea about feeding and stable management. And it is unfair to adopt sole responsibility for an animal's wellbeing if you are not really sure what you are doing.

How can you prepare for such a responsibility? Well, there are plenty of good books on the subject. Take time to read and inwardly digest. And in many places it is possible to attend evening classes in horse management. However, because such a lot of the everyday care of horses involves work of a hands-on nature, you really need to get some practical experience too. And there is no better way to do this than to watch how the experts do it and then try to emulate them.

Many people achieve this by helping out at their local riding school (provided of course that it is an efficient, well run one). Or it might be possible to work part-time for a while at a professional yard. Alternatively, if you have the time, you could enrol for a full-time stable management course of the type run by the British Horse Society. Handling horses on a daily basis, acquiring "horse sense" and learning to cope with unexpected problems all provide an invaluable grounding for the first-time owner.

Once you have the necessary practical skills, next look carefully into the costs of keeping a horse. Can you really afford it? Consider the logistics of stabling and grazing, feed and tack storage, and what would happen to the horse if for any reason you were not around for a while. Then, and only then should you set about choosing your horse. Take your time. Never be afraid to seek expert advice. Make the right choice and you will wonder how you ever lived without a horse.

MAKING THE RIGHT CHOICE

When horse-ownership beckons, the golden rule is to proceed cautiously. All too often people are carried away in their excitement and buy the first horse they see – only to find, having got him home, that he is totally unsuitable.

Before you make a move, ask yourself what type of horse or pony you really need. Imagining yourself aboard a high-spirited thoroughbred, trained to tackle Badminton-sized cross-country fences, is all very well. But if you are still at the trotting poles stage and only have time to do quiet weekend hacking, that will not be very practical. Give careful thought, therefore, to the following points and if in doubt seek professional advice. A well-qualified instructor at your riding school, who knows your capabilities, should be able to help.

How Well Do You Ride?

First assess your prowess in the saddle. It is a natural weakness in most people to over-rate their riding skills, so you must be honest.

Are you a nervous rider or a confident one? Do you like jumping or does it scare you? Are you seriously competitive or do you just want a "fun" horse to potter about on and perhaps share with other members of your family?

If you have only recently learnt to ride, look for a steady, reliable animal who has been well schooled and can help you to improve your riding.

What Type or Breed?

There are more than 150 breeds and types of horse and pony, so unless your interest lies in one specific branch of the showing circuit, the world is your oyster. Pedigree is immaterial if the horse is a safe conveyance and fit for the work required of him.

Everyone who rides dreams of having a horse of their own. But take care: buy the wrong one and the dream could turn into a nightmare.

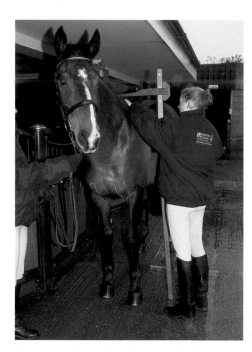

Measuring up: the horse's height is taken at his withers.

Some breeds and types are, because of their size, conformation and nature, more suited to certain activities than others, but if you just want a good all-rounder to have a little fun with – go out hacking, join your local riding club, etc – then do not worry too much about his ancestry. Your choice should be governed by other, more important, factors such as size, weight-carrying ability, temperament, athletic aptitude and, most importantly, the facilities and time which you have at your disposal.

Remember that some breeds are noted for their placid temperament while others are more highly strung. In America, for example, the

Saddlebred and the Quarter horse are both blessed with the most amiable of natures, while in Britain horses with some native pony or heavy horse blood usually make excellent first horses.

The "Schoolmaster"

The less experienced you are, the more important it is to choose a horse who has been well schooled, is willing, well mannered, a safe ride and altogether a nice person to have around. Once you have had some good, basic instruction in riding and horsemastership you will find you can learn a lot by working with a good "schoolmaster" horse with a calm, obliging temperament. He may well not be in the first flush of youth, but he will look after you, give you confidence and – most important – forgive your mistakes. Such horses are worth their weight in gold to novice riders.

Size

Generally speaking, it is best to choose a horse whose stature suits your own height. If you have very long legs, you will feel underhorsed on a small animal. Conversely, if you are short, you may feel overhorsed on a big, strapping one – and you may well find it more difficult to ride effectively. If you are a heavyweight, you must choose a horse capable of carrying you without undue effort. Generally speaking a big horse – 16hh or more – with plenty of bone (see pp.20–24) will be up to more weight

ABOVE: *Some ponies, like this lovely Connemara, make excellent mounts for adults. They are usually very hardy.*

than a small, lighter framed one. However, it should be remembered that some ponies – notably the bigger British native breeds, such as the Highland, Dales, Fell and Connemara – and some small horses – such as the little Icelandic horse – are well up to carrying adults. Since they are also economical to keep, they can be a good choice for someone on a limited budget.

Age

An inexperienced rider should never buy a novice horse – the results are almost always disastrous, especially for the poor horse. So avoid the temptation to buy a "green" youngster just because he is cheap.

As a rule, horses increase in value up to the age of about 10. Once they get into their teens their value starts to drop. Obviously the older they are the more wear and tear there has been on their limbs and the more likely they are to become unsound.

To a great extent your choice will be governed by the depth of your purse. A well-schooled seven-year-old will set you back more than a 15-year-old, but he will provide more years of active service.

If you are likely to want to sell him on in a few years time, it makes sense to opt for a younger horse because it will be easier to find a buyer. If you plan to keep him indefinitely, age is of less concern, particularly if you are not going to compete seriously. Many horses can be ridden into their late teens and early twenties with no ill effects.

Sex

Due to the growing importance of competition horse breeding programmes, more and more stallions are seen nowadays competing in sports such as show jumping and dressage. However, they require expert handling and are best avoided by the novice rider.

As to the choice between geldings and mares, it is as well to remember that mares come into season regularly during the summer months, which can sometimes be a problem, especially if you want to compete. On the other hand, if you feel that in the fullness of time you would like to breed your own foal, then a mare would be an obvious choice. Mares are often more moody than geldings and some riders avoid them rather than try to understand their little quirks. It is worth bearing in mind, though, that some of the very best competition horses, right up to Olympic level, are mares. Geldings, on the whole, are the least complicated.

Are You Competitive?

If you have a burning ambition to do, for example, competitive endurance riding or to show jump or compete in dressage, look for a breed or type of horse known to excel in such sports. A sturdy cob who will carry you well in the hunting field will not rise to the heights in dressage, while a flighty little Arab, who will happily tackle an 80 km (50-mile) endurance ride, is unlikely to trouble the best show jumpers. Bear such things in mind to avoid making an expensive mistake.

Show Jumping

Many of the German warmbloods, such as the Hannoverian, Holstein, Oldenburg, Trakehner and Westphalian, excel at show jumping, as do the Dutch and Belgian warmbloods and the Selle Français (French saddle horse). The Irish Draught, when crossed with a more refined horse such as the thoroughbred, has produced some truly outstanding jumpers, and much the same goes for the Cleveland Bay, which in its pure form is better known as a carriage horse. Show jumping at anything other than novice level does put a lot of strain on a horse's legs and back, so it is doubly important to choose a horse with good conformation.

BELOW: *For competition riding, one of the warmblood breeds might be a good choice. This horse is a Holsteiner.*

Pre-Purchase Checklist

BEFORE STARTING TO LOOK FOR A HORSE OR PONY, ASK YOURSELF THE FOLLOWING QUESTIONS — AND ANSWER TRUTHFULLY:

- **Do I know how to look after a horse?** Feeding, watering, health checks, tack fitting, general handling are all skills which take time to acquire.
- **Do I have sufficient time?** Horses, like dogs, are not just for Christmas. They need daily attention, and quite a lot of it.
- **Can I really afford to keep a horse?** It is not just the purchase price you have to think about. What about feed, shoeing, veterinary bills, rugs and other equipment, and transportation if you want to compete?
- **Do I have suitable accommodation?** Horses are selective grazers and paddocks require careful management if they are not to become "horse sick". Lack of stabling can be a problem if the horse should need to be confined, perhaps because of illness or injury. And feed and equipment require secure storage facilities.
- **Who will look after the horse if I am ill or wish to go on holiday?** Horses are notoriously accident prone. Leaving a horse in a paddock, unattended for days on end, is irresponsible and could result in real suffering

BELOW: *Always have your prospective purchase checked by a vet of your own choosing.*

Horse Trials

Although any horse with reasonably good conformation — and the right sort of fitness — can tackle the lower grade of horse trials, at three-day event level it is the thoroughbred or near-thoroughbred who usually comes out on top, because of his great courage, speed and stamina.

Dressage

Any horse can do dressage, up to a point. In fact, one or two animals with less than perfect conformation have reached the very highest level because of their aptitude and temperament — and the skill of their trainers. For many decades the top level of competitive dressage has been dominated by the Germans and to a lesser extent the Dutch, Swiss and Russians. Many of the most successful horses have come from the same breeds as the show jumpers. This is not to say, however, that the thoroughbred, the Lipizzaner, the Andalusian, the Lusitano or some of the many Russian horse breeds cannot succeed — they can and do.

Endurance Riding

Pure- and part-bred Arabians have an outstanding record in endurance riding, though any breed or type of horse can be made fit enough to take part in shorter distance rides.

Facilities

Your choice of horse or pony will be governed to a greater or lesser extent by the facilities you have at your disposal. If you have a paddock but no stabling, then you must choose an animal who is hardy enough to live out in all weather. Native ponies cope admirably with harsh conditions, finely bred thoroughbreds do not. It is unfair, if not cruel, to buy a horse who needs special facilities which you cannot provide.

RIGHT: *For the higher levels of endurance riding the Arab or part-bred Arab is a sensible choice.*
INSET: *Horses of all shapes, sizes and colours can be schooled to perform a creditable dressage test.*

There are far more complications to owning a horse than keeping, say, a dog or cat. But there are also a number of options open to the one-horse owner, so you need not abandon your dream of having your own horse just because you lack the right facilities.

Keeping a Horse at Livery

There are plenty of livery yards which will, for a price, keep your horse for you if you do not have land and stabling of your own, or simply do not have the time to care for a horse on a daily basis. In both Britain and the United States, for example, boarding horses at livery yards is a widespread practice, particularly in urban areas.

The cost is governed by the facilities on offer – some yards have extensive schooling facilities in addition to stabling and grazing – the area in which you live and the type of livery you require. Generally, the nearer you are to a built-up area, the higher the charges will be.

Types of Livery

FULL LIVERY

If you work full time, and need someone to take on every aspect of your horse's day-to-day care, including grooming – and exercising on days when you are unable to ride – then you will have to opt for full livery. Obviously, this is the most expensive type of boarding out a horse.

HALF LIVERY

With half livery, the yard will take care of most of your horse's day-to-day needs, including feeding and mucking out, but you will do all the riding. Assuming you have time, it will reduce costs if you undertake to groom your horse yourself.

DIY LIVERY

Do-it-yourself is the most economical type of livery – all you will be paying for are the yard's facilities, ie, stabling, grazing, feed storage, etc. You will be responsible for visiting your horse every day to feed, water, muck out and groom him, and to turn him out or exercise him. Remember that if you become ill or are unable to visit him because of an

KEEPING A HORSE

Horse ownership is a big responsibility and should not be entered into lightly. Before you buy your first horse, consider exactly how you are going to care for him.

ABOVE: *A good sturdy field shelter gives horses at grass some much needed protection from the worst of the weather.*

emergency, you must arrange to have him cared for, either by a friend, or perhaps by someone at the yard, for whose time you must be prepared to pay.

GRASS LIVERY

If your horse is kept out on a full-time basis, you can pay simply for grass livery. However, be sure to choose a yard which has suitable grazing, and stabling available should it be required in an emergency – for instance, if your horse is injured and needs box rest.

Quality Time

Remember that there is no better way to get to know your horse than to spend time with him on a regular basis, not just when you want to ride. Feeding, mucking out, grooming, handling him on the ground – all these things help you to get to know each other, to understand each other's personalities and to form a bond of trust and friendship.

Before you get involved in the expense of long-term full livery, ask yourself whether you really do have the time to fully enjoy a horses of your own or whether it would not be better, until your circumstances change, simply to go on riding at a

Horse Sense

Horses are sociable animals: it is cruel to deprive them of company of their own kind. Therefore, if you have your horse at home, you must provide him with at least one companion. An older, retired horse or pony or a donkey might be suitable or, if you have the facilities, you could consider taking in a livery or two – the income would help to pay your bills.

ABOVE: *Horses are sociable animals and should never be kept alone. A Shetland pony makes a good companion.*

RIGHT: *Well designed looseboxes make a suitable environment for the stabled horse.*

good equestrian centre whenever the opportunity arises. It will be far less costly, and the money you save can be put aside for the day when you really do have the time to spend with a horse of your own.

Keeping a Horse at Home

Ideally, to keep a horse at home you will need a couple of acres of suitable pasture, plus stabling and secure storage facilities for feed, bedding, equipment, tack and possibly a trailer or horsebox.

If your property has these sorts of amenities attached, all well and good. If not, you may be able to construct stabling on your premises and rent adjoining grazing. Be wary of renting unsupervised grazing elsewhere – ie, not attached to a yard. Horse theft is common and, sadly, deliberate maiming and even killing of horses is becoming more widespread in many countries.

Horses are happier if they can spend at least part of each day turned out at grass. If they can be provided with a suitable field shelter, so much the better. This will enable them to take cover from extremes of weather should the need arise. Many people find that the most convenient method of horse keeping is to stable their horse at night and turn him out for part of each day. This is called the combined method and is particularly useful if you are competing or hunting regularly, when you will want a dry, clean horse at the start of the day. It is, however, more time-consuming, because you will have the daily task of mucking out.

To keep a horse "in" all the time is even more demanding and is not to be recommended unless you have the time to give him plenty of exercise to prevent boredom setting in.

HOW TO BUY A HORSE

Buying a horse is probably one of the biggest investments you will ever make, so be sure to seek expert advice and never rush into things.

When you finally decide that horse ownership is for you, it will quickly become apparent that there are always plenty of horses and ponies for sale. This does not necessarily mean that you will find the right one immediately. Remember that the perfect horse is as rare as the perfect human. You are going to have to search around and, inevitably, there will have to be a certain amount of compromise.

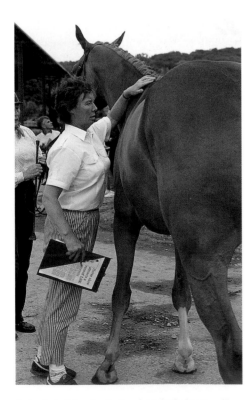

Seek expert advice when buying a horse for the first time. Have your prospective purchase checked out before you decide to buy.

Remember too, that while many animals are on the market for perfectly genuine reasons – perhaps the rider is giving up, or has outgrown the horse or pony, or is ready to take on a more challenging ride – there are just as many others who have defects, either of temperament or health. Such defects may not be immediately obvious and the vendor, you can be sure, will not be keen to bring them to your attention.

Buying by Recommendation

Finding a horse by personal recommendation is undoubtedly the most reliable method for the novice. If you have been taking lessons regularly at a reputable riding establishment, your instructor, who knows your capabilities, will be in a perfect position to recommend a horse or pony should one become available. Or you could approach your local riding club or branch of the Pony Club for advice. In Britain many wonderful children's ponies change hands by this method, never coming on the open market.

Buying from a Private Vendor

There is never a shortage of horses for sale privately. You will see them advertised in equestrian journals, local newspapers, agricultural publications and equestrian-related premises such as tack shops and riding schools. The big problem for the uninitiated is that the vendors are bound to emphasise the horse's good qualities, leaving you to find out his faults for yourself.

How to Read an Advertisement

Horse-for-sale advertisements follow a pretty standard formula. There will be a description of the horse's age, height, breeding, colour and sex, plus a short description of his virtues – such as "excellent temperament", "a perfect gentleman" – his level of schooling and, if relevant, what he has achieved competitively.

The art in reading these ads is to look for what is NOT mentioned. For example, an advert might mention that the horse is "good to catch, shoe, clip and box". Fine. But is he also good in traffic? Or he may be described as "not a novice ride". Why? Does he simply need further schooling, or is he a confirmed puller, does he buck, bolt or what?

You might fall in love with the idea of a four-year-old described in the most glowing terms. He might very well be a paragon, but at four his education will certainly not be anywhere near complete and, if you are inexperienced yourself, he would be a totally unsuitable purchase. To begin with, then, it is wise to make a list of exactly what you are looking for and only go to see animals who sound as if they come reasonably close to your "ideal".

Buying from a Dealer

Tradition has it that horse dealers are an unscrupulous lot, out to make money and willing to go to any lengths to deceive the horse buyer. Of course there have been and probably still are dishonest ones, but the vast majority are simply people wanting to earn a living. In order to do that on a long-term basis they must maintain a decent reputation and it is only fair to say that some very good animals indeed pass through the best dealers' yards each year.

For the newcomer to the horse world, the main stumbling block is getting to know who are the best dealers in their area. The wisest thing is to take advice from someone more experienced. Again your riding school proprietor, riding club or Pony Club should be able to help. Anyone who has regularly bought horses from a particular dealer and who has been well satisfied with the results will point you in the right direction.

Sales

Unless you can call on the services of someone who is thoroughly experienced in the process, it is best to steer clear of horse sales, where everything happens so quickly that you could end up buying totally the wrong type of animal. There are plenty of good, reputable equine auctions operating throughout the horse world, and the best ones are conducted under strict conditions of sale designed to protect both the vendor and the buyer. But it takes a practised eye to pick out a suitable horse when business is so briskly conducted.

If, for example, a horse has an obvious physical defect and you fail to spot it until you have taken the horse home, you cannot plead ignorance. It was up to you to see it before bidding for the horse.

If you do have expert help on hand and you decide to try your local sales, make sure that there is somewhere for you to see the horse in action. And bear in mind that each horse should have an entry form, completed and signed by the vendor – this serves as a contract between all three parties, vendor, auctioneer and buyer.

ABOVE, TOP: *Blemishes that you might miss will be obvious to a practised eye.*

ABOVE: *Many good horses change hands in the sales ring, but business is conducted at a brisk pace and it takes skill to pick out a bargain.*

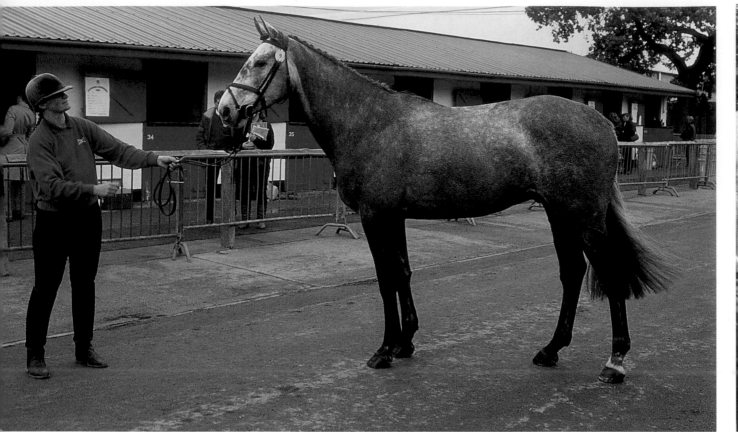

Be Prepared

Rule number one for the novice horse buyer is to take along someone far more experienced than themselves when they go to look at a horse. They are more likely to notice things which have been glossed over by the vendor. They can also act as a witness to a sale. If you do not have a friend with sufficient knowledge, it is well worth paying for an expert opinion. Rule number two is to ask the vendor as many questions as possible – in the hearing of your witness – including:

■ Is the horse safe in all types of traffic?

Ask to see him ridden on the road and then ride him yourself if you are satisfied that he is safe. On the day that you see him you may not encounter all types of traffic so still ask the question because he may have a hang-up about one type of vehicle.

■ Is he "spooky"?

A horse can be perfectly safe in traffic but still be dangerous on the roads if he spooks at every bird in the hedge or every piece of litter on the verge.

■ Is the horse easy to catch, tack up, shoe, clip and box?

Ask to see him being caught – and try catching him yourself. Ask to see him being tacked up – and try it yourself. Ask to see him being loaded and unloaded – and then try leading him in and out of the trailer or box yourself. You are unlikely to be able to see him being shod or clipped, but you could ask who has been shoeing him and get in touch with them, and you could ask to see how the horse reacts if clippers are switched on close to him.

■ Is he well mannered in the stable and when being led?

Watch how he behaves when the vendor handles him and then try for yourself. Make sure that he moves over in the stable when asked, walks calmly through the doorway – no rushing or barging – and is quiet to lead.

■ Does he bite or kick?

Watch the horse's behaviour when approached and handled by the vendor. Biting and kicking may well be tolerated by an experienced person if the horse's athletic talents make up for such rude behaviour, but it can ruin your everyday relationship with a horse if you are constantly having to dodge his teeth and heels.

■ Does he tear his rugs and/or bandages?

Some horses become extremely adept, either through boredom or irritation, at tearing or even completely removing their rugs and bandages. Sometimes it is possible to prevent them by fitting a bib – a piece of stout leather – to the underside of the headcollar noseband, but dedicated rug tearers will manage to circumvent it. If you really want the horse, you must be prepared to dip into your pocket regularly – you may well become your local saddler's best customer! Think twice if the horse is going to be kept in most of the time.

■ Does he have any stable "vices", such as crib-biting, wind-sucking, weaving, box-walking, wall-kicking or door-banging?

Make sure you ask about all such habits and get your expert adviser to check for visible signs. For an explanation of these terms, see pp. 104–5.

■ *Does he ever nap, that is refuse to go away from home or from other horses, and continually try to whip round and head back the way he has come?*

Watch the horse while he is being ridden before trying him yourself. The horse may only misbehave in certain situations, so make sure you get a clear answer to your question.

■ *Does he buck, rear or bolt?*

A little buck may be simply high spirits but some horses buck quite seriously, which can be very unnerving for a novice rider. Rearing and bolting are both very dangerous. Neither fault may manifest itself when you go to view the horse, so again be sure to get a clear "no" from the vendor before considering purchase.

■ *Is he a headshaker?*

Horses who continually shake their heads can be difficult, and sometimes dangerous, to ride. The behaviour may be caused by a dental or ear problem, an uncomfortable bridle or bit or because the horse is exceptionally sensitive to flies. This type of

headshaking problem can usually be resolved. But where no treatable cause can be found, it is a much more serious matter. Although on-going research has not yet revealed the cause, one school of thought is that it is a neurological problem. What is certain is that many horses become extremely distressed and even injure themselves as they try to relieve the irritation or pain. Some have to be put down to prevent further suffering. Keep a keen eye open, therefore, when you go to look at a horse, both in the field and in the stable, and if he is constantly throwing his head about, beware. Bear in mind that some horses headshake more at certain times of year and will no doubt not be offered for sale when the problem is most noticeable. For example, a horse who cannot tolerate flies is unlikely to come on the market at a time of year when insects are active. The owner will try to find a buyer during the winter months.

■ *Is he aggressive towards other horses?*

Occasionally you come across an equine bully, which can cause problems when you are sharing facilities. Other owners will not take too kindly to their horses

ABOVE, OPPOSITE: *You may like the overall look of a horse – but is he going to be easy to ride and look after?*
ABOVE, CENTRE: *Checking a horse's action is an important aspect of buying. He should also be well-mannered and easy to handle.*
ABOVE: *Make sure that the horse is easy to load and unload.*

being roughed up in the field. Horses who lash out at other horses when being ridden in a group are also best avoided by the first-time owner.

■ *Has he learnt to undo stable doors?*

Some horses seem to be born Houdinis, so you need to know before you get your purchase home whether you should fit your stable (and gates) with specially designed safety bolts.

■ *Does he jump out of his paddock?*

This can be a really difficult and dangerous problem unless you have exceptionally high fencing or hedges round your paddocks. However, horses who jump for fun like this will probably make good competition horses – if you can keep track of them.

WHAT ARE VICES?

The confined conditions in which the domesticated horse is kept can lead to a number of stereotypical behaviour patterns. These are known as "vices".

Weaving, crib-biting, wind-sucking, box-walking: these are just some of the peculiar sounding habits that horses may acquire because of the restrictive way of life man inflicts upon them. They are not, generally speaking, drastically harmful to the horse, though once acquired they are difficult to break. Indeed, it may well be that by trying to cure an established "vice" you are simply putting more stress on the horse.

It is usual when buying a horse to ask whether he is "vice free", so that you can be prepared if he does have any. For instance, a horse who chews wood can do damage to your stabling as well as causing wear on his teeth. If the vendor admits that the horse has one of these habits, it is up to you to decide whether you still want him.

Common Stable Vices

BOX-WALKING

Horses who incessantly walk round and round their stable are known as box-walkers. Research has shown that this habit is sometimes hereditary, but the major contributory factor is, of course, confinement. The method by which the horse was weaned as a foal has also been found to have a bearing.

Usually it is all too easy to spot a box-walker

RIGHT: *Some people supply stabled horses with toys, like this ball, to help prevent boredom.*

FAR RIGHT: *A crib-biter grasping the top of his stable door. He has been fitted with a cribbing collar.*

simply by looking over the stable door. Even if he is not on the move at that particular moment, you will see the track which he has made in his bedding.

If a horse is up for sale at a public auction, the condition has to be declared. But when you go to look at a horse being sold privately, a confirmed box-walker may well have been removed from his stable beforehand so that there is no visible evidence. He may have been turned out to grass, or be tied up to prevent him tramping round. If the horse is kept under the American barn system (see pp.120–21), he will probably be tethered on "cross-ties" (two ropes, reins or chains, one attached to each side of his headcollar) in the centre aisle for you to have a look at him.

The only way to know for sure is to watch him when he is loose in his stable, though it has to be remembered that some horses only box-walk at certain times, for example when they anticipate exercise or when they are left alone.

Horses who are kept stabled for long periods, such as racehorses, may box-walk to the extent where the muscles on one side of their body build up, while those on the other become wasted (that is if they box-walk in one direction, as many do). Some individuals will walk for so long that they become exhausted and are not fit for the work required of them.

Some people try to prevent box-walking by placing obstacles such as straw bales or old tyres in the stable, but such a ploy is only likely to increase the horse's frustration. The kindest thing is to ensure that the horse has plenty of exercise to help satisfy his need to be on the move and to turn him out to grass as much as possible, in the company of one or more really placid companions. Sometimes a complete change of environment solves the problem – a horse who box-walks in one yard may drop the habit when he is moved to another.

Whether or not you buy a box-walker depends on what you want to do with the horse and how you plan to keep him. If he can be outside a lot, it may not be a problem. If you plan to keep him stabled and to get him fit to compete on a regular basis, you may find it difficult to keep him in peak condition and you will always have a messy stable to contend with.

CRIB-BITING

A horse crib-bites by seizing hold of a fixed object with his incisor teeth and pulling backwards. It is often accompanied by a grunting sound. Some

Remember

The sensible approach to stable "vices" – and the most humane – is to tackle the underlying cause, not the symptoms.

RIGHT: *Keeping a horse "in prison" like this can all too easily lead to stable vices.*

BELOW: *A chewed stable door may indicate a diet-related problem.*

horses suffer no ill effects, though the habit can lead to digestive disorders and to the teeth wearing down. An experienced horseman will probably be able to tell from the state of the incisors whether the horse is, or has ever been, a crib-biter.

Modern research techniques, involving X-rays, have rather put paid to the traditional belief that the grunting noise signifies the swallowing of air. It appears, in fact, that air is not ingested and the noise is produced by the flapping of the soft palate as air travels from the horse's mouth to his oesophagus. Research also suggests that horses indulge in crib-biting to compensate for their inability to forage.

Fitting the horse with a special cribbing collar, designed to constrict the muscles and prevent him from arching his neck, is the traditional way to deter the horse. But by preventing him doing something which he finds necessary and pleasurable you are simply adding to his frustration — and only have yourself to blame if he becomes bad tempered. The best "treatment" is to remove the stress which causes the habit, ie, give the horse much more freedom.

When he does have to be inside, ensure that all the surfaces are completely flat so that there is nothing for him to catch hold of. Fit a metal strip over the top surface of the door.

If you like the horse, then there is no need to pass him over because of crib-biting. However, you should be prepared to give him as natural a life as possible in an effort to remove the cause. Bear in mind though that a confirmed crib-biter — like many an alcoholic human being! — is virtually impossible to cure, because he likes what he is doing.

WEAVING

A horse who constantly shifts his weight from one foreleg to the other, rocking his head and shoulders from side to side as he does so, is said to be weaving. Again, it is a form of behaviour associated with mental stress. The habit is usually most marked at moments of excitement, such as the lead-up to feed time, or the sight of a horse's friends going out to exercise without him.

Unless a metal anti-weaving grille is fitted to the top of the stable door, the horse will most likely stand with his head over the door, swaying

The tops of the stable door (and other vulnerable surfaces) should be protected with metal to prevent chewing.

from side to side. A grille will not, however, stop the determined weaver, who will simply stand with his head inside the stable and carry on weaving.

The frustration of confinement seems to be the usual cause, though there are instances of very young foals weaving even while turned out and the habit does seem to run in families.

If you merely want a "fun" horse, and can turn him out to grass for long periods, then there is no reason why you cannot manage a weaver. When he is stabled, the problem may be alleviated if you can replace part of the side walls with metal bars so that he can see and talk to his neighbours. Because, generally speaking, it is the super-fit equine athletes – who have to be kept stabled for much of the time and who undergo the stresses associated with travelling and competing – that are most prone to weaving, much will depend on what you plan to do with the horse.

WIND-SUCKING

When wind-sucking, the horse produces the same grunting noises associated with crib-biting, but he does so without grabbing hold of anything with his teeth. Crib-biters who are deprived of surfaces to take hold of may well become wind-suckers. As with the crib-biter, there is no real reason to turn down a wind-sucker – though it would be helpful to know whether he is particularly prone to colic, since both habits can lead to digestive problems.

The tops of the stable door (and other vulnerable surfaces) should be protected with metal to prevent chewing.

Wood-chewing

Wood-chewing is a rather different problem from the stereoptypic behaviour patterns of crib-biting and wind- sucking. Although the true causes are not yet understood, it seems likely that it has to do with food requirements. The horse may be trying to boost his fibre intake, or to make up for some other deficiency in his food. Horses will chew wood in their stables, but they will also do it while they are turned out at grass. The fact that the latter habit tends to be seasonal – it is most marked towards the end of the winter – leads to the suspicion that it is often diet-related. Future research may well show

that this is indeed the chief reason for the habit.

The main concern for the horse-owner, of course, is the damage done to their property. Wooden surfaces in stables can be treated with a bitter-tasting non-toxic substance which may or may not deter the horse. Where possible – for instance the top of the stable door – the wood should be covered with a metal strip. In fields electric fencing may be used to protect the boundary fencing. The other matters for concern are the damage which may be caused to the horse's teeth, which could be worn down unevenly, and possible digestive upsets.

There is no reason why you should not buy a

horse prone to wood-chewing if he is suitable for your purposes. If you have brick or breeze-block stabling, so much the better – there will be less wood available for him to attack. Otherwise you can take the preventive measures mentioned above. When stabled, or in winter when the grass is scarce, you can try ensuring that he never runs out of hay to nibble at – this might well deter him from looking for wood to chew. It is not necessary to feed him more hay. Simply feed it in a haynet with smaller than usual holes (putting one haynet inside another has the same effect) so that it takes him longer to eat his ration and thus keeps him busy.

DECISION TIME

"Trying" a horse and having him examined by a veterinary surgeon are the two most vital steps along the path to ownership.

The horse's pulse may be felt in the facial artery on the inner edge of the lower jawbone.

Even if someone you know and whose judgement you trust comes up with the "perfect horse for you", never buy a horse without first seeing him and "trying" him yourself; and always have him "vetted" by a veterinary surgeon of your choice before you part with your money.

Trying a horse

Trying a horse involves making an appointment with the vendor to see him, watching him being handled and ridden and then handling and riding him yourself. Only by doing this will you know whether the two of you really are going to get along. Always go in the company of someone more expert than yourself.

Begin by telling the vendor exactly what you are looking for and asking all the relevant questions (see pp.100–03). Ask to see the horse in his stable, being tacked up, led and stood up so that you can look at his conformation. Watch him being trotted away from you and towards you to see how he moves. He should be trotted on a loose rein – the clever horseman may well be able to mask defective action by holding a horse on a short rein.

Watch while the horse is ridden at the various paces and put over a little jump, either by the vendor or their assistant. If there is a glaring omission in what the horse is asked to do (for example, to canter on a particular rein), it may be that the animal has a problem with that. Make a mental note to try that particular movement yourself. Finally, if possible, ask to see him ridden in traffic. View with suspicion any excuse for not responding to any of your requests.

When you are satisfied that the horse is a suitable ride, first get your advisor to try him and then try him yourself. No one can pretend that it is easy to assess a horse in such a relatively short time, but you should be able to judge whether he suits your build, whether you like the way he goes, whether he is responsive to the aids and safe in whatever traffic conditions are to hand.

Ideally, you should ask to have the horse on trial at home for a short period. Some vendors will agree to this, in which case you must agree the arrangements (in writing) and organize transport. While he is with you, all costs for his maintenance – including veterinary bills – will be your responsibility. You will also be held liable for negligence.

Having a horse on trial is a great advantage, because there will be more time to assess his general behaviour and to find out whether you actually like each other. If you have any doubts, send him back and look elsewhere.

WARRANTIES

Horses bought at public auctions usually come with a warranty, that is a statement of fact made before or during the transaction. A horse may, for instance, be "warranted sound". When buying privately, make sure you acquire the same sort of written warranty from the vendor before you pay your money. Because of the trend towards litigation these days, some vendors may be reluctant to give a warranty, so you must be prepared to insist. If they have nothing to hide, it should not be a problem. The warranty should detail specific points which you have raised with the vendor, for example, that the horse is safe in traffic, is vice free, and so on.

Checking the horse's action is an important part of the vetting process.

Wise Precautions

If you are thinking of buying a particular horse and the vendor asks for a deposit, make clear conditions: for example, that the deposit is subject to a satisfactory veterinary inspection, or that you are entitled to a further trial ride on the horse. Make sure you are given a receipt for the deposit.

When you go ahead with a purchase, make sure you are given a receipt and warranty at the time and keep them in a safe place. Also ask for any breed papers that the horse may have. These may be essential should you want to show the horse. Keep them safe in case you ever decide to sell him so you can pass them to the new owner.

Having a Horse Vetted

When you decide that you have found the horse for you, tell the vendor that you will buy him "subject to a veterinary certificate" and arrange for a veterinary surgeon of your choice – not the vendor's – to inspect the horse. If possible, be present when the vet examines the horse so that you can discuss any problems.

WHAT THE VET IS LOOKING FOR:

- **The horse's general attitude and state of health:** the vet notes how he behaves in the stable, the condition of his skin, the presence of any lesions or heat in a joint or tendon, any discharge from the nostrils or eyes, etc.
- **The horse's conformation:** the vet asks for the horse to be stood up squarely on flat ground outside the stable so that he can make a thorough manual examination.
- **The horse's movement:** the horse is walked and then trotted both away from the vet and towards him to reveal any signs of lameness. The vet may also ask to see him backed for a few strides, or turned in a tight circle to either side, or lunged on a hard surface – all are devices used to reveal unsoundness.
- **The horse's wind and heart:** the horse is ridden, first at walk, trot and canter to warm him up, then at a gallop, after which the vet listens to his heart and lungs.
- **The final check:** when the horse has cooled down he is trotted out again in hand – old lameness problems sometimes reappear after fast exercise; muscular and arthritic problems, which might disappear when the horse is warm, may reappear once he has cooled off.
- **The veterinary certificate:** When the vet's examination is over, he will complete the certificate, which includes a detailed identification of the horse (this includes peculiarities of colours and markings, height, etc), his report, and his opinion regarding the suitability of the horse for the prospective purchaser's purpose.
- **Remember –** veterinary surgeons are not clairvoyant! A vet's certificate is not a guarantee, but an opinion expressed by a qualified person. It means that the horse is free of certain disorders at the time he was examined. It cannot mean that he will remain completely free from disease in future, nor does it guarantee that the horse is free from stable "vices".

7
PART SEVEN

HORSE MANAGEMENT

The world's best horsekeepers are Jacks (and Jills) of all trades: whether it is the digestible energy content of feedstufffs, the finer points of fence design, correct pasture management or the right way to hang a gate, you name it and the chances are that the competent horseman will know something (often quite a lot) about it. Whatever else it may or may not do, keeping horses certainly broadens the mind.

Horses have been kept in all sorts of different conditions down the centuries. Some have lived under the same roofs as their human masters. Others have been chained to the wall in cramped stalls. They have had their coats clipped off, or been clad all over in felt, had their ears and tails mutilated and been fed all manner of weird and wonderful concoctions.

Each age imagines it has invented the ultimate method of horse management. Most systems have their merits – and demerits. Many of the oldest tenets of good horsekeeping still hold good today. Among them are the vast majority of the principles propounded by the Greek soldier and historian Xenophon (c.430-350 BC). Among other things, Xenophon clearly understood the benefits of good stable drainage when he advocated the installation of a sloping floor. "The same care which is given to the horse's food and exercise, to make his body grow strong, should also be devoted to keeping his feet in condition. Even naturally sound hoofs get spoiled in stalls with moist, smooth floors."

However, by no means all horse-keeping methods put the horse's welfare first, certainly not his mental welfare. As the "vices" discussed in the previous chapter demonstrate, locking horses up in stables is often extremely stressful for the animals, however convenient it may be for their owners. How boring it must be to be shut up in what amounts to a small room for most of the day, especially if that room has no view. Yet that is how many horses were kept in the past, and how some are still kept for much of their lives.

Nowadays, fortunately, people are realizing more and more the benefits of turning their horses out in a paddock for at least part of each day so that they can do what comes naturally to them: wander about and eat grass. Provided their legs are protected and their environment is hazard free, they generally come to no harm and the benefit to their spirits is inestimable.

Views have also changed, and will no doubt continue to do so, on the complex subject of feeds and feeding. Age-old traditions are constantly being challenged by scientific knowledge. Where the horseman of bygone days had to rely on his instincts and his eyes to tell him whether he was feeding his horse correctly, his modern counterpart can turn to science to help remove the guesswork.

The great thing is to have an open mind. By embracing the old and the new, we can help to give our horses healthier, happier lives.

KEEPING A HORSE AT GRASS

It is unwise to underestimate the horse's desire to roam – or his uncanny knack of getting into trouble!

Boundaries

Bearing in mind that the horse is by nature a nomad, paddock boundaries – whether they comprise fencing, walls or hedges – must be strong and secure if they are to keep the occupants on the correct side and free from injury. Never risk putting your precious horse in a field with flimsy fencing, gap-filled hedges, loose strands of wire or sharp, projecting objects.

FENCING

Without doubt good quality post and rail fencing is about the best material for confining horses. Correctly erected and maintained it is strong, attractive looking and long lasting. True, it will not afford protection from foul weather, but in really exposed areas it can be effectively combined with thick hedging – the fencing being on the paddock side of the hedge – to make the perfect horse environment.

FENCING PRECAUTIONS

- To prevent damage to the fencing – horses love to rub themselves against it – it must be sturdily built.
- Use 10 cm (4 in) square posts. For a 1.2 m (4 ft) high fence, use 2 m (6 ft 6 in) long posts driven well into the ground.
- Cut the tops of the rails on a slight slope to allow rain to drain off.
- If possible, attach the rails to the paddock side of the posts. This helps to protect the horse from injury should he bang himself against the fence and also prevents the rails being pushed off should he lean on them.
- Avoid protrusions and always fix the top rail level with the top of the posts.
- Avoid right-angled corners in the paddock: curved fencing helps to prevent horses from jarring themselves by coming to an abrupt halt in a corner, or by actually colliding with the fence, should they gallop about. It will also help prevent a horse from being cornered by an aggressive companion.
- Treat the timber with a non-toxic preservative to protect it from the weather and to help prevent the horses from chewing it.

HEDGED IN

Hedges can make excellent boundaries – well maintained, they look good and afford protection from wind and wet. But they do require more upkeep than fencing. Regular trimming is required and any gaps which appear must be safely fenced off immediately, otherwise horses will be tempted to push their way through. They must also be kept clear of poisonous vegetation. Beech and hazel

Horses at grass need a constant supply of clean water. A galvanized metal trough is ideal.

make especially good, dense-growing hedges for horses, and neither is palatable.

WIRED UP

Wire mesh looks less attractive than fencing or hedges but it can be very effective, though on the debit side it may stretch if horses lean against it. Barbed wire is best avoided, horses may cut themselves if they rub against it and they can incur severe injuries should they become tangled up in it. Plain wire may be used provided it is really taut, to ensure this, it should be professionally erected.

WIRING PRECAUTIONS

- When using mesh, choose only small, V-shaped openings so that the horse cannot trap his foot in the holes.
- Use stout timber posts.
- Use proper strainers at the corners to keep the wire taut.
- With plain wire, position the strands 30 cm (12 in) apart.
- With plain wire, set the lowest strand 46 cm (18 in) above the ground – too low and the horse may put his leg through and become trapped; too high and he might try putting his head underneath to reach food on the other side.
- Make wire fencing more visible and safer by substituting a wooden rail for the top strand.

STONE WALLING

Provided they are at least 1.2 m (4 ft) high, stone walls make good boundaries; if they are any lower a horse might be tempted to jump out. Correctly maintained they look most attractive and horses like sheltering against them in bad weather.

ELECTRIC FENCING

Although it looks flimsy, electric fencing is respected by horses and can be very useful for temporarily dividing paddocks.

PLASTICS

Modern plastic fencing can provide a good alternative to wooden posts and rails, particularly if you have a horse who chews wood. Plastic may not look as good, but, unlike wood, it will not rot and it does absorb impact without injuring the horse. It

---

Safety First

- **Check all your fence boundaries regularly and have any suspect sections repaired at once.**
- **Never use bits of slack wire to block off gaps in hedges – fence them off with timber.**
- **Avoid using sheep or pig netting, both of which have holes big enough for a horse to trap his feet in.**
- **Securely fence off any treacherous areas such as potholes or deep ditches.**
- **Never use concrete or metal posts for fencing. They will cause more injury than wood if a horse collides with them.**
- **Ensure that all electric fencing is visible to both horses and humans. Try tying strips of strong plastic at intervals all along the wire.**

must be properly strained on stout wooden posts.

Gates and Gateways

Horse paddocks must have good, safe access, not only for you and your horse but also for large vehicles. There will be occasions when large machinery, such as a harrow attached to a tractor, may be required to keep the grazing in good condition. Gateways must therefore be wide and it helps, especially in winter, if the footing is firm.

POSITIONING OF GATEWAYS

For safety's sake it is best, if possible, to avoid putting horses in paddocks which open on to busy

RIGHT, TOP: *Well constructed post and rail fencing is perfect for horse paddocks. Note the sloped tops to the posts.*

RIGHT, CENTRE: *A fence made of barbed wire and sheep wire is unsuitable for horses.*

RIGHT, CENTRE: *Modern plastic fencing is a useful alternative to the wooden variety.*

roads. Not only is it hazardous leading horses in and out from such a situation, it also makes theft that much easier, since the perpetrators have an easy escape route. Gateways are best sited on well-drained ground. If possible, avoid low-lying, muddy areas.

WHICH GATE?

Gates may be made of wood or metal – either is suitable for a horse paddock provided it is sturdily built. Cross bars give added strength. Maintenance is essential: wooden gates should be treated with non-toxic preservative, galvanized metal ones should be painted regularly. A metal gate is the obvious choice if your horse is a wood-chewer.

HOW TO HANG A GATE

Unless you are very adept at DIY, leave gate hanging to the professionals. Correctly hung, a gate will give years of service. First and foremost, the posts must be very strong: they should be set some 90 cm (3ft) into the ground. Hinges must also be strong, and the gate must fasten with a catch that horses cannot undo with their teeth.

It is essential that gates are easy to open and shut. You will have enough to contend with when leading a horse through without having to wrestle with a gate which sticks, or keeps swinging shut on you, or takes a strongman to lift. A well-hung gate will neither drag the ground nor swing open the moment you release the catch.

GATE PRECAUTIONS

- Hang your gates so that they open into the field, thus making it impossible for the horse to push them open and barge through the moment you unfasten the catch.
- Avoid gates less than 1.8 m (6 ft) wide. Horses can easily injure their hips when bumping into gateposts.

Siting a water trough next to a gateway inevitably leads to poached ground.

- To deter thieves, securely fasten all gates at both the hinge end and the opening end with sturdy chains and padlocks.
- Avoid fastening gates with string which can easily be undone by both horses and thieves.
- If you must climb over a gate in an emergency, climb over the hinge end. Otherwise, avoid putting this extra strain on a gate.
- Never use rusty metal gates. They are easily broken and can cause serious injury to a horse.
- Never feed horses close to a gateway, particularly in winter. The ground will quickly become poached, making it doubly difficult to get into and out of the field.
- Site your gates so that you could, in an emergency, gain access with a large vehicle, for example a box or a trailer.

Water

Horses drink several litres of water per day, the actual amount varying according to the moisture content of their food. In the wild, where the herbage will often contain quite a high percentage of water, it is usual for horses to drink first thing in the morning and again in the evening, though in hot climates they might well need to drink more frequently.

The grass-kept domesticated horse should have access to a constant supply of fresh water. Horses will readily drink from a natural source, such as a stream, provided the water is clean. But too often nowadays water that appears clean is not as pure as it looks. You should make absolutely sure that it is not being polluted upstream before you allow your horse to drink from it. If you have any doubts, fence off any streams and rivers. The same goes for stagnant-looking ponds. Remember that horses are

A natural source of water is fine for horses provided it is pollution free.

fussy drinkers and that they are also great at escaping, so if any of your fencing crosses a stream or river, check it regularly otherwise your horse may well wander off up or down stream.

In the absence of a suitable natural supply of water, the best thing is a galvanized trough fed by the mains and fitted with a ballcock to control the water level. The ballcock must be enclosed to prevent the horses damaging it. Troughs should be sited parallel to a fence, preferably recessed slightly into the line of the fence to avoid the risk of injury from projecting corners. If it is not possible to feed the trough from the mains, it will need to be filled by a hosepipe or, assuming there is a conveniently situated tap, by bucket.

When only a small number of horses are kept together, buckets could be used instead of a trough. Being light they can be moved to different areas of the field to prevent poaching of the ground, and they are also easy to clean. On the minus side, they hold only small quantities of water and are easily knocked over. One way of preventing this is to stand each bucket or other small container in an old car tyre.

WATER PRECAUTIONS

- Check your horse's water supply daily.
- All water containers must be kept scrupulously clean. Clean out all containers at least once a week.
- To keep the water clean, avoid siting containers under trees and hedges.
- Never place water troughs in the middle or corners of a field, where they are more likely to be a source of injury.
- In freezing conditions break the ice on your horse's water at least twice a day.
- To prevent poaching of the ground, where it breaks up into muddy patches, place water troughs on hard, well drained ground – put down hardcore or concrete if necessary.
- When laying a feed pipe to a trough, bury the pipe well into the ground and lag the length above ground to prevent freezing.
- Do not allow horses to drink from streams or ponds with a sandy bottom – they may swallow sand with the water.

SHELTERS & PASTURE MANAGEMENT

Making the paddock a congenial and healthy place for horses to live is part of good ownership practice.

TOP: *Pasture management is an important aspect of good horse keeping.*

ABOVE: *A well designed field shelter, with a high, backward-sloping roof.*

Field Shelters

A well designed field shelter is a very useful facility to have. In extreme weather conditions, either very wet and windy, or very hot, it will provide horses with a welcome refuge. It also provides a dry environment for feeding horses in inclement weather.

An open-fronted shelter is by far the safest, since a horse can easily escape should he be bullied by a more aggressive companion. The shelter must be large enough to house the number of horses who graze together in safety. Too small, and you run the risk of horses being injured if they quarrel. It should be sited either on well drained ground or on a specially prepared concrete standing.

SHELTER TIPS

- Position the shelter with its back to the prevailing wind.
- Ensure that the roof is high enough to allow the horse adequate headroom.
- Slope the roof down towards the back so that water drains away from the entrance.
- Position interior fixtures, such as mangers and hay racks, high enough from the ground to prevent leg injuries.

WINDBREAKS

If you cannot afford a shelter, or have a horse who resolutely refuses to use one – and some horses do – try erecting a wooden windbreak screen. To be effective the screen should be about 2 m (6 ft 6 in) high. It can be built in conjunction with a straight stretch of fencing or you can erect a double-sided one in a corner. Alternatively, free-standing, multi-angled screens can be positioned in the open, giving protection from several directions. They must be sturdy and secured to well driven-in posts.

Remember that a horse's instinct is to shelter beside a hedge or wall, in a natural dip in the ground or beneath a tree – depending on the conditions. In this way he still retains a wide field of vision and can easily use his speed to escape from real or imagined danger. Some horses are resolutely averse to going into the confined space of a shelter, however splendid it is. It may save you money if you find out first whether your horse will actually use a shelter before you set about erecting one. If he is not keen, and his paddock is very exposed, windbreak screens may be a better bet.

Pasture Management

The best pasture for horses is one which has been sown with a mixture of "horse-friendly" grasses. Perennial rye grasses are commonly used to make up about half of the seed mix, with another quarter comprising creeping red fescue. The remainder might contain some Kentucky blue grass (smooth stalked meadow grass), crested dog's tail and Timothy (if you want to take hay from the paddock). The best mixtures include both early and late flowering varieties of grass, thus ensuring that

Worm Control

- Frequent removal of horses' droppings helps to control worm infestations.

- On large tracts of land, where removal of droppings is impracticable, regular harrowing (preferably in dry, warm weather) will help to kill the larvae.

- Grazing cattle alongside horses, or in rotation with them, helps to control worms (the cattle's digestive system destroys the larvae).

- Grazing cattle and sheep on horse pasture helps to tidy up the rougher portions of grazing which horses will not eat; in wet conditions sheep are preferable to cattle because they cause less damage to the ground.

there is good nutritional value throughout the spring and summer months.

Well drained ground produces the best grazing. Where land is poorly drained horses feet will quickly poach the ground (create muddy patches) and ruin the grazing. In such cases it may well be worth the expense of installing proper underground drainage. If drainage exists in the form of ditches, check them regularly and clear out blockages. Bear in mind that if ditches are not functioning adequately it could be that they are blocked on a neighbour's land.

Various factors – the type of soil, the amount of rainfall, altitude and prevailing winds – will affect the quality of grazing produced by even the best seed mixes. When re-seeding a paddock, always have the soil tested and, if necessary, treated first for deficiencies or imbalances. Always keep horses

off land which has been fertilized, or otherwise treated, for the recommended period.

Even the best pasture needs regular attention if it is to sustain horses in the long term. To keep the grass sward in good heart, it should be harrowed during the spring. This pulls out dead grass, making room for new growth. Grass should always be harrowed before fertilizing. Poached areas can be repaired by rolling, which helps to firm the soil.

Remember that the denser the sward of grass, and the better the condition of the ground – ie, not poached – the less chance there is of unwanted weeds such as the deadly ragwort from becoming established.

Never allow your paddock(s) to become "horse sick" through overgrazing. If you have two paddocks, graze and rest them alternately. If you have only one, dividing it into sections with electric fencing is

Cattle help to rid horse pasture of worms. They will also eat the less palatable herbage.

an easy way of managing it efficiently. On a rotation basis, one section can be rested, one grazed by your horses and a third by sheep or cattle.

PASTURE TIPS

- Well-fertilized soil prevents perennial rye grass from deteriorating after the first couple of years.
- Kentucky blue grass tolerates dry, sandy soils.
- Rough-stalked meadow grass thrives in rich, damp soils, its dense growth also keeps out weeds.
- Creeping red fescue is ideal for difficult ground conditions – which is why it is commonly seen on sports grounds.
- A little wild white clover added to the seed mix will improve soil fertility.

BEWARE POISON

Danger, in the form of poisonous vegetation, lurks all around the domesticated horse. By the time symptoms appear, it may be too late.

ABOVE: *Ragwort is lethal to horses. It must be dug out and burnt.*

LEFT: *Horses do not find buttercups especially palatable.*

There is more to keeping horses at grass than ensuring that boundaries and gates are secure and that the grazing and water supply are adequate. Equine animals are susceptible to a huge range of poisonous trees, shrubs and plants, which puts the onus on owners to be vigilant in their pasture management.

Luckily, horses tend to avoid a great many growing poisonous plants – buttercups, for instance, if eaten in large quantities when fresh are poisonous, but horses do not find them especially palatable and will normally graze round them.

There are, however, times when they are at great risk. When grazing is sparse they may be lured by hunger into eating forms of vegetation they would otherwise avoid. The succulent early spring growth of poisonous plants may prove more tempting than the scarcer growth of grass. In addition, some poisonous plants become more palat-

able after being sprayed with weed killer, which may not necessarily reduce their toxicity, or when wilted or dead, which is why great care must be taken when feeding hay.

What to Avoid

Among trees yew is one of the most lethal. All parts of the tree contain poison and the eating of even small amounts usually proves fatal. Laburnum is another tree to avoid. The roots, wood, bark, leaves, flowers, and especially the seeds, are all poisonous, though it takes quite large doses to kill a horse.

Oak trees are also potentially dangerous, since both the leaves and acorns are poisonous. The consumption of small amounts of acorns is probably harmless, but some animals – often ponies – develop an appetite for them. In a year when they are prolific they should be raked up and removed from the pasture.

Where plants are concerned, one of the biggest villains is ragwort, an opportunist weed which thrives on land that is closely grazed and of low fertility. It spreads rapidly where horses are kept in intensive conditions – ground badly poached (muddied) by horses' feet provides an ideal seed bed for weeds such as ragwort.

In Britain during the 1990s ragwort spread at an alarming rate, despite its being listed as an injurious weed. This legislation empowers the Minister of Agriculture, Fisheries and Food to serve notice on the occupier of any land on which ragwort is growing to prevent its spread to agricultural land. Some local authorities are also empowered to take action under bye-laws or the Environmental Protection Act 1990. Yet ragwort still flourished both in fields and along kilometre upon kilometre of roadside verges, whence its wind-borne seeds could travel freely to wide areas of grazing land.

Ragwort causes serious liver damage and its poisonous effects are cumulative – a small intake

Eliminating
RAGWORT

- **Practise good pasture management**
- **Apply fertilizer**
- **Control grazing levels**
- **Pull out occasional plants and BURN**
- **Spray larger areas while the plants are in the rosette stage. Spray in April or May (September or October of previous year if the pasture is to be used for hay).**
- **Remove horses from pasture before spraying and until the plants have died and disintegrated. Spray all infected paddocks at the same time.**

CLOCKWISE FROM LEFT: *Rhododendrons, acorns, lupins, foxgloves, privet, yew and horse tails are all poisonous. Trees and shrubs that cannot be removed should be fenced off.*

over a long period of time can be just as damaging as a large single intake. Young animals are the most susceptible and there is no known treatment. Its eradication on horse pastureland is, therefore, vital (see pasture management, pp. 116–7).

Symptoms of poisoning include dullness, rapid pulse and breathing, weakness, constipation – which may result in a prolapsed rectum – jaundice and wasting. Nervous symptoms – yawning, drowsiness and staggering – are also typical. Unfortunately, once clinical symptoms appear death usually follows.

Some plants, such as bracken and meadow saffron, contain poisons which may take time to build up in the system, by which time the horse is beyond help. The rhizomes (underground stems) of bracken are said to be five times more poisonous than the fronds. Bracken contains an enzyme

which induces vitamin B1 deficiency that produces neuro-muscular symptoms.

Like ragwort, foxgloves become more palatable to horses when they are dried in hay than when fresh. A few ounces may prove fatal. Symptoms of

foxglove poisoning include convulsions and difficulty in breathing and death follows in a short time.

Hemlock is a similarly devastating plant, though it takes larger quantities – several pounds rather than ounces – to cause death. All members of the nightshade family are poisonous, as is monkshood. Horsetails, which are commonly found growing in boggy areas, are very dangerous if eaten in large quantities in hay. Luckily, horses do not usually eat the growing stems.

Other hazardous plants include aconite, bryony, flax, horseradish, hellebores, lupins (especially the seeds), purple milk vetch, St John's wort, water dropwort and yellow star thistle. The stalks of potatoes, both green and dry, are also very dangerous, as are green or sprouting tubers. When potatoes are boiled, the alkaloid they contain is dissolved out into the water. The potatoes then become harmless provided the water is thrown away.

Dangerous shrubs include box, privet, laurel and rhododendron. The latter can cause death through respiratory system failure.

Precautions
AGAINST POISONS

- Learn to recognize trees, shrubs and plants which are poisonous to horses before embarking on horse ownership.
- Before you put a horse in a new field, make a thorough check of the grazing area, hedges and overhanging trees for signs of poisonous vegetation.
- If you find any poisonous plants, dig them up and burn them.
- Cut back and/or fence off any poisonous trees or hedging which cannot be

removed, making sure that they are well out of reach of horses or ponies.
- Never leave poisonous hedge or tree trimmings, or poisonous plants which have been dug up, lying about in the paddock – many plants, including ragwort, are more palatable to horses when wilted or dead.
- Regularly check all paddocks and hedges – remember

that poisonous plants can spread from adjacent land.
- If your paddock adjoins gardens, keep an eagle eye open for cuttings dumped over the fence or hedge.
- If there are poisonous trees in the vicinity, watch for fallen branches or twigs – particularly in windy weather.
- When buying hay, ask your supplier for ragwort-free hay – and always check it carefully when feeding.
- Wear gloves when handling poisonous vegetation.

THE STABLED HORSE

Living indoors is not natural for horses so it is up to the owner to ensure that the effects are not detrimental.

Boxed In

In Britain and many other European countries the most popular type of stabling is the loosebox or box stall. Looseboxes are usually built in a row or rows facing a yard. This enables the horses to see each other and take an interest in everyday activities around the stables, helping to alleviate boredom. Well built looseboxes give horses plenty of fresh air without being draughty.

Stables come in a variety of materials. Brick, breeze block and wood are all suitable, providing you bear in mind the extra fire hazard associated with wood. Metal, such as corrugated iron, should never be used because the interior of the stables will be too cold in winter and too hot in summer. Horses are also more likely to injure themselves on metal.

An alternative to the loosebox system – and one which is particularly prevalent in the United States and some countries, such as parts of Russia, where extremes of weather make it more practical – the barn system of stabling is used. As the name suggests, this comprises a large barn, housing rows of looseboxes on either side of a central aisle. Barn stabling is often preferred by humans because they can go about their daily work without getting wet or being baked by hot sun.

However, barn stabling does have its disadvantages. Many barns are made from wood, and so they pose a major fire hazard; also, disease is more likely to spread when horses are kept in such close proximity. It is important, therefore, to provide good ventilation. The centre aisle and all doorways must be wide enough to prevent horses from banging themselves when they are moved about. Sliding doors are the safest in barn stabling. Ideally, horses should be able to see out of the back of their box stalls as well as into the centre aisle. This will help to prevent them becoming bored.

A third method of housing horses under cover is the yard system, which involves keeping a group of horses loose in a large barn or partially covered area. They can be kept on deep litter, which is labour saving, and provided they are compatible, they will enjoy each other's company.

LEFT, TOP: *A "kick-over" bolt is the ideal fastening for the bottom of a loosebox door.*

LEFT: *Large, well constructed looseboxes like these provide a suitable environment for stabled horses.*

Stable Precautions

- Avoid stables that have a window positioned immediately behind the open top-half of the door – this will cut out a good deal of the light and ventilation which the window is intended to provide.
- Position light fittings well out of reach of the horse.
- Protect all electrical wiring with horse- and rodent-proof conduits.
- Fit waterproof switches – again well out of reach of the horse.
- Equip your stable area with the right fire extinguishers, hoses and sand buckets: if in doubt, seek advice from your local fire prevention officer. Remember that fire extinguishers need regular servicing.
- Check the inside of the stable frequently for splinters, protruding nails, etc, which could cause injury.
- Cover all external drains with strong grids.

Living Room

Expecting a horse to stay happy and relaxed when he is cooped up in a small space for many hours of the day is a tall order. The following are the minimum recommended dimensions for stabling although larger stables are preferable:

Small pony ....2.4 m x 2.4 m (8 ft x 8 ft)
14hh pony............................3 m x 3.7 m 10 ft x 12 ft)
Horse under 16hh ....3.7 m x 3.7 m(12 ft x 12 ft)
Horse 16hh and over.....3.7 m x 4.3 m (12 ft x 14 ft)

ROOFING

Suitable roofing materials for stables include slates, tiles, felt-covered wood or heavy duty corrugated plastic. Metal should be avoided.

Stabling should have a sloping roof, which can be either single planed or ridged, and should be fitted with efficient guttering and downpipes. There should be plenty of head clearance for the horse. If the roof is of the single-planed type, the

Well built barn stabling, with a wide centre aisle and sliding doors.

lowest point should be no less than 3 m (10 ft) high. If the roof is of the ridged variety, the eaves must be at least 2.25 m (7 ft) from the ground and the roof top should be in the region of 3.7–4.5 m (12–15 ft) high.

FLOORING

Concrete is the most widely used material for stable flooring nowadays. The surface must be roughened to prevent horses slipping – a special rubber material can be used to give even better grip. For drainage purposes, the floor should be sloped slightly to the rear – that is, away from the door. An interior drain in a stable is not a good idea. It will need frequent cleaning if it is not to become clogged with bedding material, and there is always the danger that a horse might get one of his feet trapped.

KICKING BOARDS

Lining the inside of the stable walls with stout wooden boards, known as kicking boards, adds strength to the box and helps to keep out draughts. Boards also help to prevent injury to a horse's feet if he kicks out at the walls of his box. For safety, the boards should be at least 1.2 m (4 ft) high.

ENTRANCES AND EXITS

Stable doors must be wide and high enough to allow a horse to be led through safely, with no risk of banging himself. Aim for a minimum width of 1.2 m (4 ft) and a minimum height of 2.1 m (7 ft).

Hinged doors should open outwards and be made in two halves. Except in the very severest weather conditions, the top half of the stable door should be kept open, fastened securely back to the wall. This permits the free circulation of fresh air and also allows the horse to put his head out to see what is going on outside.

The lower half of the door should fasten at the top with a horse-proof bolt and at the bottom with a "kick-over" bolt. All bolts and hinges should be checked and oiled regularly. The top surface of the lower door should be protected with a strip of metal. When the lower door is open, it too should fasten securely back to the wall to prevent it swinging shut when a horse is being led through.

Where boxes are fitted with sliding doors, the channels in which the doors run must be kept scrupulously clean to allow the doors to operate properly.

WINDOWS

As well as making stable interiors lighter, windows can be used to improve ventilation. It is customary to site a window on the same side of the loosebox as the door to avoid creating cross-draughts. If a window is fitted in another wall, it should be positioned well above the height of the horse's head. All stable windows must be protected on the horse's side with grilles.

AND SO TO BED...

The stabled horse needs suitable bedding to keep him warm and protect him from injury.

Use a skip to remove droppings from a shavings bed. Note the banked-up sides.

Bedding in a stable serves a number of purposes:

- It helps to protect the horse from injury when he lies down or rolls.
- It helps to prevent draughts and to keep him warm.
- It helps to reduce jarring to the horse's legs which can result from standing for hours on an unyielding surface.
- It encourages many horses to lie down to rest, thus relieving strain on their legs.
- It encourages horses to stale (pass urine). Male horses are often reluctant to urinate on a bare floor.
- It helps to keep both the horse and his rugs clean.

Types of Bedding

WHEAT STRAW

PROS: Economical, warm, free-draining, easy to dispose of; it can be burnt or used as mushroom compost.

CONS: May be dusty or contain fungal spores which can cause an allergic reaction in some horses, may only be available in big, difficult-to-handle bales, may be palatable to greedy horses.

WOOD SHAVINGS

PROS: Dust free – if the supplier has put them through a dust extractor – hygienic, non-palatable, packed in strong plastic bags so easy to store.

CONS: May contain "foreign objects" such as nail fragments (though not if good quality), may cause skin irritations if wood has been chemically treated, bales heavy to handle and shavings likewise when wet, difficult to dispose of (being slow to rot).

SHREDDED PAPER

PROS: Cheaper than shavings, most dust free of all bedding materials, warm, light, so easy to handle.

CONS: Saturates more quickly than shavings and straw, if made from printed paper staining may occur on horse's coat, muck heap more difficult to control especially in windy conditions.

HEMP

PROS: Dust free, very absorbent, economical to maintain, easy to dispose of (it rots down to usable compost in a few weeks).

CONS: Initially expensive to lay down, free-flowing so less easy to bank up sides of bed.

RUBBER MATTING

PROS: Totally dust free, low-cost maintenance, easy to muck out with hosepipe.

CONS: Unless used in conjunction with another form of bedding, provides less warmth and protection from draughts and injury than other materials, does not absorb urine or droppings, so horses tend to lie in them, soiling their coat and rugs.

Bed Making

Stables can either be mucked out daily, or horses can be kept on the deep-litter system. The latter involves the daily removal of droppings and regular topping up with fresh bedding. A deep-litter bed will provide extra warmth in winter and, correctly managed, can stay down for about six months before the whole stable is cleaned out. This system is best suited to large, well ventilated stables, especially if the horses are turned out by day, thus giving the bed more chance to dry out. The disadvantages are the heavy work involved in eventually cleaning out the stable and the tendency of the bed to smell and for wooden walls to deteriorate.

Tips and Tools
FOR BEDDING

- When putting down a straw bed, banking the sides with new straw then covering the banks with a layer of the used straw will help to deter the horse from eating his bed.

- If the horse is to stay in the stable even for a short time after mucking out (perhaps while he is prepared for exercise), scattering a thin later of bedding, or "standing litter" over the floor will prevent him from slipping.

- Picking up droppings regularly throughout the day in a special container known as a skip helps to keep the bedding – and the horse – clean.

- You will need a fork to sort through the bedding and a sturdy, hard-bristled yard broom to sweep the floor. Depending on how adept you are, straw can be mucked out with a four-, three- or two-tined fork – the more tines, the heavier the fork. There are special forks, with close-set prongs, for shorter bedding materials such as shavings.

- If you use a wheelbarrow to cart the droppings and soiled bedding to the muckheap, you will need a lightweight shovel for loading it. The shovel can usually be dispensed with if you use a muck sheet because you can fork and sweep most of the droppings and used bedding on to it, using your hands, provided you wear gloves, to scoop up any remains. Remember that the less tools you have around, the less likelihood there is of a horse injuring himself if he makes an unexpected movement.

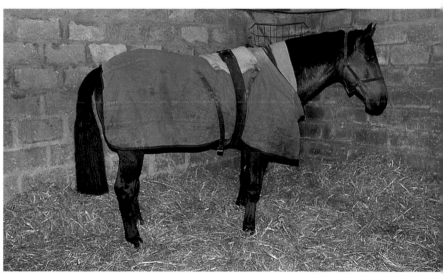

TOP: *Shredded paper is the most dust-free bedding material. It is also cheap, and light to handle.*

ABOVE: *Straw is warm and free draining, but it can cause an allergic reaction in some horses.*

LEFT: *A selection of mucking-out tools. Choose the ones that best suit your bedding material.*

In daily mucking out, the droppings and wet straw are removed and the floor swept clean. The remaining clean bedding is used to cover the floor area. Fresh bedding, as required, is banked up the sides of the walls. Banked sides help to prevent draughts and can help to prevent a horse becoming "cast" if he rolls; a horse is said to be cast if he rolls over so that his legs are so close to the wall that he is unable to get up

The most effective mucking-out method is to clean out one dry, corner of the stable and pile the retained bedding there. The rest of the floor can then dry properly while the horse is turned out. Taking the bed up totally in this way is easier with light materials such as paper and straw. The alternative is to remove all bedding from one wall of the stable each day, so that each bank of bedding is moved regularly.

Muck Heap Management

Site your muck heap conveniently close to, but downwind of, the stables. A level, dry approach will make life easier for you. And remember that there should be good drainage away from adjacent paths. A three-sided bunker constructed of breeze blocks makes an ideal container. A muck heap contained in this way will be easier to keep tidy than a free-standing one. If you are going to have the muck heap removed periodically by a contractor, there must be adequate access for a large vehicle.

FEEDS & FEEDING

Feeding the domesticated horse is both an art and a science: like humans, horses and ponies vary a good deal in their requirements.

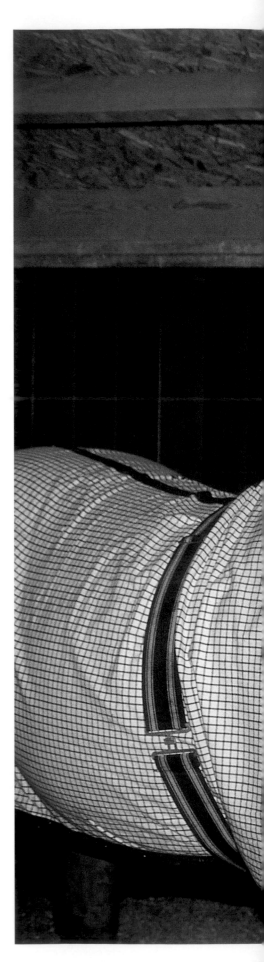

The most important thing to remember when feeding horses and ponies is that they are not designed to eat a limited number of set meals a day. The equine animal is what is known as a "trickle feeder". He has a small stomach in relation to the size of his large intestines, and needs to keep topping up with food. Little and often are the three most important words in horse nutrition.

Horses living under natural conditions, roaming freely and eating the grasses and herbs which form their staple diet, will graze for the greater part of each 24 hours. In summer, when food is plentiful, they put on condition; in winter, when food is scarce, they use up their bodily reserves, chiefly in keeping warm.

Humans want the domesticated horse to work and to maintain condition throughout the year. To enable him to do both he requires additional "fuel", since grass alone is not, in most cases, sufficient. This takes the form of various feedstuffs, some of which are old, tried and tested favourites such as oats, while others are of more recent origin, such as horse and pony nuts or cubes.

ABOVE: *Meadow hay (left) is usually greener and softer than seed hay (right).*

OPPOSITE: *Feeding hay in a net saves wastage.*

> **When feeding hay to horses at grass, prevent squabbling by dividing it into well spaced-out heaps, always providing more heaps than there are horses.**

Rolled oats.

Barley.

Bran.

Roughage

The traditional way of feeding the all-important roughage which all horses and ponies need throughout the year is in the form of dried grass, otherwise known as hay. Seed hay, made from top quality grasses sown as a crop – the grass is ploughed in and re-sown on a regular basis – is usually more nutritious than meadow hay, which is cut from permanent pasture and may include weeds. Meadow hay can usually be distinguished from seed hay by its greener colour and softer texture. Horses in hard work are best fed seed hay. For those doing less work or resting, meadow hay is sufficient. Seed hay has the disadvantage of being more expensive, and it may also lack some of the minerals contained in meadow hay, which usually comprises a far wider range of plants.

A modern method of feeding roughage is to use haylage, which is made in a similar way to silage, that is, produced from wilted (not dried) grass from which the air has been excluded. Haylage is sold in vacuum-packed plastic bags and it is important to ensure that the bags are not punctured during storage. Haylage can be used in conjunction with or instead of hay and is better than hay for horses with respiratory problems.

Another recent invention is the grass "cube" which, being high in protein and carbohydrate, falls somewhere between true roughage and the other main type of equine feed, concentrates. Cubes are made from grass which is cut at intervals during the growing season and immediately put into a drier. They should be soaked before being fed to the horse.

To prevent wastage, hay is often fed in a haynet tied to a ring in the stable wall, but it is not natural for a horse to eat for long periods with his nose high in the air. Ground feeding is far better: it aids drainage of the horse's respiratory tract, and so helps to minimize the effect of dust inhalation. Ground-level feeding is obviously the most natural for the horse, though care must be taken to prevent contamination of the hay, for example from soiled bedding. A useful compromise is a specially designed low-level manger fitted in the corner of the stable. Grass-kept horses should be fed their hay on a clean – not dusty – area of the field.

Chaff or chop is hay, or hay mixed with oat or possibly barley straw, which has been chopped into small lengths. It is added to concentrate feedstuffs to promote good digestion by encouraging the horse to masticate his food properly. Large stables may have their own chaff cutting machine, but chaff is also available ready-chopped.

Concentrates

Energy-giving food, such as cereals and legumes, are known as concentrates. The quantity an individual horse needs is governed by the amount of work he does, and his individual make-up and temperament.

OATS

Highly palatable and easy to digest, oats have long been considered the ideal cereal for horses, though it should be borne in mind that some animals (particularly ponies) can become too "fizzy" and unmanageable on an oat-rich diet. Before feeding, oats should be lightly rolled to further aid digestibility. Once rolled, the seeds will quickly begin to deteriorate, so rolled oats should be used within a couple of weeks.

BARLEY

Barley is harder and less digestible than oats and must not be fed whole to horses. It can be fed cracked, rolled, steam-flaked, extruded (cooked at high pressure and flash dried) or micronized (cooked in a similar way to popcorn, and then rolled). The cooking process tends to increase digestibility. Barley has a slightly higher digestible-energy content than oats and should be fed more sparingly.

MAIZE

Weight for weight with oats and barley, maize has more digestible-energy content but a lower fibre level. It may be fed whole, steam-flaked, extruded or micronized (as is usual in Europe) or – as is sometimes the practice in the United States – fed on the cob, in which case its fibre level will be higher.

BRAN

Bran, a by-product of wheat, can either be fed dry with other concentrates or in the form of a mash (damped with boiling water, covered and allowed to cool). Traditionally a part of the stabled horse's diet, its suitability is now disputed as more and more horse owners adopt the scientific approach to equine feeding which asserts that bran, with its poor calcium to phosphorus ratio, can lead to bone problems. Also, the poor quality of modern-day bran – as opposed to the large-flaked product of former times – makes it less digestible.

SUGAR BEET

Sugar beet cubes or shreds for equine consumption are made from the remains of the root vegetable once the sugar has been extracted. Sugar beet is high in digestible fibre and is a good source

Sugar beet.

Alfafa.

Pony nuts.

of digestible energy. It must be fed soaked. Fed dry, it will expand inside the horse and is likely to cause fatal colic and/or intestinal blockages. Sugar beet should always be soaked for several hours, according to the manufacturer's instructions; cubes need longer soaking than shreds. Cold water – two to three times water to cubes is the usual recommendation – is essential: hot water can cause potentially dangerous fermentation. Mixed with other concentrates, soaked sugar beet helps the digestion process by making the horse eat more slowly.

LEGUMES

Peas and beans can be fed to horses, being both palatable and a useful source of protein. They are particularly rich in lysine. They should be micronized or steam-flaked.

MOLASSES

A by-product of sugar, molasses is very palatable and is therefore useful for mixing with other concentrates to tempt shy feeders or to disguise unpleasant tasting feed additives or medicines.

COMPOUND FEEDS

For the first-time horse owner, compound feeds, prepared for particular needs, are a great boon. Produced in the form of nuts or cubes or coarse mixes, they help to take the guesswork out of feeding. They contain a variety of ingredients, including some or all of the concentrates already mentioned, and are formulated by feed experts to suit different horses: there are feeds for competition horses, broodmares, elderly horses, racehorses and so on. A good feed merchant will help horse owners to choose the right feed for their particular animal.

How Much?

There are no hard and fast rules as to how much food an individual animal needs, but there are useful general guidelines:

Height	Daily feed requirement
Under 12 hh	6.3–7.2 kg (14–16 lb)
12–13 hh	7.2–8 kg (16–18 lb)
13–14 hh	9–10 kg (20–22 lb)
14–15 hh	10–11 kg (22–24 lb)
15–16 hh	11–12 kg (24–26 lb)
over 16 hh	12–12.5 kg (26–28 lb)

Each horse or pony varies in his requirements and, like humans, some animals put on weight more quickly than others. Irrespective of height, the horse's build will also have a bearing on his food requirements as, most importantly, will his workload.

It is the workload which determines how much of a horse's food should be made up of roughage or bulk feed to concentrates. A horse in hard work, such as regular eventing, will need in the region of 70 per cent of his total feed as concentrates and 30 per cent as bulk. A horse in regular but less strenuous work – up to around 10 hours a week – including hacking, some dressage and/or jumping and schooling sessions, will need 50 per cent concentrates to 50 per cent bulk. A horse doing around an hour's light work a day, hacking or a little schooling, may need no more than 30 per cent concentrates to 70 per cent bulk. If the digestive system is to function properly no horse, however hard he is working, should receive less than 25 per cent of his daily ration as bulk.

If the weather is good and the grazing of good quality, a horse or pony may be able to sustain a small amount of light work – say quiet hacking – on a diet of grass alone. But it is wise to check his weight on a regular basis to ensure that he is coping.

The following is a useful formula for calculating a horse's weight if you do not have access to a horse weighbridge:

$$\text{Weight (kg)} = \frac{\text{girth}^2 \times \text{length (cm)}}{11,900}$$

To measure the horse's girth, run the tape measure around his barrel immediately behind his elbow. Always take the measurement just after the horse has breathed out. Length is measured from the point of the shoulder to the point of the buttock.

Succulents and Roots

Ideally, every horse should be turned out to graze for at least part of each day. In practice, particularly with competition horses, this is simply not possible, so a good way to help make up for the lack of natural succulents in their diet is to feed fruit and vegetables. These can include apples, carrots, turnips, parsnips, swedes and dandelion leaves. To prevent a blockage in the oesophagus – a condition known as choke – avoid cutting carrots and parsnips into rings: they should be sliced lengthways or grated.

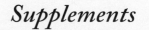

Supplements

Cereals such as oats and barley have a low calcium-to-phosphorus ratio. Horses fed primarily on these cereals may need a calcium supplement.

Where to Feed

The stabled horse should be given his concentrate feed in a manger designed for the purpose and fitted safely in the corner of the loosebox, with no dangerous protrusions on which the horse will injure himself.

The most convenient method of feeding concentrates to a horse at grass is to use a plastic manger designed to clip on to the rail of a fence. Buckets or bowls on the ground can be used but the horse is much more likely to tip them over, wasting his feed. They are also a potential cause of injury.

If a haynet is used, it must be tied high enough to prevent the horse from catching a foot in it when it is hanging empty. Feeding hay on the ground, or in a low-level manger, is more natural.

Good Feeding Practice

- Feed little and often.
- Feed at the same times every day — horses are creatures of habit.
- Never leave uneaten remains of a feed in the manger when you give the horse his next feed. If he regularly fails to "eat up", you may be giving him too much, or there may be something wrong either with the feed or the horse.
- Keep mangers scrupulously clean — wash them out regularly.
- When feeding concentrates, divide the daily ration into several small feeds of no more than 1.8 kg (4 lb) each. The stabled horse should have his concentrates in at least three feeds per day.
- Mix concentrates with chaff to encourage mastication and aid digestion.
- Never feed immediately before exercise. Allow up to two hours between food and work.
- Always feed concentrates before hay, and give the bulk of the hay at night.
- Never leave your horse for long periods without food.
- Soak hay in clean water for a few hours before feeding to help prevent the horse from inhaling mould spores. For horses with respiratory problems it is essential always to soak their hay before feeding.
- Avoid making sudden changes to your horse's diet. If you want to introduce new feedstuffs, do so gradually over a period of a week or two.
- Worm your horse regularly — your veterinary surgeon will advise on a suitable worming programme.
- Have your horse's teeth checked regularly. If he is to chew his food efficiently, any sharp edges will need rasping down.
- Ensure that your horse has ready access to salt. Special salt licks are available.
- Add limestone flour and vitamin/mineral supplements to your horse's concentrates to correct any imbalance — check on the required amounts with an equine nutritionist. Feed all such supplements on a daily basis, not just once or twice a week.
- Store hay under cover. Protect it from damp ground.
- Store all other feedstuffs in clean, dry, rodent-proof containers.

Water

The horse's natural food — grasses and herbs — is high in water content. Hay and concentrates are not. It is therefore vital that the stabled horse has free access to water to counteract the dryness of his feed. The average stabled horse will drink around 36 litres (8 gallons) of water a day. Depending on his diet, work routine and state of health, as well as the weather conditions, he might be happy with as little as 22.75 litres (5 gallons) or need in excess of 45.5 litres (10 gallons).

Water makes up approximately 60 per cent of an adult horse's body weight — rather more in the young horse. It is present in all his body fluids and is essential if his blood and digestive and excretion processes are to function normally.

WATER IN THE STABLES

Water may be provided in buckets or by means of automatic drinking bowls. Large, heavy duty rubber or metal buckets are both suitable, although metal is more likely to cause injury if the horse is in the habit of messing about with buckets. Plastic buckets are lighter to carry but are less advisable since they tend to split and, again, may injure a horse.

Some horses get into the habit of knocking their buckets over, either through playfulness or clumsi-

ness. A safe way of preventing this is to stand each bucket in a rubber tyre, provided the stable is large enough. Alternatively, you can fix the buckets to the stable wall with special clips. Buckets are best positioned in a corner of the loosebox, with the handles away from the horse.

health. Leaks will ruin his bedding. Care must be taken, too, to ensure that feed pipes do not freeze in winter.

WHEN TO WATER

Traditionally, horses were watered according to the old maxim, "water before food" and often they were not allowed access to water once they had started eating, or for several hours before very hard work such as racing.

Up-to-the-minute research into the effects of water – and lack of it – on competition horses has brought about a change of thinking. Generally speaking, it is considered better for horses to drink when convenient during long periods of work in order to prevent dehydration. Thus horses taking part in endurance rides are encouraged to drink their fill at suitable places during the ride and eventers are allowed a small drink – just a few mouthfuls – after finishing one phase of a horse trials and before beginning another.

The modern school of thought is that so long as horses are normally allowed free access to water, they will not want to drink vast quantities immediately before the start of a competition or other work. It is, therefore, not necessary to remove their water supply several hours beforehand. An hour or so is probably sufficient if the horse is to do very fast work, less if he is going to do something less strenuous.

GOOD WATERING PRACTICE

- Supply all horses, stabled or at grass, with a constant supply of clean water.
- Avoid asking a horse to do hard work immediately after a long drink.
- After very hard work, offer a horse about 2.25 litres (half a gallon) of water every quarter of an hour until he has cooled down (a horse swallows approximately a third of a litre in one go). Once he is cool and his pulse and respiration are back to normal, he can be given free access to water.
- Keep all water utensils scrupulously clean. However thirsty they are, horses will often refuse to drink if the water is not really fresh tasting.

Automatic drinking bowls are labour saving and are therefore favoured by some large yards, but they are quite small and so horses cannot enjoy a deep drink. It is also difficult to judge how much a horse is drinking – unless the bowl is fitted with a meter – and the quantity of water a horse drinks is a useful indicator of his state of health. A drinking bowl must have a plug to facilitate cleaning and should be recessed to prevent the horse interfering with it. Drinking bowls must be checked daily for any malfunction that could be caused by horses fiddling with them. Lack of water will be detrimental to the horse's

MAIN PICTURE: *Feed time! The horse's feeds should be measured out into a clean bucket and given at the same times each day.*

INSET: *An automatic drinking bowl.*

GROOMING

A well groomed horse is a pleasure to behold – but grooming does far more than just please the eye

A horse that is kept outside should not be groomed too thoroughly. His head and the saddle and girth areas should always be cleaned before you put the tack on – this keeps your tack clean and helps to prevent skin sores. But the rest of the horse should be tidied up just for appearance's sake rather than given a thorough grooming. This is because he needs the natural grease and dirt in his coat for warmth and to keep his skin dry.

The stabled horse is a different matter entirely, particularly if he is being asked to undertake hard work. During hard work the horse's skin excretes waste matter in the form of sweat and to ensure that this excretion system is kept in good working order, his skin and coat must be kept clean. Strenuous grooming also helps to improve the horse's muscle tone. And, of course, a clean horse means clean tack and rugs.

Essential Kit

BODY BRUSH

The body brush has short, fine bristles. It is fitted with a loop for your hand and is used on the horse's entire body and legs. Leather-backed body brushes are more comfortable to hold than wooden or plastic ones and are less likely to hurt the horse if you happen to knock him.

CURRY COMBS

The teeth of the metal curry comb are used for cleaning the body brush – never the horse. A curry comb made of rubber or plastic and fitted with a loop for the hand, can be used to removed dried mud from the horse's coat. They are particularly useful for tidying up thick-coated grass-kept horses. Take care not to knock bony areas.

DANDY BRUSH

A brush with longer, stiffer bristles than the body brush. Useful for removing caked mud and bedding stains from the horse's legs. It is too harsh to use on the horse's body, mane or tail.

WATER BRUSH

A brush with softer bristles than a dandy brush and usually with a wooden back. It is used for dampening the mane and tail.

SPONGES

For cleaning the horse's eyes and nostrils, under the tail, and the sheath of a male horse. Always keep separate sponges, one for the front end, one for the rear.

HOOF PICK

Essential for cleaning out the underside of the horse's feet. The end should be blunt to prevent damage to the foot.

SWEAT SCRAPER

A metal frame with a handle and a rubber blade, used for removing excess water from a horse's coat after he has been washed down. Take care not to knock bony areas.

STABLE RUBBER

A piece of cloth, chamois leather or sacking used, when damp, to add a final gloss to a horse's coat.

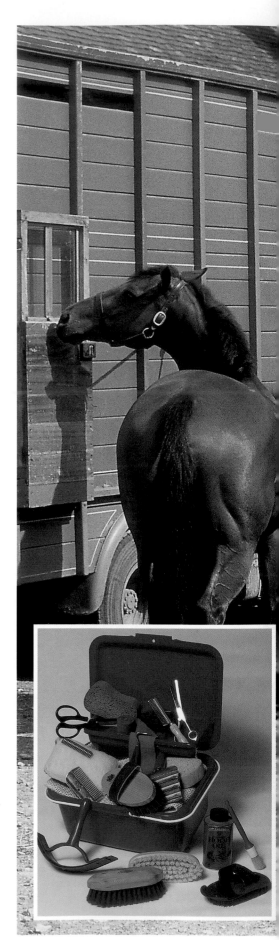

RIGHT: *Grooming is an essential part of the care of competition horses.*

INSET: *A well-stocked grooming kit. Each horse should have his own and all items must be kept clean.*

Tool Tips

- Tie a piece of brightly-coloured baler twine or string to your hoofpick so that you can easily find it again if you drop it in the horse's bedding.
- Stand wet wooden-backed brushes bristle-side down while they dry – the sooner the wood dries, the longer it will last.
- Store your brushes bristle-side up – they will last longer.

How to Groom

Using the hoofpick, clean out the horse's feet thoroughly – into a skip, not on to the bedding. Always use the pick from the heel towards the toe, and take care not to damage the frog.

- With the body brush in one hand and the metal curry comb in the other, give the horse's entire body a thorough brushing, starting with the neck on one side, working down the shoulder and foreleg, over the body and hindquarters and

down the hindleg, then repeating the process on the other side.

- Stand slightly away from the horse and use firm, brisk strokes.
- After every few strokes draw the bristles of the body brush across the teeth of the metal curry comb. Every now and again tap out the dirt from the curry comb – either at the stable door or outside, not into the horse's bedding.
- Release the horse's nose from the headcollar noseband and gently brush his head with the body brush, not forgetting the underside.
- Carefully brush the mane and tail with the body brush, if necessary untangling knots with your fingers first. Hold the tail away from the horse's body so that you can brush out one section at a time.
- Dip the water brush in water – a separate grooming bucket, not the horse's drinking water – and lightly damp down the topside of the mane and the top of the tail.
- Using clean water, gently sponge the eyes and nostrils. With the second sponge, clean under the dock (tail).
- Clean a gelding's sheath every couple of weeks to remove any accumulated greasy discharge which may cause the horse discomfort. Use mild soap and warm water, or a specially prepared solution. If you can, catch the horse when he is staling. If not, gently insert the sponge into the sheath. Rinse thoroughly and dry with a towel. With a strange horse be on your guard in case he objects and tries to kick you.
- A thorough grooming will take in the region of 45 minutes.

Quartering

Preparing the horse for morning work usually involves a briefer tidying up known as quartering. The horse's rugs are unfastened and turned back over his loins so that his front half can be given a

LEFT, ABOVE: *The correct way to clean out a horse's foot, using the hoofpick away from the heel.*

LEFT: *For all-over grooming of the horse's body use the body brush, and clean the bristles on a curry comb.*

quick brush over. Then the rugs are turned forward so that his hindquarters can be cleaned. Stains or bedding marks are removed with a sponge or water brush and the damp areas dried with a cloth or towel. His mane and tail should be brushed and damped down and his feet picked out.

Quartering will take about 15–20 minutes.

GROOMING PRECAUTIONS

- To prevent the risk of spreading infection, have a separate grooming kit for each horse.
- Wash and disinfect all grooming tools regularly.
- In cold weather do not totally remove a horse's rugs while grooming. Turn them back as for quartering.
- Avoid standing directly behind a horse.
- Avoid kneeling or sitting on the ground while grooming – always squat so that you can quickly get out of the way if he moves unexpectedly.
- Never try to groom a sweaty horse. Walk him around on a lead rein until he has dried off.
- Shake blankets and rugs thoroughly at least once a week to remove dust and hair.
- To help dry off a wet horse in the stable, place a layer of straw on his back and hindquarters and put a sheet or rug – preferably one made of "breathable" material – over the top. This is known as "thatching".

Washing

A very muddy or sweaty horse may be washed all over but only if he can be dried off quickly to prevent chilling. Use a sweat scraper to remove the bulk of the water. He should be walked around until he dries off. If the weather is cold (for example, during the hunting season) let the mud and sweat dry ("thatching" will speed up the process) and then brush the horse clean. Before a special occasion, such as a show, the horse may be washed with a special equine shampoo, but again only in mild weather.

To give the horse's tail a thorough cleaning, use a bucket of water with equine shampoo or mild soap. Rinse the tail several times in clean water to remove all traces of suds. Stand to the side of the horse if you are not sure how he will react. A greasy mane may also be shampooed. Take care not to get suds in the horse's eyes or ears. To wash dirty hooves, use a water brush and a bucket of water to clean both the wall – the outer side – and the underside of the hoof. Take care not to wet the heels.

Trimming

MANES

A horse's mane can be shortened, levelled and kept looking neat and tidy by means of "pulling". This involves plucking out excess hair until the mane is the desired length and thickness. It is best done when the horse is warm and the pores open, when the hairs will come out more easily, so making it less uncomfortable for the horse. The mane will lie flatter if the hair is pulled primarily from the under side. It should be damped down afterwards.

Most horses tolerate having their manes pulled, provided you spread the job over several days to avoid making them sore. If a horse really objects, his mane can be tidied up with a thinning comb. Scissors should never be used – the result is never satisfactory looking.

- Take hold of a SMALL section of the mane with the fingers of one hand, holding the hair taut.
- Using a special mane comb in the other hand, back-comb the hair up towards the roots, so that only the longest hairs remain between your fingers.
- Wrap these remaining few hairs around the mane comb.
- Pluck out these hairs with a short, sharp pull on the comb.

TAILS

The bottom of the horse's tail will need trimming from time to time to prevent it becoming too long. The tail can either be levelled (known as a "bang" tail) or left in its natural, unlevel shape (a "swish" tail).

The top of a bushy, untidy tail can be neatened by removing some of the excess hair as in mane pulling. The hair should be taken primarily from the sides of the dock, less so from the top. Remove only a few hairs at a time and spread the whole job over several days to avoid making the horse sore. If he objects, you may have to stand outside the stable, with his tail over the stable door, so that he cannot kick you. Proceed carefully and avoid mak-

ABOVE: *Manes are trimmed by "pulling", using a mane comb.*

RIGHT, TOP: *Take care when brushing out the tail. Always use a body brush, not a dandy brush.*

RIGHT, BELOW: *To tidy up a bushy tail, pull hairs from each side of the dock.*

ing his dock sore, otherwise he will be more difficult next time. Fine-coated horses such as Thoroughbreds rarely need to have their tails pulled – they look better left in their natural state.

Never pull the tail of a horse who lives permanently outside. He needs the hair on his dock to protect him from rain and snow.

To shorten and level the bottom of the horse's tail, raise the dock (the bony part) until it is in the position in which he carries it when on the move. Slide your other hand down the length of the tail hair and cut off the excess length. When this is done correctly, the bottom of the tail will be parallel to the ground when the horse is in motion.

To neaten the top of the tail, quickly pull out a few hairs from either side of the dock, either using the mane comb if the hair is long enough, or your fingers if it is not. Wear rubber thimbles to give your fingers sufficient grip.

LEGS

Excess hair can be trimmed from the horse's fetlocks using a comb and a pair of sharp, round-ended scissors.

Comb the hair upwards, against the direction of growth, and snip off the excess hair which protrudes through the teeth of the comb. Take care to avoid leaving "steps".

HEADS

Bushy hair on the outsides of the ears may be snipped off with sharp, round-ended scissors. Never remove the interior hair because it serves a vital purpose in protecting the ears from dirt and insects. Whiskery hair under the jaw can also be removed with scissors. The whiskers on the horse's muzzle act as sensors and should never be removed.

CLIPPING

Removing part or all of a horse's winter coat helps to keep him comfortable and healthy.

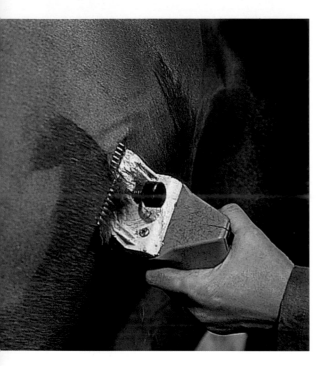

The clippers should be used in long, sweeping strokes against the lie of the coat.

If a horse is required to do hard work while wearing a thick, winter coat, he will quickly lose condition through excessive sweating. He will also be uncomfortable and may well catch a chill if he is not dried off properly after exercise. The solution is to clip off the horse's thick winter coat and provide him with blankets and rugs as a substitute to keep him warm. If a clipped horse is to be turned out for part of each day, he will need to be rugged up well with a warm, windproof and waterproof New Zealand rug.

Types of Clip

FULL CLIP

This is when the horse's entire coat is removed, that is from his body, head and legs. It is usually only necessary for a horse with an exceptionally thick coat and then only on the first occasion of clipping.

HUNTER CLIP

A hunter clip involves removing all the hair except that on the legs and the area under the saddle. Leaving the hair on the legs affords some protection from injury, while a "saddle patch" prevents soreness.

BLANKET CLIP

Removing the hair from the neck, shoulders, belly and all or part of the head, but leaving the hair on the horse's back, loins and hindquarters, is known as a blanket clip. It is suitable for horses doing medium to hard work.

TRACE CLIP

A trace clip is often the best option for a horse who is mainly kept out and only doing moderate amounts of work, or a stabled horse in steady, but not strenuous, work. For the outdoor horse a low trace clip is the most suitable, the hair being removed only from the underside of the neck, between the forelegs, and from the belly and the upper part of the hindlegs – that is, the areas most prone to sweating. For a stabled horse in steady work it is better to use a medium or high trace clip, removing rather more of the body and neck hair.

CHASER CLIP

So called because it is used on many fine-coated Thoroughbred racehorses, the chaser clip involves removing the hair from the head, the lower part of the neck, the chest, the belly and upper part of the hindlegs. If the horse objects to having his head clipped, it is better to leave it unclipped, particularly if the hair growth is not dense. It is less stressful for the horse, even if it does not look so smart.

How to Clip

- Having decided on the type of clip, mark the outlines on the horse's coat with a damp piece of saddle soap or a piece of chalk.
- Begin clipping on the neck or shoulder, using the clippers against the lie of the coat. Use long, sweeping strokes. Make each stroke parallel to the one above or below, and slightly overlapping the previous one.
- Clip the body and finally the hindquarters.
- When removing the coat from the horse's hindquarters, clip a neat inverted "V" at the top of the tail.
- When clipping the head, start on the cheeks, placing the slippers (switched off) against the cheek for a moment or two first so as not to take the horse by surprise. Clip underneath, from the chin to the throat, and then over the forehead. Use the clippers as lightly as possible and take great care when going round the eyes and ears.
- Hold each ear in turn and run the clippers lightly along the outside edge.

Clipping Tips

- To mark a saddle patch, put the horse's usual saddle on his back, without girths or stirrup leathers. Ensure that it is lying in its normal position when he is being ridden, then draw round it. Make the saddle patch a little larger than necessary to allow for any mistakes when clipping.
- To achieve the right position and angle of clip at the top of the forelegs: for the "V" at the front, measure one hand's width from where the foreleg joins the chest; for the back of the leg, measure two hands' widths below the elbow. Join these two points together in a sloping line with chalk or saddle soap.
- To achieve the correct position and angle of clip at the top of the hindlegs: for the front, measure four hands' widths below the top of the stifle; for the back, measure two hands' widths above the point of the hock. Join the two points together in a sloping line with chalk or saddle soap.
- When clipping the soft skin on the inside of the top

of the foreleg, get an assistant to pick up the leg and hold it forward to stretch out the folds of skin.

- When clipping between the hindlegs, keep hold of the horse's tail to help prevent him from kicking out if you tickle him.

- When clipping the delicate skin in the stifle area, straighten out the folds with your spare hand.

- Never try to clip a horse who is sweaty or dirty.

- Allow the horse's coat to grow fully before giving him his first clip.

- Take care as clipping horses is hard work and can be dangerous. If in doubt, seek expert help.

CLIPPING PRECAUTIONS

- If you have never clipped a horse before, learn how to do it under expert tuition.

- Never try to clip a horse on your own.

- Clip in good light conditions.

- Put your hand on the underside of the blades every few minutes during clipping. If they feel hot, switch off the clippers and allow them to cool before carrying on.

- To ensure efficient running, clean and oil the blades every 10–15 minutes during clipping.

- Keep the horse warm during clipping by throwing a rug over the clipped areas. A horse who is cold will tend to fidget and you or he could end up being injured.

- Accustom a nervous horse, or one who has never been clipped before, to clippers by first running non-motorized ones over him.

- If a horse is known to be nervous or difficult to clip, ask your veterinary surgeon to administer a sedative. In such circumstances, the quicker the clipping job is done the better, so it is best left to an expert.

- Have clippers serviced regularly.

- Have blades reground regularly and replace with new ones as necessary.

RIGHT, TOP: *The blanket clip is suitable for horses in medium to hard work.*

RIGHT, CENTRE: *The hunter clip, with correctly positioned, protective saddle patch.*

RIGHT: *The high trace clip is useful for the stabled horse in steady work.*

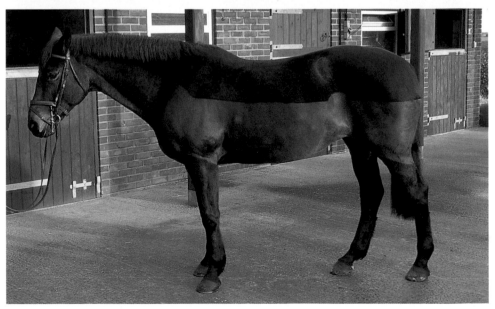

8
PART EIGHT

ESSENTIAL EQUIPMENT

In theory, all you need to be able to ride a horse is some means of control, in other words a bridle. In fact, it's possible to train a horse to take you where you want, and to jump too, without even a bridle (but that's one for the experts – please don't try it at home!).

Of course, as in most walks of life, things are not quite so simple in practice. The modern rider demands comfort and security, so a suitable saddle is a must. And if you decide to compete in a sport such as horse trials, which involves doing dressage one day and jumping another, the time will come when you will want a different type of saddle for each phase. If you are going to enter show classes, you may need a double bridle and other specialist gear. And whatever you do with your horse it is always nice to have one set of everyday tack and another for "best". It is surprising how quickly it all mounts up.

Elsewhere, the horse needs as much specialist equipment as a new-born baby, only on a much grander scale: rugs and blankets to keep him warm in the stable, dry in the field and clean in the horsebox; bandages for his legs and tail; boots to protect his leg joints; creams and potions of all descriptions; brushes, combs and polishing cloths. Add to that buckets, mangers, feed storage bins and mucking out tools, and you will begin to appreciate the complications of keeping a horse. The list is endless and for the one-horse owner with limited space it can present storage problems of nightmare proportions. If you have never yet tried to dry a muddy New Zealand rug in the depths of winter, you have a rare treat in store!

So why do we surround ourselves with quite so much equine paraphernalia? Is it really necessary? Much of it is, certainly. Horses are valuable animals. We keep them in an unnatural, restricted environment and expect them to do work for which they were never intended, so protecting their limbs and body makes good sense on all counts.

Where tack is concerned, however, many people accumulate so much gadgetry that they end up not seeing the wood for the trees. When it comes to dreaming up new methods of controlling the horse, it seems that man's imagination is boundless. Whatever the problem, someone somewhere will have devised a bit or another piece of tackle with which to address it. As soon as a horse stops doing what we want when we want there is a tendency to reach for the latest item of high-tech equipment, just because it is fashionable. What we should be doing is getting back to basics: making sure that the horse's education has not been skimped, that he really does understand what we want of him and is in a fit condition to do our bidding. Where some riders are concerned, there is no doubt that if they got the three equine R's right in the first place, they would have more space in their tack rooms.

ARE YOU SITTING COMFORTABLY?

Apart from the horse itself, your biggest financial commitment when you first become a horse owner will be a saddle. For everyday riding you need a general–purpose saddle complete with girths, stirrup leathers and stirrup irons. A good quality saddle that fits both horse and rider will last for many years so it pays to buy the best you can afford and to look after it carefully.

ABOVE, TOP: *Girths must be strong – your life could depend on them! Check the stitching and buckles regularly.*

ABOVE: *The three main types of saddle (from left): dressage, general purpose and jumping.*

Saddles

Saddles are usually made of leather and are built on a frame known as a tree, traditionally made of laminated wood, although nowadays synthetic materials are sometimes used to replace both wood and leather. A "spring-tree" saddle, which has an inset strip of springy metal on either side of the tree, gives a more comfortable ride than a "rigid-tree" saddle.

The general-purpose saddle is suitable for everyday hacking, schooling, cross-country riding and jumping. The flap – the long, flat piece of leather on which your leg rests – extends forwards towards the horse's shoulder sufficiently far for you to be able to ride with slightly shorter stirrups for faster work and jumping and still be comfortable. Most saddles are fitted with knee rolls, an area of padded leather at the front of each flap which gives support to your knee.

THE JUMPING SADDLE

Riders who want to show jump or ride across country at the higher competitive levels will need a special jumping saddle, which has a longer tree and more forward-cut flaps that enable you to ride with much shorter stirrups.

THE DRESSAGE SADDLE

Saddles for the dressage specialist are designed with a much deeper seat and straight flap, allowing you to use a long length of stirrup and to have more of your leg in contact with the horse's side.

SADDLE FITTING

The importance of correct saddle fitting cannot be over-emphasised. Great discomfort and actual damage can be caused to the horse's back through an ill-fitting saddle. Whether you buy a brand new saddle or a second-hand one, always have it professionally fitted by a qualified saddler.

There are several key points to be taken into consideration. The panels – the parts of the underside of the saddle which rest on the horse's back – must be evenly stuffed so that the rider's weight is spread evenly over the horse's back. The larger the weight-bearing area, the better for the horse.

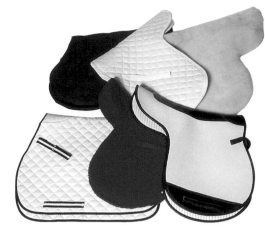

ABOVE: *Numnahs are designed to keep your saddle clean and add to the horse's comfort.*

RIGHT: *For safety, always run the stirrup irons up the leathers when saddling up and unsaddling.*

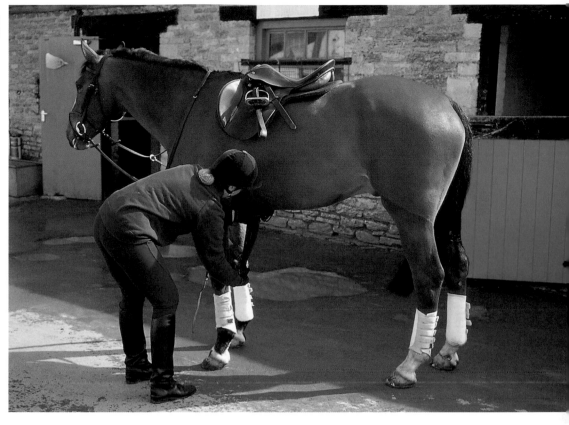

When a rider is mounted, if you look along the horse's spine, you should be able to see clear daylight along the full length of the gullet – the space between the two panels. The gullet must be high and wide enough to avoid any pressure on the withers or spine. The saddle should not sit so far back that it lies over the horse's loins, nor should it slide forward on to his withers. The panels must not impede the movement of the horse's shoulders.

Fitting a saddle to a horse is rather like fitting shoes to your own feet: no two horses are the same size and shape so you will have to shop around to get the best fit. To take into account the fact that horses change shape from time to time, as they become fitter and leaner, or the reverse, some modern saddles are made with adjustable trees.

NUMNAHS

A numnah, or saddle pad, helps to keep the underside of your saddle clean and should be more comfortable for the horse's back than the leather panels of the saddle. However, it must be stressed that numnahs should never be used to correct the deficiencies of an ill-fitting saddle. Nor should they be made of synthetic materials. They must be of natural fibres so that they "breathe" and absorb sweat from the horse's skin to prevent soreness. The cen-

tre of the numnah must be tucked well up into the gullet of the saddle to prevent pressure on the spine. All numnahs and saddle pads must be washed frequently.

SADDLE AND RIDER

Although the way the saddle fits the horse should be your prime concern, there is no point in choosing a saddle which is not comfortable for you, too. If you sit badly because your saddle is the wrong shape and size for you, you will not ride effectively and will probably cause your horse discomfort or even pain. Riders come in a vast variety of sizes and shapes, and a good saddler will take into account the length and dimensions of your legs when recommending a saddle. If you can afford to have a saddle made specially for you, it can be fine-tuned to give a perfect fit to both you and your horse.

GIRTHS

Girths, which hold the saddle in place, must be both strong and comfortable for the horse. They are made in a variety of styles and materials and you should choose the one which best suits your particular horse's conformation. Some girths, such as the Balding and Atherstone styles, are cut away in

the area behind the horse's elbows, to ensure that he has complete freedom of movement. Leather girths are very strong, though they do have the disadvantage of not being absorbent and in hot weather those made of materials such as lampwick or cotton string may be more comfortable for the horse.

As an added precaution, particularly if you are doing very fast work or strenuous jumping, when a broken girth could be more likely – and very dangerous – a surcingle affords extra security. This is an additional webbing or elasticated strap which passes over the top of the saddle and lies over the girths.

STIRRUPS

Always use strong, good quality stirrup leathers and stirrup irons. Your irons should be made of stainless steel and should be 2.5 cm (1 in) wider than your boots. Any wider and there is the chance of your foot sliding through the iron and becoming trapped. Any narrower and your foot may fail to slide free in the event of a fall. You can opt for special safety stirrups. These have a gap in the outer side that is closed with a rubber loop designed to detach itself from the retaining hook in an emergency. Rubber treads fitted to the bottom of your irons will help keep your feet in the correct place.

BRIDLES, BITS AND PIECES

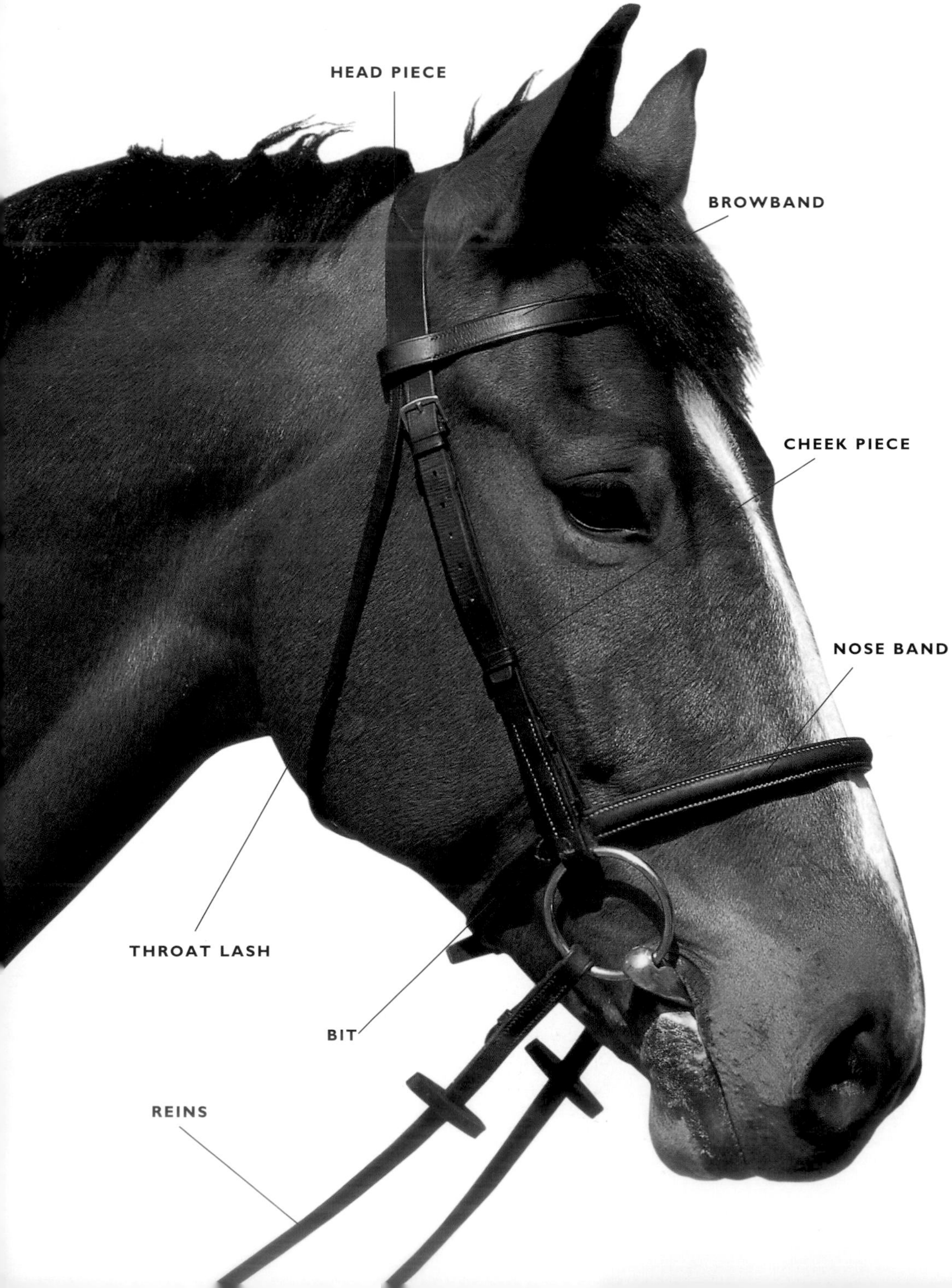

There is a key to every horse's mouth – finding it is one of the enduring fascinations of horsemanship.

HEAD PIECE

BROWBAND

CHEEK PIECE

NOSE BAND

THROAT LASH

BIT

REINS

Put simply, the bridle is a series of straps – usually leather – devised to hold a bit in the horse's mouth – the bit being the means by which the rider steers. In practice, the function of a bridle is usually more complicated than that, because by fitting it with a noseband – of which there are a number of different designs – it is possible to affect the way in which the horse responds to the bit and the way he carries his head. As for the part that actually goes into the horse's mouth, whole books have been and continue to be written on the complex subject of bits and bitting. The best advice for the novice rider is to keep things as simple as possible and if problems develop to seek expert advice from a good instructor

Bridlewise

The basic components of a bridle are: the headpiece, a broad leather strap which lies behind the horse's ears and which divides into two straps on either side of the horse's head. One – the throatlash or throatlatch – passes under the horse's throat, fastening with a buckle on the nearside. It prevents the headpiece from slipping forward over his ears. The other ends of the divided headpiece rest on either side of the horse's cheekbones and are attached to the cheekpieces, short straps which fasten round the rings of the bit to hold it in place in the horse's mouth. It is usual to fit the headpiece through a browband – a strap with a loop at each end. This lies over the front of the horse's head, in front of his ears, and prevents the headpiece from sliding down his neck.

NOSEBANDS

Different nosebands perform different functions. The popular cavesson, a broad leather band fitted a couple of inches below the cheekbones, is mainly used for appearance's sake. Many horsemen believe a horse does not look properly dressed without one. It is, however, essential if you wish to fit a standing martingale (see p.143).

The drop noseband, a narrow strap which fastens below the bit rings (but must not be fitted so low that it interferes with his breathing), is designed to keep the horse's mouth closed and prevent him from crossing his jaw and thereby evading the action of the bit. A similar effect is obtained from the Grakle – which has two straps, one fastening above the bit, the other below it – and the flash, which is a combination of a drop noseband and a cavesson.

The Kineton noseband, comprising a nosepiece with a metal loop on either side which is fitted under and around the side of the bit, is a more severe device. It exerts pressure on the bit and the nose and is often effective on a hard-pulling horse. It should only be used by an experienced rider.

BITLESS BRIDLE

It is perfectly possible to ride and control a horse without him having a bit in his mouth. Indeed, there may be occasions when it is essential, for instance if the horse has suffered a mouth injury or tooth problem, or if he has a mouth which is difficult to fit with a bit.

In the absence of a bit the horse is controlled through pressure and leverage on his nose and chingroove. There are various designs of control nosebands. The novice rider should, however, be wary of using them and should take expert advice first. Some have a very severe action if used incorrectly and are certainly not suitable for inexpert hands.

Reins

Reins should be made of strong leather, of a width which is comfortable for your particular hands. They come in pairs and fasten to the bit rings with neat stud billets. At the other end – the rider's end – they fasten with a buckle. Although they must not be too short, the reins should not be so long that you catch your foot in the spare end.

The reins may be covered for part of their length with rubber, which gives greater grip in wet weather or on a sweaty horse.

Bits and Bitting

The bit lies on the bars of the horse's mouth, that is, the part of the lower gums where there are no teeth.

When you buy a horse you should, if possible, find out what sort of bit he has been ridden in by his previous owner. If he goes well in that, there is no reason to change to anything else.

By far the most commonly used bit is the snaffle, which may consist of a single bar of metal or rubber – fitted with a metal core for strength – or may be jointed in the middle. A thick single-bar snaffle has the mildest action, particularly if it is slightly curved. The jointed snaffle is intended to give greater control through its more severe "nutcracker" action in the horse's mouth, which exerts pressure on the corners as well as on the bars of the mouth.

An eggbutt snaffle – one where the rings to which the cheek pieces of the bridle are attached are fixed – is less likely to cause pinching of the lips than a loose-ring one. Some snaffles have long vertical pieces of metal on either side – known as cheeks.

DOES IT FIT?

Whatever bit you use, it is essential that it fits the horse's mouth – any old bit simply will not do. It must be neither so narrow that it pinches his lips nor so wide that it slides about in his mouth. Not only the width of his mouth, but also the size of his tongue and the shape of the roof of the mouth

A selection of snaffle bits, showing a few of the many different types of mouthpiece. Materials used include stainless steel, copper, rubber and Nathe – a soft pliable off-white synthetic material with a flexible inner core.

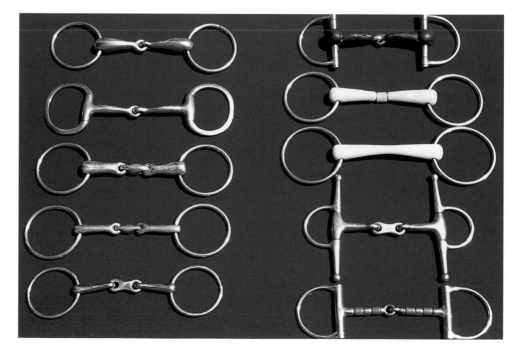

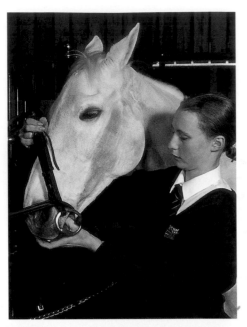

Bridle Care

Horses quickly become headshy and difficult to handle if they are treated roughly: always be patient and gentle when putting on or taking off a bridle.

LEFT: *To prevent the horse from becoming headshy, be quiet and gentle when putting on the bridle. Inserting your thumb between the corners of his lips will encourage him to open his mouth and accept the bit.*

BELOW: *Use both hands when sliding the bridle off.*

must be taken into consideration when choosing a bit for a particular animal.

Bits are measured according to the width of the mouthpiece, which may be as narrow as 10 cm (4 in) for a small pony or as large as 15 cm (6 in) or more for a horse. Mouthpieces are measured in increments of 6 mm (¼ in) and to fit correctly a jointed mouthpiece needs to be slightly wider than that of an unjointed one.

If in doubt, ask an experienced person such as your instructor or a good saddler to measure your horse's mouth in order to find the right bit for him. Horse's mouths vary a great deal and if you start having difficulties of any kind in controlling your horse, look to his mouth first to see if there is a problem there – either an ill-fitting bit, or something wrong with his gums or teeth. If he is in discomfort or pain, he will soon become a "difficult" ride.

The double bridle differs from the snaffle bridle in that it has two bits, not one. It comprises a snaffle bit, known as a bradoon, and a curb bit with a port (a half-moon shape) in the centre which accommodates the horse's tongue. The depth of the port governs the amount of pressure put on the bars of the mouth by the bit.

Attached to the curb bit is a curb chain, which may be leather-covered and which passes under the horse's chin groove. The severity of the curb bit depends upon the length of the cheek – the longer the cheek the greater the leverage.

The double bridle has two pairs of reins, one attached to the bradoon, the other to the curb. Because of its more complex action upon the

horse's mouth it should only be used by the experienced horseman.

Putting on a Bridle

Stand on the nearside of the horse, who should be tied up. Unfasten the headpiece of the headcollar, release his nose from the headcollar, then re-fasten the headpiece around his neck so he cannot wander off.

Holding the headpiece of the bridle in your left hand, place the reins over his head and neck with your right hand. Slide your right arm under the horse's head until your right hand is above his nose and take hold of the bridle, below the browband, with your right hand.

Using your left hand, guide the bit into the horse's mouth; then use both hands to guide the

headpiece gently over the horse's ears, taking care not to knock his eyes.

Gently pull his forelock over the browband, which should be level; check that his mane is lying flat. Make sure that the bit is level in his mouth.

Buckle up the throatlash – not too tightly – you should be able to place the width of your hand between it and the horse's cheek.

Fasten the noseband, if used. With a cavesson noseband, there should be room for your fingers between the noseband and the horse's nose.

If the horse is reluctant to open his mouth to take the bit slide the thumb of your left hand between his lips. Make sure you do this in the corner of his mouth, behind his incisor teeth so that he cannot bite you. Use the same trick if he is reluctant to let go of the bit when being unbridled.

Taking Off a Bridle

Unfasten the noseband, followed by the throatlash. Use both hands to slide the headpiece – together with the reins – forward over the horse's ears.

Allow the horse to let go of the bit.

Martingales

A martingale is a leather strap that passes from the girth, between the horse's front legs, and is attached to the bridle.

The type most commonly used is the running martingale. The strap through which the girth passes divides at the base of the horse's neck. Each of the two ends is fitted with a metal ring through which one of the reins passes. The martingale is kept in place by another strap fastened loosely round the horse's neck.

The standing martingale, most often seen on polo ponies, consists of a single strap which attaches to the underside of a cavesson noseband.

Both martingales should be adjusted so that they have no effect on the reins/noseband unless the horse raises his head excessively high. They should never be shortened in an attempt to force him to carry his head lower than normal.

The running martingale, and a little gadget known as an Irish martingale – which consists simply of two rings joined by a strip of leather – are useful for preventing both reins ending up on the same side of the horse's neck, which can happen if a horse throws his head about or if the rider loses hold of the reins for any reason, perhaps because the horse jumps a fence awkwardly and the rider is nearly unseated. Ending up with both reins on one side of a fast-moving horse's head can, obviously, be a potentially dangerous situation.

Headcollars

The headcollar is an indispensible item of tack, used when handling the horse in the stable and, provided he is quiet, when leading him around outside. It may be made of leather, nylon or webbing. Leather headcollars look the smartest and are generally considered the safest because if a horse were to get his headcollar hooked up on something, and

ABOVE: *How not to fit a standing martingale: this short, it prevents the horse from carrying his head in its natural position.*

BELOW: *A correctly fitted headcollar.*

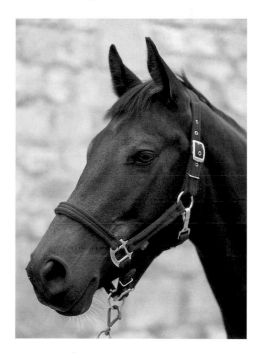

then panicked and pulled backwards, leather is more likely to break than nylon, thus saving the horse from injury. The best headcollars are fully adjustable – the headpiece, noseband and throatlash are all fitted with buckles.

To lead the horse about or tie him up in his stable for grooming, etc, you need a sturdy lead rope fitted with a trigger clip or spring clip, which fastens to the metal ring on the underside of the noseband. For safety, the clip should be fastened with the opening part facing away from the horse's chin.

RUGS, BOOTS & BANDAGES

To complete his wardrobe, your horse needs a selection of warm clothes and protective legwear.

Because grooming deprives the horse of natural insulation in the form of dirt and grease, and clipping deprives him of his own "fur coat", he must be kept warm by other means. The stabled horse will need rugs and blankets and, for when he is turned out to grass, a waterproof New Zealand rug.

Rugs

STABLE RUGS AND BLANKETS

Stable rugs are made in a huge variety of materials ranging from the traditional wool-lined jute to the equine equivalent of a duvet or quilt. Shaped to fasten in front of the horse's chest, they can be held in place by means of a roller – a broad, buckled strap which goes around the horse's entire body – or by a cunning system of self-righting straps situated underneath the rug and devised to keep it in position even if the horse rolls. If a roller is used, it must be well padded where it rests on the horse's back. There should be no pressure whatsoever on the spine.

The modern lightweight alternatives to jute are easier to handle and probably more comfortable for the horse, though it is advisable to choose one with a cotton lining as some horses, like humans, are allergic to synthetic materials.

In very cold weather the horse may need an extra layer of clothing. A blanket under his rug will keep him snug. A roller will be essential in this case to prevent the blanket from slipping back. Alternatively, some rugs now come with detachable quilted linings.

DAY RUGS

Smart day rugs, often made of wool, are usually kept for special occasions, for example when going to shows. Many people like to put their initials on the rear corners of the rugs and, if they compete in a sport where they have their own "colours" sometimes have matching rugs.

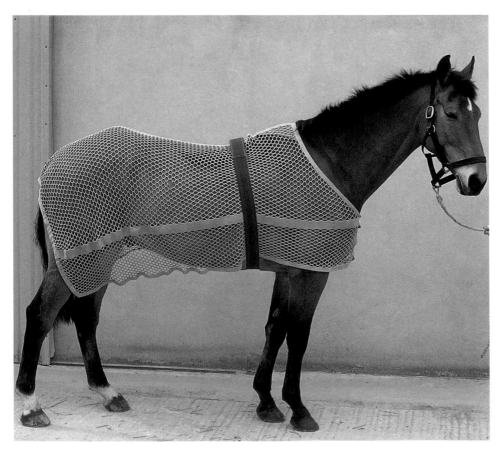

The equine equivalent of a string vest helps a hot horse to dry off more quickly.

section and is fitted by turning up the front corners either beneath the saddle or under the girth straps. It should have a fillet string attached to each rear edge. This lies under the horse's tail and prevents the sheet from blowing about in windy weather.

NEW ZEALAND RUGS

Horses who are kept on the combined system, that is stabled by night and turned out by day, those who are turned out for the odd hour or two on a daily basis and some who live out permanently will need special protection from the weather. Being both windproof and waterproof, the New Zealand rug is the perfect solution. Again a system of self-righting straps keep the rug in place.

LEFT: *A smart day rug fitted with an anti-cast roller. Ideally there should be additional padding under the roller.*

BELOW: *A summer sheet held in place with a matching roller and breastgirth.*

ANTI-SWEAT RUGS

An anti-sweat rug or cooler is a useful item for putting on a hot horse while he is cooling down. It enables him to dry off without becoming chilled. It should be made of an absorbent material such as cotton or one of the up-to-the-minute "breathable" fabrics now available. In hot climates a lightweight cooler which covers the horse from just behind his ears to the top of his tail is a useful means of protecting him from the sun and from flies.

SUMMER SHEETS

Made of heavyweight cotton, a summer sheet is a good alternative to the horse's normal stable wear in hot weather, keeping his coat clean without making him too hot. It should be kept in place with a roller.

EXERCISE SHEETS

A light woollen or cotton exercise sheet, often known as a paddock sheet – because racehorses wear them during the pre-race preliminaries – is ideal for putting under your saddle when exercising a clipped horse during cold weather. It is designed to keep the delicate area over the loins warm. It has a square front instead of the usual front-fastening

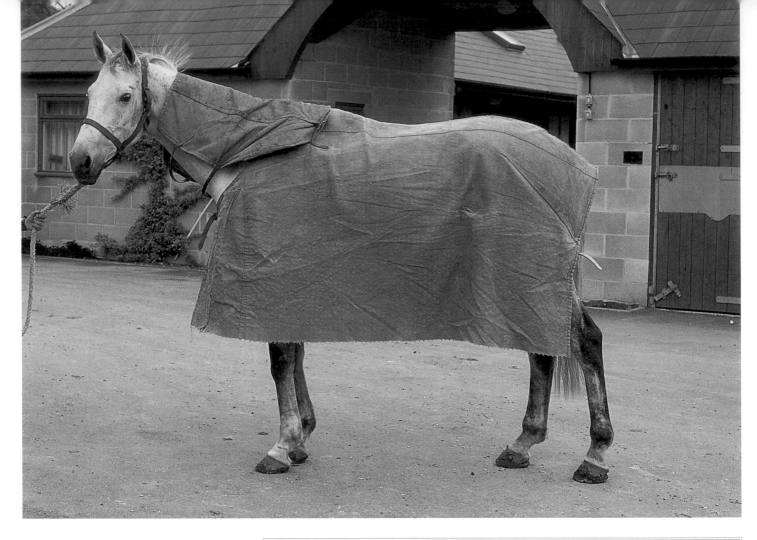

A weatherproof New Zealand rug and neck cover give excellent protection against the elements.

New Zealand rugs used to be made of heavy canvas but lightweight modern materials are more suitable, since they are less likely to cause pressure sores. Careful fitting is essential if the rug is to give adequate protection. It must be shaped to fit the horse and reach well down the legs and over the hindquarters. Some rugs are fitted with a tail flap and neck protector for use in particularly harsh weather. A New Zealand rug will need reproofing periodically.

Bibs and Head Covers

However well fitting their rugs, some horses become chafed on the chest and shoulders. Horses who live out and wear weatherproof rugs for long periods are particularly susceptible to chafing. One way of preventing it is to fit the horse with a rug bib, a stretchy garment which fits over his shoulders and chest and fastens with a belly strap.

In very severe weather and for horses who feel the cold more than most, there are also stretchy head and neck covers.

Waterproofs

A waterproof sheet is an indispensable item to have on hand when you go to competitions. There is usually a good deal of waiting about, which in wet weather can be miserable for the horse and ruinous to your saddle. By throwing a waterproof sheet over them, you can protect both horse and saddle in one go – and ensure that you have something dry to sit on when you do mount up. As with human rainwear, avoid noisy materials which might startle the horse, and remember to keep an eye on him to make sure he does not start sweating – the disadvantage of many waterproof materials is that they do not "breathe".

Boots

TENDON BOOTS

There are various designs of tendon boots aimed at protecting the horse's legs from injury. To a limited extent they also give support to the legs. They are particularly useful when a horse does fast work and for jumping and may be used on either the forelegs or the hindlegs or both. Foreleg tendon boots help to protect the vulnerable area at the back of the legs from blows from the toes of the hindfeet. Tendon boots come in various materials and are fastened either with buckles and straps or with Velcro or quick-release clips.

KNEE BOOTS

When exercising on the roads, where the surface is so often slippery, it is a sensible – but all-too-often neglected – precaution to fit your horse with knee boots. The padded leather or polypropylene kneecap is fastened round his leg by means of an elasticated strap, which should be just tight enough to keep the boot in place. The lower strap is there to prevent the boot from flipping upwards as the horse moves and should be fastened loosely so as not to interfere with his action.

FAR RIGHT, TOP: *A correctly fitted hock boot.*

FAR RIGHT, BOTTOM: *Easy-to-fit tendon boots.*

RIGHT: *Kneeboots. They should always be fitted for roadwork.*

BELOW: *Brushing boots and overreach boots.*

BRUSHING BOOTS

Brushing is the term used when a horse strikes his leg, usually in the fetlock region, with the hoof or shoe of the opposite leg. It is most likely to happen during strenuous work and may be the result of a conformational defect or sometimes of faulty shoeing. Horses are also more likely to strike into themselves when they are unbalanced or tired. It can result in serious injury so horses who are inclined to brush should wear specially designed boots to protect the vulnerable areas. If the horse knocks his legs higher up towards the knee or hock, the term is speedy-cutting.

OVER-REACH BOOTS

One of the commonest equine injuries occurs when the horse strikes the heels of his forelegs with the toes of his hindfeet. Over-reach injuries can be deep and difficult to heal and are particularly likely to occur when a horse is jumping, especially in deep going when he may have difficulty in getting his front feet out of the ground after landing. Over-reach boots, constructed of strong rubber or Neoprene and fitted around the front pasterns, cover the vulnerable coronet and heel areas. Those constructed of overlapping sections known as "petals" give good protection as they do not invert during use. Damaged "petals" can be replaced. Boots which fasten with straps or Velcro are far easier to fit than the pull-on variety.

HOCK BOOTS

Hock boots are made and fitted in a similar way to kneeboots, and are a wise precaution for a horse in transit. They are particularly recommended for a horse who is inclined to kick while he is in a trailer or horsebox, and by the same token are useful for horses who kick in their stables. Some horses object to hock boots when they are first fitted, so care should be taken to introduce them gradually.

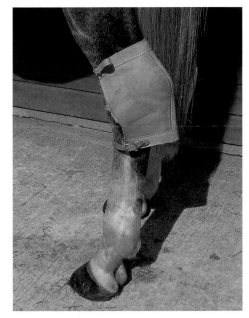

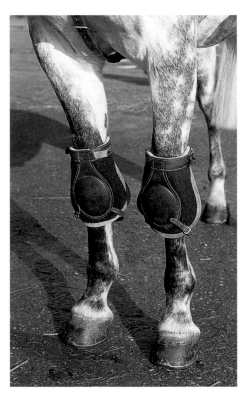

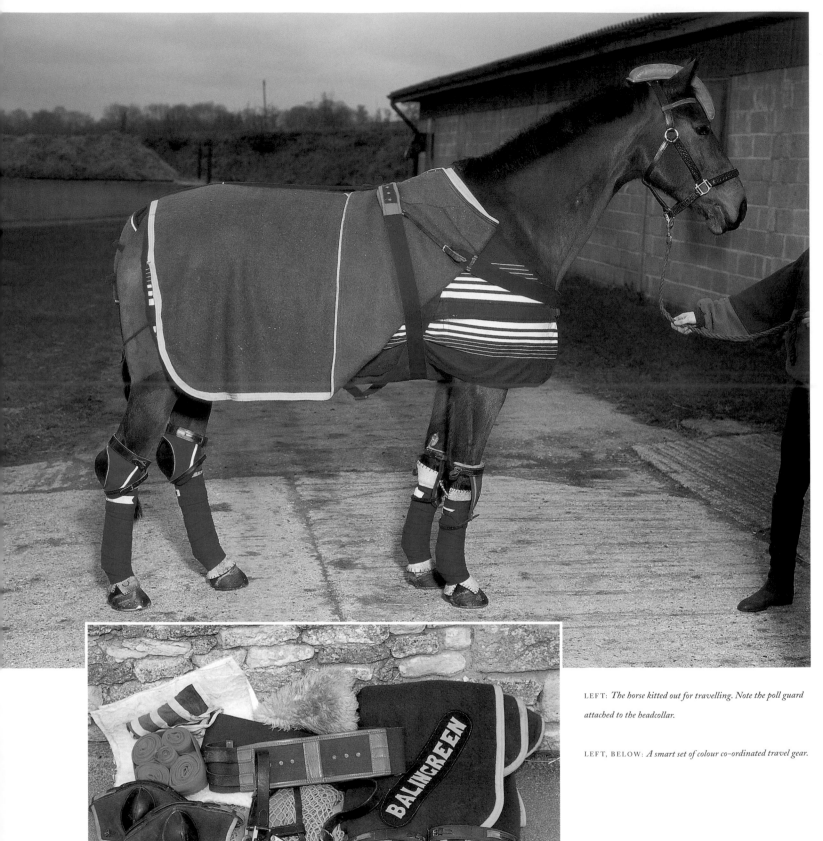

LEFT: *The horse kitted out for travelling. Note the poll guard attached to the headcollar.*

LEFT, BELOW: *A smart set of colour co-ordinated travel gear.*

Travelling Gear

Horses are particularly vulnerable to bangs and bruises when they are being transported, no matter how careful the driver. It makes sense, there-

Bandage Tips

- Make sure that the horse's legs are clean before applying any bandage, otherwise you could make him sore.
- If the bandages fasten with tapes, always tie them on the outside of, which causes pressure on the tendons.
- Never tie tapes tighter than the bandage.
- Tuck away the loose ends of tapes.
- On competition horses, secure the bandages with needle and thread or with strong tape, which is easier to remove.
- Apply bandages in an anti-clockwise direction on the nearside legs and a clockwise direction on the offside legs, if a bandage does happen to come undone while the horse is moving, the loose end will be on his outside and he will therefore be less likely to step on it and trip.
- Keep bandages clean – wash them in mild, non-biological soap powder – and replace padding regularly.
- If a horse is confined to his stable with a leg injury, bandaging his opposite "good" leg will help support it and prevent strain.

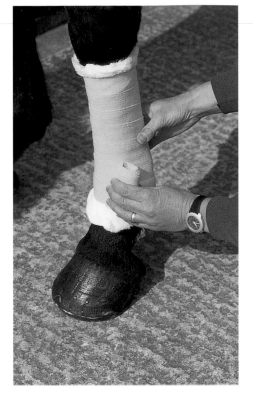

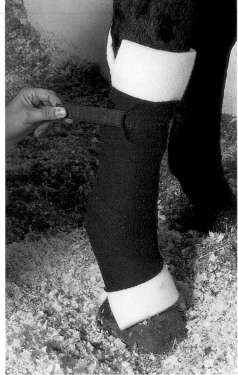

ABOVE, LEFT: *Exercise bandages are designed to protect the legs and give support. They need to be fitted with great care.*

ABOVE, RIGHT: *Stable bandages afford protection and warmth. They should be less tight than exercise bandages.*

fore, to fit them with the best in protective gear. The legs should be bandaged and fitted with knee and hockboots or alternatively you can use specially designed leg protectors which cover the horse's entire lower legs, including the pasterns and coronets. These protectors are very convenient because they normally fasten with Velcro and are therefore easy and quick to fit and remove. If bandages are used, they must be fitted over a layer of Gamgee tissue which should extend down over the coronets, and must not be too tight.

Like his legs, the horse's head is also very vulnerable during transit and it is wise to attach a padded poll guard to his headcollar. Care must be taken to keep the horse comfortable during his journey by giving him the right sort of sheet or rug

for the type of weather. He must not be cold but you do not want him to break out into a sweat, either. It is wise to make frequent stops during a long journey so that you can check on him and adjust his clothing as necessary. Rugs and sheets should be kept in place with a roller. To prevent him rubbing the top of his tail, fit a tail bandage with a tailguard over it. The tailguard attaches to the back of the roller to keep it in place.

Bandages

Bandages are used on horses' legs for a number of reasons: to help support the tendons, to afford protection from injury, and to give warmth. Bandaging is something of an art; wrongly applied, bandages may do more harm than good, so you should always seek expert tuition before trying it yourself, especially where exercise bandages are concerned.

STABLE BANDAGES

These are used primarily to provide warmth and are particularly useful if the horse has had his legs clipped. They are about 11 cm (4½ in) wide and may be made of traditional wool or of one of the more modern fabrics, including thermal. They should always be used over a layer of padding, such

as Gamgee tissue, and care must be taken not to apply them too tightly, otherwise they may interfere with the horse's circulation. The Gamgee should extend beyond the top and bottom of the bandaged areas. The leg should be bandaged from below the knee or hock to just above the coronet. Stable bandages should not be left on for prolonged periods. They should be removed and re-applied at least twice a day.

EXERCISE BANDAGES

Exercise bandages are used to protect the legs from injury and to give them some support. They are about 8–10 cm (3–4 in) wide and, like stable bandages, should be fitted over a layer of padding. To support the legs they must be fitted more tightly than stable bandages and should finish at the fetlock joint so as not to impede the horse's movement.

9 FIT FOR THE JOB

Horses must be brought to the right degree of fitness at exactly the right time if they are to fulfil their potential. Unlike human athletes, they cannot tell their trainers in so many words how they are feeling, so it is up to the trainers to learn as much as they can about the complex business of getting their partners fit. Nowadays this often means plugging into the wonders of science.

As an example, it was the sight of three-day event horses suffering from severe heat stress at the 1990 World Equestrian Games, and again at the Barcelona Olympics two years later, which highlighted the urgent need for a greater understanding of the effects of climate on the competition horse. With the prospect of the 1996 Olympics in Atlanta looming, it sent the Fédération Equestre Internationale (FEI) scurrying to commission high-level research into the problem in order to safeguard the horses – and equestrian sport's good name.

The results of the detailed scientific research undertaken prior to Atlanta, and the actual Atlanta experience, taught veterinary surgeons and riders alike a great deal about the fitness training and care of the equine athlete required to work in an inhospitably hot, humid climate. But such research does not benefit only the top echelon of competition horses. It invariably produces valuable spin-offs - in this case a better insight into the stress suffered by any horses – not only eventers – being transported, or competing, on a summer's day.

The rider has a great responsibility towards his horse when it comes to getting him fit to do the work required of him and caring for him both during and after work. He needs to have his body fine tuned if he is not to be plagued by injury.

Getting and keeping horses fit is both a science and an art. Science has taught the modern horseman a great deal about nutrition, and of course the progress made in veterinary science over the past few decades has been as dramatic as that in the field of human medicine. The sport of endurance riding, in particular, has given the horse world at large invaluable insights into equine fitness and the importance of water and electrolytes.

But science alone will not produce winning performances. Successful riding also involves a less easily definable skill – the art of horsemastership. The expert horseman does not need scientific tests to tell him when a horse is ready to compete or, conversely, is "under the weather". He can tell from the "feel" the horse gives him, whether he is raring to go, or not as the case may be.

Horses, like people, are individuals. One will thrive on one diet, another may not. One needs X amount of exercise, another may need Y. Each horse reacts to work and stress in a different way. Trying to discover how to bring the best out of each individual animal is all part of the fascination of working with horses.

EXERCISE AND FITNESS PROGRAMMES

Like human athletes, horses need to follow a carefully planned programme to reach the fitness necessary for the work required of them.

Fitness training programmes for horses can be divided into three clear phases. First there is the all-important slow, strengthening work; this is followed by a period of more concentrated "serious" schooling; finally, and particularly for horses taking part in sports which require speed and stamina, there is the fine-tuning required to prepare them for a peak of activity on a particular day or days.

Slow Work

If you want your horse to stay sound, never skimp on the slow preparatory work. The prospect of doing nothing but walking exercise day after day for two or three weeks – preferably longer – may seem boring, but it is this steady build-up which provides the solid foundation for everything which follows. If you try to go too fast too soon, the horse – and particularly his legs – will simply not stand the strain.

When a horse first comes back into work after a rest at grass he will need about three-quarters of an hour's walking exercise a day to begin with. He will undoubtedly feel sluggish at first, but you must nevertheless concentrate on riding him correctly, that is keeping him going forward, straight and in rhythm.

In Britain, roadwork has always been the traditional way of getting horses back into work after a lay-off. The level surface reduces the likelihood of injury to his legs and feet and, indeed, is believed to '"harden them up". If you can vary your route each day, there will be plenty for the horse to look at, so he should start to take a keen interest in his daily excursions.

Over a period of several weeks you can gradually increase the daily walking exercise to two hours. By this time the horse should have more of a spring in his step and will be feeling as if he wants to do more.

During the third or fourth week you can start steady, controlled trotting. At this early stage always walk for the first half hour. Keep the trot periods short to begin with and never trot flat out on the roads, even when the horse is fit, as this will jar his legs and may cause lameness. Uphill trotting is recommended as it puts less strain on the forelegs than trotting on the flat. Avoid trotting downhill. Remember to change diagonal at regular intervals. Gradually increase the length of the trotting

Hillwork is one of the finest ways of building up the horse's muscles.

Showing a clean pair of heels! Like humans, horses need a daily period of relaxation.

periods. Always finish roadwork at walk so that the horse returns to his stable dry and cool.

When the horse has been back in work for about four weeks he should be ready for some short (about 20 minutes) schooling sessions. This should be done mainly at walk and trot with only a little canter work. Always take him for a hack afterwards so that he can relax.

Hillwork is one of the finest ways of building up muscle and this can be introduced during the fifth week. Continue with the short schooling sessions and hacking. During week six he should be ready for some faster work at canter. Keep the canter

controlled, but let him stride out. Again, uphill work will be the most beneficial.

Serious Schooling

Once the horse has completed his slow-work pro-gramme, more serious schooling can commence. You can start to introduce suppling exercises – circles, serpentines, etc – and gymnastic jumping over small grids and on circles. Keep the schooling sessions short to start with, gradually increasing them as the horse becomes fitter and more athletic. Remember to finish every schooling session on a good note, that is after the horse has performed a movement really well, and allow him to relax both his body and his mind by going for a hack.

Fine Tuning

The final preparation of the horse will depend on your chosen sphere of activity. If, for example, you are going to compete in horse trials, which call for speed and endurance, the horse will need longer periods of canter work. These should be introduced gradually and you must always do this type of work on good going to avoid putting undue stress and strain on the horse's limbs. If you have nowhere of your own on which to do long canters and the occasional short gallop (known as a "pipe-opener"), try to find someone in your vicinity who has their own "all-weather" gallop which you could use from time to time. It is vital not to subject the horse's legs to strain during his build-up fitness programme.

SHOES

Your horse's feet have to stand up to an enormous amount of stress. Never under-rate the value of looking after them.

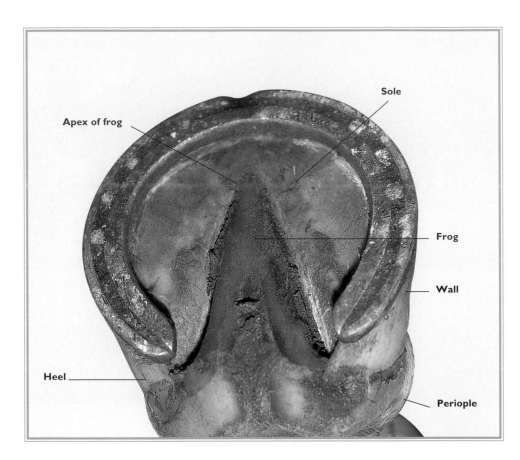

Considering the amount of weight the horse's feet have to carry – not only his own bodyweight but also that of a rider – it is not surprising that foot lameness is so common in the domesticated horse. Regular trimming and re-shoeing by a qualified farrier is essential if your horse is to stay sound despite the work required of him.

ABOVE: *The underside of the foot.*

RIGHT: *The hoof wall. The front clip helps to keep the shoe in place.*

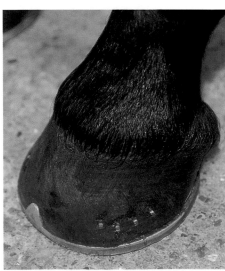

What is a Foot?

The term "foot" is used to describe the hoof – the dense horny covering – and all the structures which are contained inside it. The outer part of the hoof, which is insensitive, comprises:

THE WALL: an outer, protective layer.

THE SOLE: a plate of hard horn just under 2cm (1in) thick, which protects the sensitive inner structures and helps support the horse's weight.

THE FROG: a wedge-shaped mass of soft, elastic horn, situated in the hollow behind the heels. It performs similar functions to the sole, as well as providing grip. Importantly, it also helps to reduce concussion by expanding when weight is placed on the foot.

THE PERIOPLE: a thin layer of epidermis between the hoof wall and the skin, designed to control evaporation from the underlying horn.

The internal part of the hoof comprises:

THE SENSITIVE LAMINAE: these are interlocking leaf-like structures which attach the hoof to the pedal bone. The hoof contains hundreds of sensitive, or primary, laminae which dovetail with thousands of horny, secondary, laminae growing out from the interior of the hoof wall.

THE SENSITIVE SOLE: attached to the lower surface of the pedal bone, the sensitive sole is a thin layer of tissue corresponding to the horny sole and supplying it with nutrition.

THE SENSITIVE FROG: this supplies nutrition to the digital cushion on which it is moulded.

THE PERIOPLIC CORIUM (OR RING): situated just above the coronary corium, the perioplic corium supplies nutrition to the periople.

THE CORONARY CORIUM: this is a thick structure situated above the sensitive laminae. Lying in the coronary groove, it supplies nutrition to the wall of the hoof.

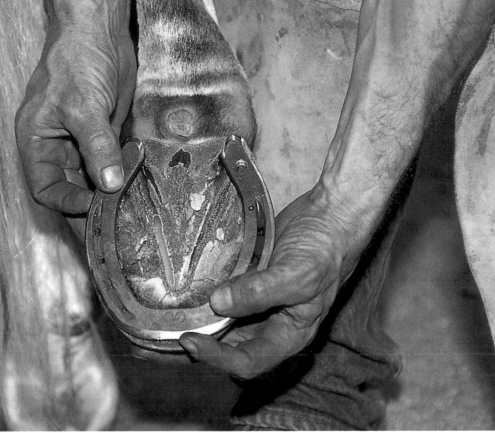

The White Line

On the ground surface of the sole, where the sole meets the wall of the hoof, there is a narrow band of soft plastic horn. It is known as the white line and is of immense importance to the farrier since it indicates the position of the sensitive structures of the foot and the thickness of the wall. It helps determine where nails can be driven into the hoof wall to hold shoes in place without touching the sensitive areas of the foot.

Fitting the Shoe to the Foot

The horn of the hoof is constantly growing. In the wild the horse's feet wear down naturally because of his nomadic existence. However, the domesticated horse's feet are subjected to far more wear and tear because he is required to work and to carry or pull a weight. Without shoes to protect them, his hooves would wear down far more quickly than they would naturally regenerate. As a result he would become lame.

This is where the farrier comes in. Fitting the horse with shoes, usually metal ones, protects his feet. But of course the horn still continues to grow, so it is essential to have the shoes removed regularly and the feet trimmed and kept in good shape. A skilled farrier is worth his weight in gold.

Shoes may be fitted hot or cold. Hot shoeing ensures a more perfect fit, because the shape of the shoe can be adjusted during the actually shoeing process. The hot shoe is placed against the insensitive hoof for a short time and the imprint it makes shows the farrier whether any fine tuning is required.

The farrier fitting a hind shoe. The heel is tapped (has a hole) to take a stud. The clips on hind shoes are set to the side to minimize the risk of injury if the horse strikes his foreleg.

The golden rule of shoeing is always to fit the shoe to the foot, not alter the foot to fit the shoe.

When to Shoe

The horn of the horse's foot grows, on average, about 5–9 mm (¼–⅜ in) each month, so to ensure that his shoes continue to fit correctly the horse should be re-shod every four to five weeks. If the shoes are not too worn, they can be refitted after his hooves have been trimmed. Refitted shoes are known as "removes".

Horses who are resting may be left unshod, but they must continue to have their hooves trimmed regularly. Confinement in a paddock is not the same as living wild, and their hooves will not wear down to the same extent.

Getting a Grip

Studs are fitted to shoes to give a horse extra grip in certain situations. Three-day eventers and show jumpers, for example, must be able to gallop and jump without slipping. Different types of studs are fitted according to the ground conditions. Pointed ones give better grip on very hard ground, large square or round ones are suitable for soft going. They are screwed into specially provided holes in the shoes shortly before the horse competes. When the studs are removed the holes should be plugged to protect the screw threads.

There are two schools of thought on the fitting of studs. Some people believe that it is best to fit only one stud on the outside of each shoe. Others feel that this may cause the foot to be thrown out of balance and that studs should be fitted to both sides of each shoe.

For everyday riding, particularly on slippery roads, smaller roadwork studs may be permanently fitted to the shoes. They are usually made with a tungsten core and are very hard wearing.

A–Z of Ailments

AZOTURIA

Also known as setfast, tying-up or Monday morning disease, azoturia is a painful condition of the large muscles. It occurs after exercise, especially following a period of rest. The horse sweats profusely, becomes stiff and is reluctant to move. The muscles, particularly those of the back and hindquarters, become hard and painful. The horse will appear restless and will have increased respiration and pulse rates and a raised temperature. Dark reddish urine may be passed, sometimes with difficulty. The condition occurs in horses being fed on highly nutritious diets and is believed to be the caused by an accumulation of lactic acid which destroys muscle fibres. The horse must be rested. The veterinary surgeon will prescribe painkillers and anti-inflammatory drugs.

COMMON AILMENTS & INJURIES

An owner needs a knowledge of routine equine health care and to be able to recognise when to call the vet.

BRUISED SOLE

Horses who are ridden, particularly at speed, over hard or rough ground may suffer from bruised soles or stone bruises. The forefeet are particularly susceptible. Lameness may be moderate to severe and will be more marked several hours after the horse finishes work. The horse must be rested until the problem resolves.

CAPPED ELBOW/CAPPED HOCK

A bursal enlargement at the point of the elbow or hock. A capped elbow is often caused by the horse's shoe catching his elbow when he lies down or gets up. A capped hock may occur if a horse kicks the wall of his stable or the ramp of a horsebox or trailer while he is in transit. The swelling is soft and unsightly; it may also become quite large but is not usually painful. If necessary, the condition can be treated by draining off accumulated fluid and giving an injection of a corticosteroid. A protective ring known as "sausage boot" fitted on the horse's pastern will allow a capped elbow to heal.

CHRONIC OBSTRUCTIVE PULMONARY DISEASE

Known as COPD for short, this chronic respiratory condition is caused by hypersensitivity to dust and is believed to be the most common cause of chronic coughing in horses. It is most often found in stabled animals and is brought on by exposure to dust in the atmosphere and mould in straw and hay. Symptoms include a non-productive cough,

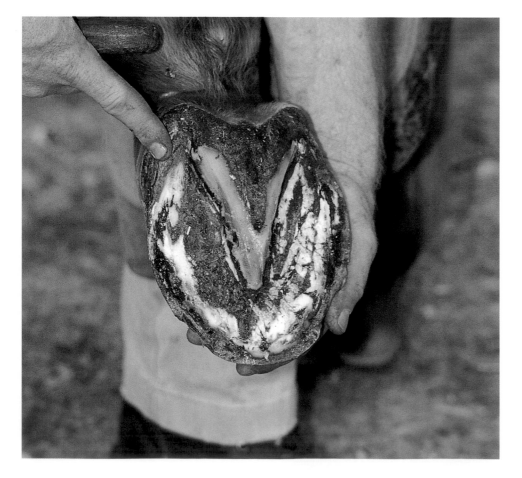

The farrier indicates the site of a bruise to the foot. The horse will need rest while it heals.

The swelling associated with a capped hock looks unsightly but there is usually no pain.

The Healthy Horse

- **The normal temperature of the healthy horse is about 38°C (100.5°F). The temperature is taken with a clinical thermometer which is inserted into the rectum and held there for about a minute.**
- **An adult horse's heart rate is about 38 beats per minute; it may be slower at rest and increases markedly during periods of stress.**
- **An adult horse's respiration rate can vary from about eight to 18 breaths per minute. It tends to increase in hot weather.**

---

often prompted by a change from a warm environment to a cold one. The horse may become restless and sweaty and there may be a nasal discharge. In time his respiratory rate at rest may increase. The vet may prescribe antibiotics and the horse must be given rest, fresh air and dust-free feed and bedding – such as paper. If he is fed hay, it should be soaked in water first. COPD can be prevented by giving the horse a dust-free environment in the first place.

COLIC

If a horse stands looking round at, or trying to kick, its flank, starts sweating and/or repeatedly lying down and rolling, and has a generally anxious look, he is suffering from colic, a condition which may be fatal. Colic may be caused by a sudden change in a horse's diet, by migrating worm larvae, by food impaction in the intestines, by a tumour or, more rarely, by a twisted gut. The horse should be sta-

bled on a deep bed to protect him from injury should he roll, and veterinary help should be sought immediately. Depending on the type of colic, the vet may administer a lubricant, such as liquid paraffin, or a pain-relieving or relaxant drug. If the colic is the result of a major obstruction, usually the result of over-eating or a sudden change of diet, the horse's condition may deteriorate rapidly as toxins are released into his system. In such a case surgery must be carried out as quickly as possible.

CORNS

Bruises of the soles in the angle of the heels. Corns, which are most common in the front feet, may result from faulty or too infrequent shoeing or from a stone becoming wedged in the foot. Excessive pressure results in haemorrhage in the sensitive corium which in turn leads to poor hoof growth. Infection sometimes sets in. Ill-fitting shoes must be removed immediately and the corn trimmed away. Poulticing may be necessary if there is infection. Regular trimming and re-shoeing helps prevent corns.

GRASS SICKNESS

A painful and almost always fatal disease, which is not yet fully understood, although research shows it is associated with a malfunction in the nervous control of the horse's intestinal tract. It occurs most frequently in the summer months and is only seen in horses and ponies out at grass. It often occurs when the weather is dry, or when cold, wet weather follows a warm, dry spell. Acute cases show similar symptoms to those of colic. In addition the horse has difficulty in swallowing and the fluid contents of his stomach are regurgitated down his nose. There may initially be diarrhoea. There is also uncontrollable muscle-trembling. In acute cases death follows after only a few days. Chronic cases may linger for several weeks or even months, gradually losing condition. The horse has little appetite and his droppings are hard and dry. Typically he will stand with his feet brought together under his body and with his back dipped.

INFLUENZA

Equine flu is a serious and highly infectious acute respiratory disease. There are two main types and

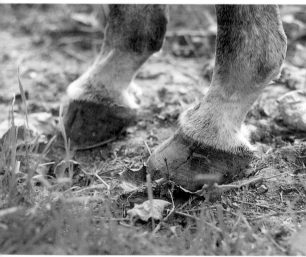

numerous subtypes. The symptoms include a raised temperature, a clear nasal discharge, a cough, shivering and a lack of appetite.

The horse must be kept in a well-ventilated environment and treated with antibiotics. An extended period of rest – at least six weeks – is essential. Too fast a return to work may cause heart and liver damage. Vaccines against equine flu are widely available and are compulsory for most sports horses.

LAMINITIS

A painful condition of the feet resulting from inflammation of the sensitive laminae. Also known as founder. In acute cases the horse sweats and trembles and is generally distressed. Because the front feet are usually more severely affected than the hindfeet, the horse tries to relieve the pain by leaning back, with more weight on his hindfeet. In milder cases the horse may simply keep shifting his weight from one foot to another. Laminitis can be caused by any condition resulting in toxaemia. Retention of the afterbirth in broodmares is a common cause, as is over-eating. Or the condition may be brought on by excessive concussion. A major problem with this disease is rotation of the pedal bone, caused by changes within the structure of the

foot. The tip of the rotated pedal bone presses on the sole which in turn is pushed out of its natural shape. Immediate treatment by a veterinary surgeon is essential to minimise the irreversible changes which take place in the laminae during the early stages. Treatment includes the administration of anti-inflammatory and pain-relieving drugs – Phenylbutazone is commonly used. In a very mild case the horse may be given a little light exercise on a lead rein to stimulate the blood supply to the feet. Otherwise he will need rest. He should be stabled on a surface of sand and peat, which provides essential support for the soles of the feet. Corrective trimming helps to restore the structures of the feet to their normal alignment and special shoes may be fitted.

MUD FEVER

A bacterial skin infection (Dermatophilus congolensis) chiefly affecting the lower legs and heels, when it is known as cracked heels. It is most often seen in horses whose legs are exposed to wet, muddy conditions. The skin becomes sore and

oozes serum. Treatment necessitates removing the scabs that form; if this proves too painful sedation may be necessary, cleaning the area with an antibacterial wash and, once the skin has been thoroughly dried, applying an antibiotic ointment.

NAVICULAR DISEASE

A degenerative disease of the foot affecting the navicular bone, a tiny, shuttle-shaped bone which acts as a pulley for the deep flexor tendon before it attaches to the under side of the pedal bone. Navicular disease is thought to result from a combination of factors: poor foot conformation, degeneration of the navicular bone and/or a loss of blood supply to the bone. It causes lameness which, in the early stages of the disease, may wear off during exercise. As the disease progresses, the periods of lameness increase and become more prolonged. Typically the horse will point the affected foot forward when at rest and he may stumble when on the move and become less willing to jump. Corrective trimming and shoeing can help by correcting the faulty hoof/pastern axis.

Anti-coagulants have been used with some success and anti-inflammatory drugs are helpful in the short term to control pain. Surgical procedures include sectioning the nerves in the affected area of the foot – but serious complications can occur – or sectioning the navicular suspensory ligaments which can help to produce a better blood supply.

OVER-REACH

An injury to the heel of a forefoot caused by the horse striking himself with the toe of his own hindfoot. There is often extensive bruising and over-reaches can be slow to heal. The wound should be kept clean. An antibiotic dressing will help prevent infection.

PEDAL OSTITIS

Inflammation of the pedal bone. Pedal ostitis may result from the jarring the horse's feet undergo

while in strenuous work on hard surfaces. It usually occurs in both forefeet and the horse will have a pottery action. The condition is irreversible, but special shoes and non-steroidal anti-inflammatory drugs can provide relief.

PRICKED FOOT

If the farrier mis-directs a nail so that it penetrates the sensitive area of the foot, the resultant wound is known as a prick. Pricks may occur because the horse is restive, or because the wall of the hoof has been rasped excessively. The nail must be removed at once and the hole treated with an antiseptic. Antibiotics may be required and the horse's tetanus vaccination status must be checked.

RAIN SCALD

Caused by the same bacterial skin infection as mud fever, and affecting horses exposed to prolonged periods of wet weather, rain scald occurs on the upper parts of the body. It must be treated by removing the scabs and using antibacterial washes. The skin must then be kept dry.

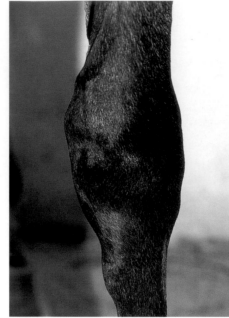

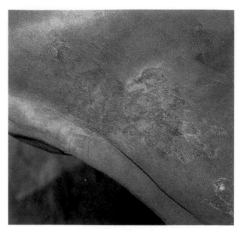

ABOVE: *Hairless skin lesions caused by ringworm.*

LEFT: *A splint (bony enlargement) just below the knee.*

FAR LEFT: *Enlarged glands, a classic symptom of strangles.*

RINGWORM

A fungal disease affecting the skin and one which may, in some cases, be transmitted to humans. The first sign is usually a single round, hairless lesion which bursts and develops a crusty scab. The lesion grows and multiplies. Lesions are most often found in areas where tack or rugs and blankets rub. Treatment involves the use of antibiotics, and special antifungal washes, which should also be used on any equipment which has been in contact with the affected horse. Since the disease is contagious, great care must be taken not to spread it by using the affected horse's grooming tools, tack or other equipment on other horses. Even a rider's boots can spread the infection. The affected horse(s) should be isolated and all his equipment and his previous stable thoroughly cleansed.

SANDCRACK

A break in the hoof wall, anywhere between the coronet and the ground surface of the foot. A crack which starts at the coronary band and goes down the foot is more serious than one which starts at ground level and extends upwards. The horse will be lame if the crack extends into the sensitive part of the hoof wall, and infection may set in. Causes include injury, neglect of the feet, over-rasping by the farrier or poor nutrition. Once any infection has been eliminated, a bad crack may need filling with synthetic resin and fixed with sta-

ples. For less severe cracks starting at ground level, correct trimming and balancing of the foot are usually all that is needed.

SPLINTS

Bony swellings which develop between the splint bones and the cannon bones. Usually found on the inner side of the forelegs, splints can also occur on the outside of the cannon bones and on the hindlegs. They are caused by concussion and are frequently seen on young horses when they first come into work. Initially they feel warm and may cause lameness. In time they become hard and cold to the touch and usually reduce in size, causing the horse no further problem, although in the showing world they are considered a blemish. Rest and the application of anti-inflammatory lotions can be beneficial in the early stages.

STRANGLES

An extremely contagious infection of the lymph glands under the jaw caused by the bacterium Streptococcus equi. Early symptoms include depression and a high temperature. There is a nasal discharge and the glands under the jaw and behind the ears become tender and swollen. The horse finds it difficult to swallow and may be unwilling to eat. He should be kept warm and fed soft, palatable food. The abscesses in the glands must be encouraged to burst by constant bathing with hot water

or the application of heat pads. Once they do burst the horse's condition generally improves rapidly. Because the pus from the abscesses is highly contagious, all affected horses must be kept in isolation. In a few cases, especially if the victim is either very young or old, the infection may spread to the lungs, brain or abdomen. This is known as bastard strangles and is a much more serious disease, with only a poor chance of recovery.

SWEET ITCH

A dermatitis believed to be caused by hypersensitivity to the saliva of certain types of midges. Sweet itch affects the horse's mane and the root of the tail, spreading to the neck and hindquarters in more serious cases. Because it is so irritating, an affected horse will rub himself continuously on any convenient object until he has rubbed out the mane and tail hair and his skin is raw. Eventually the skin becomes ridged and scaly. Sweet itch occurs in the spring and summer and horses who are regularly affected may eventually develop skin ulcers which will not heal. Prevention is far better than any currently available cure. If a horse or pony is known to be susceptible, he should be stabled during the late afternoon and night in spring and summer. Screens, made of mosquito netting, and insecticide strips should be used to prevent midges entering the stable. Special insecticide sprays are now available, designed to kill the midges before

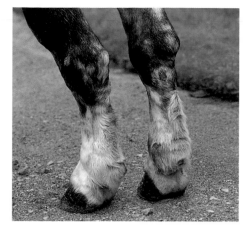

ABOVE: *A horse with windgalls and capped hocks.*

RIGHT: *Wounds, however minor, must be well cleaned.*

FAR RIGHT: *A rubbed tail is symptomatic of sweet itch.*

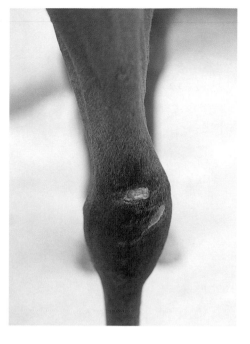

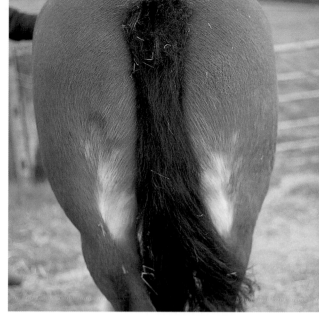

they can bite the horse. His entire surface should be sprayed regularly – he will need spraying more frequently than normal in wet weather. Long-acting corticosteroids are used to control the itching. Various lotions can be applied to the sore areas, but their effect is only temporary. It is hoped that research may lead to the development of an effective vaccine.

TENDON INJURIES

The horse's tendons – rope-like structures which connect the muscles to the bones – are all at risk due to the degree of strain put on his legs, particularly when he jumps at speed. Especially vulnerable are those in the forelegs. Injuries to the superficial and deep flexor tendons (running down the back of the cannon bones), the suspensory ligament (immediately behind the lower part of the cannon bone) and the check ligament (below the knee) are both common and serious. Sudden stress causes the tendon fibres to tear, resulting in pain, heat and swelling. The injured leg should receive immediate cold treatment in the form of an ice pack bandaged to the limb to help reduce the amount of blood and fluid accumulating at the site of injury. Anti-inflammatory drugs help and the leg will need immobilising once the horse is back in his stable, if necessary by putting it in a cast. Rest is the only long-term cure for tendon injuries. Many horses have successfully returned to strenu-

ous work after a lay-off of betwen twelve and eighteen months and a gradual and very careful re-introduction to exercise to help strengthen the damaged limb.

TETANUS

A disease caused by the bacterium Clostridium tetani, which can live in the soil and so gain entry to the horse's system via wounds. An early sign of the disease is the closing of the third eyelid over the eye. The horse's muscles begin to stiffen and, as the disease progresses, become paralysed. He stands in a stretched-out position, and drinking and eating become difficult. If he reaches the stage where he is unable to stand, death will follow fairly quickly. Caught in its early stages, tetanus can be cured. The horse must be kept in a warm, dark, quiet stable – any excitement will cause further muscle spasms – and will need treatment with antitoxin. A tranquilizer will help the horse to relax sufficiently to be able to drink and eat. Quite a high percentage of cases do recover if treatment begins promptly, but it is best to guard against tetanus in the first place by having your horse vaccinated and then maintaining his immunity by ensuring that he has regular boosters. Your vet will advise.

WINDGALLS

Soft swellings of the joint capsule above and behind the fetlock. Windgalls are generally caused by wear

and tear. They often diminish in size during work only to reappear when the horse is at rest. They do not cause lameness.

WORMS

All horses carry internal parasites. They may include large strongyles, small strongyles, roundworms, bots, threadworms, pinworms, lungworms and tapeworms. It is impossible to eradicate worms from the horse's system completely, but regular dosing with wormers helps to prevent the horse's health being affected. Consult your vet for advice on a suitable worming programme.

WOUNDS

All wounds, however minor, should be cleaned with cold water as soon as possible. If the bleeding is profuse, the application of pressure – using, say, a clean handkerchief as a pad – will help staunch the flow until the vet arrives. A large wound may require stitches. Puncture wounds, which can occur anywhere but are particularly common in the foot, are often the most dangerous: they are sometimes hard to detect and there is more likelihood of infection developing because of lack of drainage. The horse should be given antibiotics and if the wound does become infected, it must be poulticed frequently. If the horse is not already vaccinated against tetanus, he should immediately be given the appropriate injection.

10
PART TEN

THE HORSE IN SPORT

There's a saying in the equestrian world: the horse is a great leveller. One day you're up, the next you're down. Prince or pauper, all riders enjoy the same thrills, suffer the same humiliations – and share the same risks. There is no room for complacency or self-agrandissement. The inflated human ego does not survive for long when there are horses about.

Among non-equestrian enthusiasts there is often a misguided perception that horses equate with riches and "the upper classes". As those involved know, nothing could be further from the truth. Certainly, there are well-heeled riders. But for every millionaire there are a thousand "ordinary" people working hard and making endless sacrifices to support their horses. Dukes rub shoulders with shopkeepers, princesses compete on level terms with humble grooms. Farmers' sons become world champions. It is a world where everyone helps everyone else, rejoicing at their rivals' successes, commiserating with their failures. Thanks to the horse, the old precepts of true sportsmanship are still very much alive.

No one knows for sure when man first sat astride a horse, but one thing seems pretty certain: given the human being's inherent competitive streak, it cannot have been long before our ancestors started pitting one animal against another to see whose was "best". A simple form of racing must have been on the agenda very early on. Certainly organized driven races were a very popular form of entertainment in the ancient world.

Although ridden racing did not take off quite as quickly – the first recorded ridden race was in 624 BC at the Greek Olympiad, it is now without doubt the strongest section of the horse world. Not only does it employ a huge work force, it also provides governments with a valuable source of income through the taxes levied on betting. Through racing, millions of people who might otherwise have no contact with horses learn to appreciate their enduring value in the mechanized world. Another of the beauties of racing is that you don't have to be a professional to enjoy its thrills and spills. There are still plenty of race-riding opportunities for the true amateur.

As modern man gains more and more leisure time, so equestrian sports continue to gain in popularity. Carriage driving has enjoyed a world-wide resurgence, thanks to the many competitive opportunities; women are riding side-saddle again; small children can have a go at everything from gymkhana games to polo; cowboys still hone their cattle-working skills and compete at rodeos. A selection of the world's most popular horse sports is included in the following pages – this is only a small sample of the diversity of sports open to anyone who can ride. Why not get out there and have a go?

The term "horse show" encompasses just about everything, from a local get-together in one small field to a week-long affair at a state-of-the-art permanent showground featuring the crème de la crème of the equestrian world. Many shows now include jumping as an added attraction, but the showing classes on which all horse shows were traditionally based are still a major feature of many fixtures. Indeed, there are a fair number of shows (particularly those devoted to a particular equine breed or breeds) which include nothing else.

Show horses and ponies are judged on their conformation, movement and, in some cases such as hunters and hacks, their suitability for their designated job. A show hunter may never actually have been hunting (show horses should be free from blemish, so it would be too risky) but he should be the epitome of the best type of horse for that particular job.

Anyone with a horse who does not have too many obvious imperfections can enter an appropriate show class, though it is as well to bear in mind that showing does revolve very much around the judges' opinion: never be too disappointed if your horse, who may be the apple of your eye, fails to win a ribbon. If your equine partner is not designed for the show ring, you can still have immense fun watching those who are – and pitting your judging skills against those of the experts.

Something for Everyone

There are show classes for ridden (including sidesaddle), in-hand (led) and driven horses and ponies; for specific types such as riding horses, hunters, hunter ponies, children's riding ponies, hacks and cobs; and for specific breeds such as Arabians, Quarter horses, Hackneys, Palominos, Mountain and Moorland ponies, Shire horses, Clydesdales, Appaloosas and many, many more.

For the horse or pony who is perhaps just below top show standard but is a good athlete there are "working" classes, such as those for working hunters. Here the horses are required to prove their jumping ability over hunting-type obstacles as well as being judged for conformation.

Then again there are classes designed to test

SHOWS & SHOWING

The aim of show classes is to maintain and improve the quality of exhibits – they are the "shop windows" of the horse world.

In show classes good conformation is usually a pre-requisite and the judge will also check the horse for blemishes.

not the beauty of the horse but the rider's skill. The equitation division seen at shows in the United States is an excellent training ground, for here the young riders are judged on their performance and style both on the flat and over fences. If more countries adopted this idea, the standard of junior riding (particularly jumping) could be improved a good deal.

In Britain smaller shows often include classes for the useful rather than beautiful horse. "Ordinary" riders can have great fun competing on their "ordinary" mounts in competitions designed to find the best "family horse" or the best "handy horse". In the latter competition the entries might have to open a gate, or stand still to be mounted and dismounted from both sides, be loaded into a trailer or complete other similar "tests".

What Happens in the Ring?

In ridden classes such as those for show hunters, the judge first has a chance to see the horses with their regular riders as the whole entry circles the arena at walk, trot and finally at canter. The horses are then called in to form a preliminary line-up, after which the judge will ride each in turn. Lastly the horses are stripped (have their saddles removed) so that they can be assessed individually for conformation. When making a final choice, the judge will

Dress Code

The dress rules for show classes are quite complicated and can vary according to the size and status of the show and the time of day of the class. Newcomers to the showing world can do no better than study the experts – they usually get it right – and check the rules for the class well in advance of the show. In most classes it is the horse who is being judged, so as a general rule the prime requisites for the rider are to be neat, tidy and unostentatious (large floral buttonholes and eye-catching bows of ribbon are definitely out). Clothes should be clean, boots well polished and long hair neatly fastened up in a hairnet.

ABOVE, RIGHT: *An elegant turnout at the top of the line.*

BELOW: *A class of ladies' hacks turned out to perfection. The "quarter marks" are applied by brush and stencil.*

take into account the horse's conformation and movement, and the quality of ride he gave. Once the judge has had a chance to ride the horses, it is not unusual for him or her to shuffle round the preliminary order – the best-looking horse may not necessarily give the best ride on the day.

Hack classes differ from hunter classes in that each horse is also required to give a short individual show with his rider. Since hacks are meant to be paragons among riding horses, riders often perform their show one-handed, and include movements such as the rein-back and canter strike-off on a chosen leg. Children's riding ponies, which of course are too small to be ridden by the judges, are also required to give an individual show. In their case it will usually include a gallop. Manners play an important part in showing, and nowhere more so than with children's ponies. Misbehaviour is (or should be) severely penalized by the judge, since a badly behaved pony is not a suitable ride for a child.

In-hand classes, which include those for youngstock and broodmares, are judged on conformation, and movement at walk and trot. In the case of broodmares, superficial blemishes are not consid-

ered unduly detrimental.

Various classes are held for driven horses and ponies. They include pure show classes, for example those for Hackneys, where conformation and action are the criteria; classes where the turnout of horse and vehicle are taken into consideration, and scurries, which are obstacle races that test the agility of the animals and the skill of the "whip" or driver.

THE ART OF DRESSAGE

In the theatre of horsemanship, dressage is the ballet
– with the horse the star performer.

It is one of the wonders of nature that, despite his tremendous size and weight, the horse is such a marvellous athlete, endowed with perfect balance, exquisite grace and extraordinary gymnastic abilities. Watch him at play as he strides round his paddock: the harmony of his movements, the superb acceleration, the ability to stop "on a sixpence" and change direction with lightning speed. When he shows off,.who can fail to admire his proud bearing – head up, neck arched, tail high – or the poise of his high-stepping "slow motion" trot, or the breathtaking way in which he extends his limbs and seemingly floats over the ground?

The object of dressage – which, remember, merely means training – is to enable the horse to regain that wonderful natural balance while carrying a weight on his back. It involves teaching him to shift weight further back on to his hindlegs to compensate for the fact that the presence of a rider puts an unnatural amount of weight on to his forehand.

Competitive dressage is designed to show the horse carrying out, on request, the movements which he performs without thinking while running loose. At its highest level, where horse and rider achieve total harmony and the rider's aids are barely perceptible, it can take your breath away.

A Brief History of Dressage

Horses must have undergone various training methods, many of them no doubt pretty crude, since man first started riding them. More than 2,000 years ago the enlightened Greek general, Xenophon (c.430–350 BC) wrote brief works on the subject of horse keeping and training – many of his humane, commonsense principles hold good today. Xenophon's works were rediscovered during the Renaissance and in 1550 Federico Grisone, an Italian, founded a riding academy in Naples where he expanded upon the Greek's teachings. Grisone is acknowledged as the first of the great classical riding masters.

In the centuries which followed, several Frenchmen, included Antoine de Pluvinel and François de la Guérinière, and the French-based Englishman William Cavendish, Duke of Newcastle, and later François Baucher, James Fillis, and the German Gustav Steinbrecht, developed and perfected the training system on which modern-day competitive dressage is based.

Actual dressage competitions date from only the last quarter of the nineteenth century and were initially intended to demonstrate the correct training of the military horse. Dressage was first staged at the Olympic Games in Stockholm in 1912.

The Arena

Dressage competitions take place in an arena of a specified size: 20 × 40 m (22 × 44 yards) for the lower levels; 20 × 60 m (22 × 66 yards) for the higher levels. The sides of the arena are marked out at intervals by letters of the alphabet, the choice of which is, intriguingly, shrouded in mystery.

The rider enters at the centre of one of the short sides of the arena. This point is marked with the letter A. In a large arena, starting from A – and moving in a clockwise direction – the other letters are K-V-E-S-H-C-M-R-B-P-F. C is in the centre of the short side facing A, while E and B face each other mid-way down each of the long sides. The letters for the short arena are the same except that V, S, R and P are omitted. Further letters are used to indicate five other positions on the centre line – the line that divides the arena in half lengthwise.

"The Marquis of Newcastle Giving Captain Mazin a Riding Lesson", from William Cavendish's **The Method and New Invention of Dressing Horses.**

These letters must be learnt as they cannot be marked on the actual arena surface. The letter X marks the halfway point of the centre line. Letters D and L are on the centre line and midway between K/F and V/P, respectively. I and G are midway between S/R and H/M, respectively.

In both large and small arenas there is a distance of 6 m (6½ yards) from each corner to the first letter on the long side. In a large arena the other letters on the long sides are 12m (13 yards) apart, while in a small arena they are 14 m (15½ yards) apart).

At the higher levels of dressage the arena will have an artifical surface, such as sand, which is levelled at regular intervals during the competition to ensure that all the competitors have virtually the same ground conditions on which to perform.

The Dressage Test

Generally speaking, in a dressage competition all the horses and riders must perform exactly the same test. This comprises a written series of instructions which must be followed exactly. Each test is divided into a number of movements which must be performed at designated places in the arena, for example: A – enter in working canter; FX – half pass (right); or R – flying change of leg. The test is devised either by a country's national federation (for classes at national level) or by the Federation Equestre Internationale (FEI). FEI tests are always used in international competitions and may also be used at national level. Tests are re-written periodically. This helps

Dressage at Olympic standard: the 1996 gold medallists, Isabel Werth and Gigolo.

to prevent horses and riders from becoming stale and provides a more interesting spectacle for the audience.

The movements required and the length of each test depend on the level of training of the horse, starting at preliminary and novice levels and going right up to Olympic, world and regional championships, where the Grand Prix and Grand Prix Special tests are used. The Grand Prix Special, used in individual championships, lasts for around seven to eight minutes. It usually takes several years to train a horse to this level, which is physically and mentally very demanding.

Holland's Anky van Grunsven and Olympic Bonfire
demonstrate the half-pass.

The Rules

Each rider is given a few minutes in which to ride around the area immediately outside the arena just before the bell rings signalling that they must go in for their test. This riding-in period gives them a chance to accustom their horse to all the strange new sights and sounds. At the highest levels of competition, where there is a large crowd, the atmosphere around the dressage arena can be electric and this can have a detrimental effect on the performance of a horse who is nervous or distracted and not listening to his rider.

The use of the voice while competing is forbidden and the rider must keep both hands on the reins except when saluting the judges and when leaving the arena.

In some national classes – though not usually those for juniors and young riders – a whip may be carried, but at international level it is not allowed.

If the rider has a lapse of memory and either misses out a movement or performs one in the wrong place or sequence, the judge rings a bell and the rider must stop and recommence the test from the point where the mistake or omission was made.

The Scoring System

Each movement in a test is awarded marks from 0 (movement not performed) up to 10 (excellent). The latter is rarely achieved! Marks are also given for the overall performance of the horse and the way in which the rider has ridden the test. Marks are deducted for errors of course. The final score is given as a percentage – a score of 70 per cent or above is very good indeed. Depending on the level, there may be only one or two judges or as many as five.

Dressage to Music

The relatively recent introduction of freestyle dressage to music has done an enormous amount to make the sport more accessible to the general public. The annual Dressage World Cup, an indoor championship held during the winter months and comprising a series of qualifiers culminating in a final, has brought dressage to a far wider audience than previously and the varied programmes and choice of music have been much appreciated.

Riders must include certain prescribed movements in their test, according to the level at which the horse is competing, but the actual choreography of the test is up to the individual. The whole performance can be significantly enhanced if their choice of music – either specially composed, or arranged – really suits a particular horse's way of going.

The judges' task, never an easy one in this sport, is even more difficult in the freestyle, for here they are required to allot marks for artistic presentation as well as for technical execution (as with the other tests, marks are awarded out of 10 for each movement). Artistic presentation criteria are: rhythm, energy and elasticity; harmony between the rider and horse; choreography, the use of the arena and inventiveness; degree of difficulty and the taking of well-calculated risks; the choice of music and the interpretation of it. If competitors finish on equal scores, it is the artistic presentation mark which is the deciding factor.

If any proof were needed that the freestyle to music had come to stay, it was given in 1996 when it was introduced at Olympic level in Atlanta. The enthusiastic response from the crowd left no doubt of its popularity.

The Movements

At beginner's level the test will require the horse to perform only simple movements at walk, trot and canter. As the degree of difficulty increases collected and lateral work are introduced. By the time international championship level is reached, the horse is required to show passage (a slow, elevated trot), piaffe (trotting on the spot), full canter pirouettes (the horse turns through 360 degrees, with his hindlegs remaining virtually on the same spot), and flying changes of leg at canter at every stride.

There are international competitions for pony riders, juniors and young riders as well as adults.

The piaffe – one of the most difficult of dressage movements.

Dress Code

- **Neatness of turnout is vital in dressage in order to complement the hoped-for elegant performance of the horse.**
- **At the lower levels, from preliminary to advanced medium, riders may wear any normal riding hat, such as a crash hat with a dark cover, a hunting cap or a bowler hat. A tweed coat can be worn with a shirt and tie or hunting tie (cravat), or a dark coat with a hunting tie. Breeches and jodhpurs should be white, cream or beige and riding or jodhpur boots may be black or brown. Gloves should always be worn.**
- **At advanced level many riders like to change to a tail coat with a top hat, although it is also acceptable to wear a dark riding coat with an ordinary riding hat. At this level black boots with light-coloured breeches are required. For official international shows, a black or dark blue tail coat with a top hat is obligatory for adults, unless they are entitled to wear a uniform, such as that of the police or armed services.**

HIGH, WIDE & HANDSOME

For colour, spectacle and drama there is nothing to beat the sport of show jumping at its highest level.

French rider, A Ledermann flying high at the Olympics in 1996 for which she took the bronze medal.

In international show jumping, horses of all shapes and sizes, and riders of either sex, compete on equal terms for some of the biggest prizes in the horse world. It is not surprising that the sport has gained such popularity with spectators for it is the most accessible of equestrian activities, thanks to its easy-to-follow rules and often nail-biting climaxes.

For those horses blessed with that special extra talent for jumping high and wide, the sky is the limit. Prize purses have increased so dramatically that the past decade has seen the arrival of that rare phenomenon outside the world of racing, the equine millionaire, and both horses and riders have become household names.

But show jumping is not just for the elite of the equestrian world. Huge numbers of amateur riders have a great deal of fun at the lower levels. There are endless opportunities, year in and year out, in all corners of the globe, for the "ordinary" rider with their "ordinary" horse and pony. All of which helps make show jumping a great sport.

Show Jumping History

Jumping was not a skill which most riders bothered with until enclosure of the land began in Britain, and some other European countries, at the beginning of the eighteenth century. Whether you were a sportsman following hounds or a member of the cavalry in the field, suddenly it became imperative for your horse to be able to negotiate, with safety, obstacles such as fences and hedges in order to travel across country. Such is man's competitive nature that it was only a matter of time before riders began to pit their horse against those of their friends. First came cross-country racing. Then, towards the end of the nineteenth century, the first "leaping" competitions.

The earliest records of such events are found in Ireland in 1864, when the first of two trial horse shows held in Dublin included a high jump and a wide leap. These were intended primarily to test the qualifications of the hunters. In 1900 "prize jumping" contests were included in the Olympic Games in Paris, and seven years later London's International Horse Show staged the world's first Nations Cup (team jumping competition).

The single most important influence upon the development of the sport was the "invention" of the forward jumping seat by a member of the Italian cavalry, Federico Caprilli (1868–1907). Previously, most riders, including the cavalry, were taught to throw their weight back when tackling a fence. It was Caprilli who convinced the world that the horse could jump more effectively if the rider shortened his stirrups and freed the horse's loins and back of weight. Although they met resistance at first, Caprilli's enlightened ideas were subsequently

Walking the course to assess the fences and the distances between them is an essential element of show jumping.

adopted by riders from all continents. It is no exaggeration to say that he changed the course of horsemanship and in the process laid the foundations of the sport of show jumping as we know it today.

In the decades before the Second World War the sport grew by leaps and bounds, with more and more international shows being staged throughout Europe and in North America. The military were still a dominant force, although some civilians, including women, did compete, not without success. In the post-war years, with most of the world's armies having been mechanized, the sport was opened up to all and sundry.

What's the Score?

The modern scoring system is a model of simplicity. Each time a horse knocks down a fence he is given 4 faults; there is no penalty if he knocks down a lower part of the fence in the same vertical plane – this does sometimes happen where a horse jumps awkwardly and hits a lower pole with his foot.

If he refuses or runs out at a fence, the penalty is 3 faults for the first disobedience, 6 faults for the second, and elimination for the third. If the horse disturbs an obstacle when refusing, the bell is rung and the clock is stopped. Six time penalties are awarded and the rider must not re-start until the

fence has been rebuilt and the bell rung again.

Each course is measured and given a "time allowed". This is based on the speed that the horse is required to maintain, which in turn is governed by the level at which he is competing. Time penalties are given for exceeding the time allowed.

The rider is eliminated for: starting before the bell sounds; not starting within 45 seconds of the bell sounding; failing to go across the start and finish lines; taking the wrong course; exceeding the time limit (twice the time allowed). A fall of horse and/or rider usually incurs elimination (but not in one or two major international competitions, such as a Nations Cup).

In jump-off competitions, those on clear rounds or equal faults go through to a timed jump-off, where the winner is the one with the lowest score in the fastest time. In some speed competitions time penalties are awarded instead of faults (e.g. 4 or 5 seconds per fence down). These are added to the time taken to complete the round, giving the rider a total score in seconds.

Dress Code

Broadly speaking, show jumping clothes are based on hunting attire, but there is a good deal of variation in coat colours because riders from different

Derby courses include cross-country type obstacles, such as this enormous bank at Hickstead in the south of England.

distances'', that is fences placed within six or seven strides of each other. These are not combinations but the siting of one fence only a few strides from another does mean that the horse's striding between those fences becomes crucially important.

Another ploy available to the course designer is the positioning of different types of fence. A classic problem is the siting of a vertical immediately after a big water jump. To clear the spread of the water the horse needs to lengthen his stride during his approach. Only the well schooled, well balanced horse will get his weight back on to his hindlegs quickly enough to be able to jump the following vertical faultlessly. Fences placed immediately after a turn pose another problem for the rider – any lack of balance and impulsion round the turn will cause mistakes at the fence.

In a jump-off the course designer can incorporate various potential pitfalls, such as a long gallop between two fences, or an invitation to riders

nations dress according to the dress rules of their own federations. For example, international riders from Ireland traditionally wear green jackets; those from the United States wear red; British men wear red, whereas British women wear either black or dark blue. Also, some riders wear coats in their sponsors' colours.

White or (for women) fawn breeches are worn with black boots. Men may wear boots with brown tops. A hard hat is compulsory and in the interests of safety some national federations now insist that a chin harness is worn. White shirts are required at international level, worn with a hunting tie or ordinary white tie. Women may dispense with the tie if they wear a shirt with a high round collar.

At the lower levels of the sport less formal clothes are usually worn, for instance a tweed or other light-coloured jacket with a pastel coloured shirt. Junior riders normally wear jodhpurs and jodhpur boots.

Course Design

Because there is a limit to how high and wide a horse can jump, course designers cannot simply go on building bigger and bigger fences in order to produce a result. If horses were faced with this every time they competed, even the most eager and generous would soon become disheartened. It is, therefore, the job of the course designer to devise other ways of sorting out the wheat from the chaff.

At the top level of the sport, where there are now so many talented, purpose-bred horses, and gifted riders, courses have had to become much more ''technical'' in recent years. Technical courses are designed to test the rider's horsemanship and the level of training to which he has brought his horse. They incorporate such things as ''long'' or ''short'' distances in combination fences – where the rider must be able to lengthen or shorten his horse's stride instantaneously – and ''related

Champions All

The principal events of the show jumping calendar, comprising both team and individual championships, are:

- **The Olympic Games**
- **The World Equestrian Games (even years between the Olympics).**
- **The World Cup (annual indoor championship for individuals only).**
- **The Pan-American Games (the year before the Olympics).**
- **The European Championships (the years between the Olympics and the World Equestrian Games).**
- **There are a number of other continental games and championships which take place on a regular basis: these include the Asian Games, the Balkan Championships and the Central American Games. There are also continental championships for pony riders, juniors and young riders.**

to cut inside one fence in order to save time on the approach to another, or to jump a fence at an acute angle. Although luck always plays a part in show jumping (a late draw, especially when jumping against the clock, is usually an advantage because the rider knows exactly what score he must beat to win) it is the best schooled horse who often emerges triumphant.

The Nations Cup

Nations Cups are among the most important events of the show jumping calendar. They are for teams of four riders, each of whom jumps the same course twice. Each nation discards its worst score in each round and the winner is the team with the lowest total score after both rounds.

Generally speaking countries are entitled to stage one official Nations Cup each year, though a very large country such as the United States is granted two.

The Puissance

An old-established competition designed to test the horse's ability over a limited number of large obstacles, the Puissance is a popular crowd-puller, though it is somewhat less popular with many riders and Puissance classes usually have only a small number of entries. This is because the true Puissance horse, who has the ability – and courage – to clear a wall at 2.15 m (7 ft) or more, is a rarity, and few riders are inclined to risk their Grand Prix horses – landing over a fence of this height can cause tremendous strain on their forelimbs. To protect the horses, the competition is limited to one round, followed by a maximum of four jumps-off. If there is still equality, the riders divide first prize.

The greatest height to have been cleared over a Puissance wall is 2.40 m (7 ft 10½ in). This was achieved by Optiebeurs Leonardo, ridden by Germany's Franke Sloothaak, at Chaudfontaine, in Belgium, in 1991.

An international-level horse clearing a big vertical

fence in immaculate style.

Derbies

The Derby is an unusual competition, which is both challenging for the horse and rider and intriguing for the spectator. It takes place over a course that is a good bit longer than a Nations Cup course and incorporates a number of "natural" obstacles such as banks and ditches which would normally be encountered when going across country. The horses need to be extremely

fit, as tiredness towards the end can lead to jumping mistakes. Most well schooled show jumpers cope perfectly well with the unusual fences.

The oldest event of this type is the Hamburg Derby, created by the well-known German rider Eduard F. Pulvermann in the years after the First World War. In 1961 Douglas Bunn introduced the British Jumping Derby at his All England Jumping Ground, Hickstead, and since them many other countries have followed suit.

HORSE TRIALS HEAVEN

The exciting and immensely popular modern sport of horse trials, or eventing, stems from a competition originally devised to test the all-round training of the military horse and rider. Indeed, in Europe it has down the years been widely referred to as "'The Military". Now, of course, military competitors are rarities and the winning horse in the world's toughest event is as likely to be ridden by a sylph-like young woman as by a man.

The concept of the sport has, however, remained the same. It tests the all-round skills of both horse and rider. At the lower levels, which are run on one day, it includes a dressage test, show jumping test and cross-country test (normally in that order). At the higher levels - two-day events and three-day events, there is a steeplechase and also two sections of roads and tracks, the first designed to warm the horse up, the second to enable him to recover after the steeplechase and before tackling the cross-country.

The sport of horse trials is designed to test the all-round skills of horse and rider. Although cross-country riding provides the ultimate thrill and spectacle, dressage and show jumping are important too.

A History of Eventing

In Europe from the 17th century onwards it was part of cavalry training to undertake long-distance rides across country, with speed and endurance the prime requisites. There is little evidence of any systematic jumping schooling.

The three-day event as a competitive endurance test incorporating jumping originated in France in the early 20th century. A competition held in Paris in 1902, exclusively for officers and military chargers, included dressage, a steeplechase, a long-distance ride and show jumping. As interest in the sport increased, the long-distance element was shortened and a cross-country course introduced. An early form of the sport was included in the Olympic Games of 1912 and 1920 and by 1924, broadly speaking, the formula used today had been arrived at.

The tremendous growth of the sport in Britain, where during the last two decades riders from New Zealand and Australia have based themselves and gone out to conquer the world, did not begin until after the 1948 Olympics. These Games were awarded to London, with the three-day event being run at Aldershot. After watching the event the Duke of Beaufort wrote: "It seemed to me that this was just the sort of activity for a good English hunter" and, little knowing that he was about to change the face of the sport, he decided to run a similar event at his Gloucestershire estate as a means of preparing the British team (who failed to complete at Aldershot) for the following Olympics.

Horse trials dressage at its best: Britain's Ian Stark with Stanwick Ghost.

Thus it was that Badminton Horse Trials came into being.   Originally viewed with suspicion by the average British rider, more used to riding to hounds than to performing a dressage test, Badminton was destined to become the world's premier three-day event. But competing at top level obviously could not be achieved overnight. There had to be some sort of step ladder to bring on promising young horses and less experienced riders. Accordingly, a system of less demanding one-day events gradually evolved, with different levels of difficulty to suit a whole range of competitors.

The Dressage Test

Although horse trials dressage does not include the technically difficult movements seen in Grand Prix dressage, it is nevertheless a challenging part of the sport. Gone are the days when a rider could "catch up" after earning a poor dressage mark by going brilliantly across country. To be a successful all-rounder, the event horse must be correctly schooled on the flat.

Often the biggest challenge for the rider on dressage day is getting the horse to concentrate on the test, whatever the level and degree of difficulty, when he is feeling as fit as a flea and longing to go galloping and jumping. One of the great arts of event riding is to know exactly how much work the horse needs to have him calm, relaxed and "listening" just as he goes in to do his test. Even the top riders do not always manage to get it right. If the horse is overworked, he will go "off the boil" and fail to sparkle; if he is underworked, the rider may find himself sitting on a hooligan.

Show Jumping

The show jumps in eventing are small in comparison with those encountered in true show jumping events, but they still pose a considerable problem and many a good cross-country horse has failed to achieve his potential because he is inaccurate over coloured poles. The difficulty lies in teaching the horse not to rattle show jumps when he knows perfectly well that he can often get away with knocking cross-country fences. In the two- and

The event horse must be a true all rounder, as adept over show jumps as over cross-country fences.

three-day events the show jumping test can be particularly demanding: any stiffness or tiredness resulting from the rigours of the cross-country will quickly catch the horse out.

Scoring

In an effort to make the sport easier to understand by all concerned – not least the public – the Fédération Equestre Internationale (FEI) introduced a new, streamlined scoring system in 1999. In most countries rules for national competitions have traditionally followed those laid down by the FEI, but there may for a while be some discrepancy between the way the big international three-day events are scored and the smaller national horse trials.

All dressage test movements are each marked out of 10. The judges' marks are then averaged and subtracted from the maximum possible mark to give a penalty score. Under the new FEI rules the resultant scores will then be rounded to the nearest whole number instead of using decimal points as in the past.

In show jumping each fence knocked down incurs 5 penalties; 10 penalties are given for a first refusal and 20 for the second. A third refusal, jumping an obstacle in the wrong order and an error of course not rectified all incur elimination. Under the new FEI rules, time faults are given at the rate of one per second over the time allowed (previously the penalty was 0.25 penalty per second)

Dress Code

DRESSAGE

At the lower levels riders may wear a dark blue or black hunting coat over a shirt with a collar and tie, or a collarless shirt with a white hunting tie. A crash hat (with a dark blue or black cover), hunting cap or bowler hat may be worn. Breeches should be fawn, and boots black. For advanced one-day and intermediate three-day levels upwards riders wear a dark blue or black tail coat with a top hat. Gloves are always worn.

SHOW JUMPING

At novice, pre-novice and junior one-day levels, a tweed coat is acceptable, worn over a shirt with a collar and tie. For all other classes a dark blue or black coat is worn over a collarless shirt and white hunting tie. In all cases a hat to the recommended safety standards is compulsory.

RIDING TO HOUNDS

For many riders there is nothing to compare with the challenge of a day spent following hounds.

Hunting may not be to everyone's taste – at least not the kind which involves the killing of animals – but the hunting field has long been considered as good a place as any to teach a horse to look after himself across country, to cope with different types of terrain and to jump unfamiliar obstacles boldly. A competition horse who has become jaded, or lacks confidence because of an injury or fall, will often perk up remarkably if he is taken hunting a few times. After all, being a member of a herd comes naturally to him.

For the riders – whose knowledge of, and interest in, hounds and the way they work varies considerably from individual to individual – hunting offers other rewards. For many, chief among them is the unique privilege and thrill of riding over countryside that would not otherwise be open to them, often at speed, and tackling obstacles of which – unlike in the competitive world – they have no prior knowledge.

Hunting History

Man has been a hunter from the very earliest times, the need for food spurring him on to track and kill other species in order to survive. When primitive man decided to make the dog his companion it proved to be an inspired choice. This animal, descended mainly from southern races of the wolf, was of course already a skilled hunter in his own right, and humans soon learnt to put their four-legged friends' superior scenting powers to good use. Add to this successful alliance the domesticated horse, and in due course man had a means of transport (the chariot) by which to accompany his hunting dogs with the least inconvenience to himself.

As early as 2,000 BC the Egyptians had developed hunting breeds of dog such as the greyhound: they can be seen in their wonderful wall paintings pursuing their quarry in the company of both horse and hound. Successive civilizations followed their example and it was only a matter of time before hunting for pleasure, not mere necessity, and riding rather than driving, became established practice. Julius Caesar records that the Gauls hunted for sport, and modern experts on the subject of venery give more than a passing nod to ancient France when discussing the fount of present-day hunting.

Down the centuries different breeds of hunting dog evolved, the quality of riding horses improved, and the nature of the quarry changed, often as a result of man-imposed changes to the environment. Hare, deer and boar – all of which were good to eat – and that much-feared predator, the wolf, were traditional European beasts for hunting. In France, with its large tracts of forest, hunting enthusiasts

ABOVE, LEFT: *The ancient Egyptians used horse-drawn chariots when pursuing their quarry.*

*Mounted followers with the foxhounds of the
Westhills Hunt, California.*

remained loyal to the deer. In Britain, on the other hand, the fox had begun to emerge as an alternative quarry as early as the 14th century. By the middle of the 18th century aristocratic landowners all over the country were hunting the fox over their huge tracts of land. Subsequently the Industrial Revolution produced a new type of "gentry" during the 19th century, and the sport became financially accessible to far more people.

Today in Britain packs of foxhounds far outnumber other packs of hounds, as they do in the United States, and it is possible to ride to hounds of one type or another in Canada, Australia (where foxes were introduced from Britain), New Zealand and a number of European countries.

Drag Hunting

If the chasing and killing of animals is not your cup of tea, you can still sample the excitement of the chase by following a drag hunt, in which a pack of hounds hunts an artificially laid scent, or bloodhounds, who hunt a human scent.

Hunter Trials

It is not necessary to hunt to take part in the fun sport of hunter trials, which are particularly popular in Britain and are also seen in the United States. Run in classes for different levels of horse and rider, hunter trials give people of all ages and abilities the chance to compete over a cross-country course. For the beginner the fences may be as low as 2 ft 6 in (76 cm), while for the experienced horse and rider in open classes they rise to 3 ft 6 in (106 cm)

or 3 ft 9 in (114 cm). A good way of getting started is to enter a pairs class together with a more experienced rider.

Hunter trials are judged on a combination of clear rounds and time – you are expected to tackle the course at a fair hunting pace (a good canter or slow gallop). Some courses include non-jumping tests, such as opening and shutting a gate, which adds to the fun.

Team Chasing

Team chasing is a more recently introduced variation of hunter trials. Teams of three or four riders compete over a hunter-trial type course. Depending on the rules for the particular event, each team's riders may be permitted to jump each fence one after another or they may be required to tackle certain fences "upsides", that is abreast.

HORSEBALL

Imagine rugby on horseback, with a dash of basketball thrown in, and you have the high-adrenalin sport of horseball.

When the word went out during the 1970s that the French Equestrian Federation was looking for a team game that could be played from Pony Club right up to senior level, Bordeaux-based riding instructor Jean-Paul Depons leapt at the idea of amalgamating his two great passions: riding and rugby. He envisaged what he described as a natural marriage between the two sports. The ingenious and highly successful result was horseball, a sport which has been described as "a cross between the Charge of the Light Brigade and the Five Nations Cup – a downright impossibility!"

Horseball, like polo, is a team game played at a fast and furious pace, but there the similarity to that highly exclusive pastime ends. Horseball, unlike polo, is accessible to everyone who can ride, men and women, boys and girls alike.

Each player needs only one horse, and the field

of play has deliberately been kept fairly small – the recommended ideal dimensions are 65 × 25 metres (213 × 82 ft) – so that play can take place equally well in indoor arenas as well as outdoors. A sand or sawdust surface is preferable since it affords both ease of movement for the horses and safety for the riders.

The aim is to gain possession of the ball, without dismounting, and to put it into the goals situated at either end of the ground. Each goal comprises a metal frame, 1m in diametre, painted white and fitted with a white net. The goal is positioned 3.5 m (11½ ft) above the ground.

Each team comprises six players, of which a maximum of four are on the ground at any one time, with the other two being used as substitutes if required. There is no limit to the number of substitutions a team can make during a game, but permission must be asked of the referee. There are two referees, the senior one being mounted, while

the other – known as the touch judge – occupies a stationary position on the centre line.

The ball, the size of a junior football, is encased in a net fitted with six strong leather handles to facilitate picking up. To snatch it from the ground, riders must lean out of the saddle Cossack style, which calls for considerable athleticism and which can bring a player's head perilously close to the flying hooves of other horses. Strength is needed to steal possession of the ball form an opponent, and dexterity to pass it and shoot at goal from the back of a galloping horse. Above all, players must be skilled riders, since for much of the time they have their hands off the reins, using just their legs and weight to control their mounts.

Although the sport has superficial links with basketball, because of the type of goals used, the elements of physical contact and passing of the ball make it more akin to rugby.

What are the Rules?

A minimum number of three consecutive passes, involving three different players, must be made by the same team before a goal may be scored. The three-pass count begins again as soon as the ball drops to the ground or is intercepted by the opposing team. Every touch of the ball is considered to be a pass. When necessary, the ball is put back into play in the same way as in a rugby lineout. The ball must not be held for more than 10 seconds by the same player.

Players are permitted to try to steal possession of the ball from an opponent by using one hand only and must not hang on to any part of the tack or body of the horse. Players in possession are not allowed to switch the ball to their other hand whilst possession is being disputed.

ABOVE, LEFT: *With its elements of physical contact and passing of the ball (a junior-size football) horseball has much in common with rugby.*

Dress Code

- **Riding helmet with chin strap (obligatory).**
- **Jerseys in team colours, numbered from 1 to 6 on the chest and back.**
- **Riding boots.**
- **Riding breeches or all-in-one suits in the team colours.**
- **The wearing of protective supports is recommended.**
- **Spurs are optional.**
- **Whips are not permitted.**

Marking, as a means of defence, is allowed and consists of bringing one's horse into contact with the horse of the opponent carrying the ball in order to slow it down, put it off course and to seize hold of the ball. A player may push his opponent with the weight and momentum of his horse, and with his shoulder and arm, on condition that his elbow remains in contact with his body. Seizing hold of an opponent, pushing or tugging with the hand or making contact with the fist, forearm, elbow or head thrust forward are not allowed.

Unsporting behaviour may be punished by the issuing of a yellow card or sending off.

Three different types of penalty are awarded, their severity depending on the infringement. Penalty number 1 gives the offended side a free shot at goal from a stationary position on the 5-metre line; number 2 awards a similar shot from the 10-metre line (or the offended riders may employ the three-pass rule if they wish); number 3, used for all minor infringements, is awarded at the precise spot where the infringement took place.

Playing Time

The game is played in two halves, each of 10 minutes, with a three-minute break between. If a large number of matches are scheduled for the same day, the halves may be reduced to six minutes each. Each team is allowed to call two breaks in play at times of its own choosing for both tactical reasons and to enable it to make substitutes.

Scoring

The team scoring the most goals wins. In knock-out competitions, in the event of equality the game is decided by a series of shots at goal.

The sport of endurance riding has opened up competitive horsemanship to a whole new generation of owners. Everyone can have a go, provided they have a sound horse, a knowledge of fitness training – and the ability to read a map.

GOING THE DISTANCE

Long-distance riding is nothing new: once humans had tamed the horse and learnt to ride and drive him they were in a position to tackle feats of exploration unheard of in their pre-equestrian days. A willing and amiable partner, the horse long ago enabled man to travel beyond the confines of his own small world, whether it was to hunt, trade or conquer new lands.

Throughout history the horse has played a vital part in mankind's movements around the globe, covering countless miles as the mount of the explorer, the merchant or the soldier, as a pack animal, or as a means of traction. Although horses may on occasion have been expendable – as in

BELOW: *Finland's Baron Mannerheim, who undertook an epic ride across Asia in 1906–08.*

times of war – they were always an essential adjunct to human life and generally valued as such. Getting and keeping them fit would have been second nature to all horse-owning peoples.

It is only in the 20th century, after the horse had for the majority of people become a luxury rather than a necessity, that riders again began to value the skill involved in covering long distances on horseback and to turn it into a competitive pastime.

A History of Endurance Riding

There is recorded evidence that long-distance riding was a normal means of training for many cavalry regiments. One of the earliest records is of a 28 km (17½-mile) ride undertaken by the Austrian cavalry in the last quarter of the 17th century. They rode at an average speed of 16 km (10 miles) an hour.

By the 19th century army officers from several European countries were undertaking much longer rides, including in 1892 the famous one from Vienna to Berlin, a distance of 592 km (370 miles). This was a competitive event, completed by the winner in a time of just under three days – including a rest period. By no means all the horses who completed the ride recovered from their exertions.

In Britain during the 1920s rides were organized by the Arab Horse Society to demonstrate to the military the tremendous stamina and recuperative qualities of Arabian horses. They were ridden over a distance of 483 km (300 miles) over a period of several days and veterinary inspections were an integral part of the test. There are records of similar events in the United States during the 1930s.

Competitive endurance riding, open to anyone with a suitable horse, is one of the most recent of equestrian sports and a truly amateur one right up to international level. The American Wendell T. Robie is generally credited with "inventing" the sport in 1955, when he inaugurated the 100-mile (160 km) Western States Trail Ride for the Tevis Cup. The Tom Quilty Ride in the Blue Mountains of New South Wales, in Australia, which dates from 1966, and Britain's Summer Solstice Ride – first run in 1975 – were both modelled on the Tevis Cup.

The Structure of the Sport

There are two divisions within the sport: the true endurance ride, which is in effect a race in which the fastest horse home is the winner, and the competitive trail ride. The latter is not a race, the aim being to test the rider's skill in training the horse and completing the ride, at a set speed, with the horse in good condition. In countries such as Britain and the United States, many riders use the competitive trail ride as a ladder to the more demanding and more exciting activity of race riding, at the top levels of which the challenge is to complete 160 km (100 miles) in one day. For the complete beginner there is no better way to get started than to enter a few "pleasure rides" of, say, 32 km (20 miles) and then gradually work up to the longer distances.

LEFT: *Competitors in a World Championship 160-km/100-mile endurance ride setting off at dawn.*

That all-important final vetting must be successfully negotiated before the corks can come out of the Champagne bottles!

Best Condition Award

One of the most coveted awards in the sport is that for the horse judged, usually by a panel of vets, to be in the best condition after an endurance race, in other words the horse most capable of continuing with work. At the bigger events judging may be carried out on the morning after the ride. To earn this prestigious prize is to receive the ultimate accolade, to know that your preparation of your horse for the ride was correct and your riding of the actual competition appropriate.

Strength and Stamina

More or less any horse (or pony) can be made fit enough to successfully complete the shorter-distance rides. After all, 32 km (20 miles) is less than a fit horse might cover in a day's hunting. But as the distances become longer there is a premium on stamina and it is then that the Arabian horse (or the part-Arabian) comes into his own.

Arab horses are ideally built for covering long distances at speed, being athletic and light of build. Big, heavily built horses are at a distinct disadvantage when asked to compete in hot conditions. It is more difficult for a horse to keep cool if he has a big body volume and weight, and keeping cool is an essential attribute of the endurance horse, otherwise he will more than likely fail to return a sufficiently low heart rate to pass the vet.

The better the horse's conformation, the more likely he is to withstand the rigours of the sport. Good, sound feet are absolutely essential. Bear in mind too, that the better the conformation the more likely the horse is to give a comfortable ride, and no one wants to ride an uncomfortable horse for 160 km (100 miles).

Temperament should not be overlooked, either, since a highly strung animal may tire more quickly than a relaxed, laid-back character and a "buzzy"

The Rules

The welfare of the horse is paramount and under the rules of some governing bodies it is compulsory to complete a set number of low-distance rides before moving up to the more demanding ones. This ensures that horses new to the sport are not pushed to the limit by inexperienced riders.

Inspections of the horses by veterinary surgeons are an important element of the sport and take place before and after the ride and, at the longer-distance ones, during the ride as well – vet "gates" have to be successfully negotiated at set intervals, the number depending on the length of the ride.

At the vet gates the horse's heart rate is checked, and provided it meets the specified criterion he then starts what is known as his "hold time". The hold time involves the horse remaining at the vet check for a specified period – every horse in the competition is held for the same amount of time. It is during the hold period that the horse is given a metabolic and soundness examination by the vet and either passed fit to continue or

"spun" (disqualified). Judging exactly when to present a horse at a vet gate – which means being fully familiar with his rate of recovery after exertion — is one of the most important skills of the endurance rider: the sooner the horse passes the heart-rate check, the sooner he starts his timed rest period and, provided he passes the veterinary examination, the sooner he continues on the course.

At short-distance rides horses may only be vetted before the start and after the finish and there will be no hold times. At the top end of the sport, over a 160-km (100-mile) course, horses are normally given a total of three hours "hold time", divided between several vet checks. These breaks give the horse the opportunity for essential re-fuelling – both eating and drinking are vitally important – and enable the rider and their back-up crew to cool the horse down and make any necessary equipment adjustments. In theory they also give the rider the chance to rest, eat and drink – in practice the rider will more likely be overseeing the welfare of the horse.

Unlike in other forms of racing, crossing the finish line first may not necessarily mean success.

Arabian and part-Arabian horses tend to excel at the sport of endurance riding.

Dress Code

- **Appropriately for a sport with such recent origins, endurance riders are less conventional in outlook than other riders when it comes to clothes and happily embrace the latest ideas on fabrics, styles and colours. Comfort becomes a major deciding factor when you are going to spend many hours in the saddle (160-km/100-mile rides often start at dawn and do not finish until the evening) and most riders favour modern riding tights which fit like a second skin, are stretchy and have padding in all the right places. Tights are often worn with half-chaps. Suitable footwear is vital and although riding or jodhpur boots can be worn, they are not really suitable for the longer distances when riders usually give the horse an occasional breather by jumping off and running beside him. Many competitors opt for riding "trainers" which are specially designed for the job.**

- **A loose-fitting shirt with a collar and sleeves is a more sensible choice than a T shirt, particularly when riding in a hot climate, and a natural fabric is always preferable to a synthetic one. Taking along a lightweight waterproof but "breathable" coat is a sensible precaution.**

- **Protective headwear can be, quite literally, a headache, for the endurance rider since conventional crash hats tend to be too heavy and hot for all-day wear. A lightweight ventilated helmet is usually the preferred choice of the serious competitor. Specially designed to be worn for long spells in hot weather, this type of hat has a ventilated shell and liner and may also be equipped with a detachable see-through peak.**

horse may well have an erratic heart rate which can make the vetting procedures a nightmare.

Although Arab blood is definitely desirable, there are plenty of other breeds which have a place in the production of successful endurance horses. In Britain the Arab/Thoroughbred/native pony cross has proved a particularly good one, while in the United States the Arab/Appaloosa cross is popular. Trakehners crossed with Arabs or Thorougbreds produce tough horses possessed of tremendous speed and Quarter Horses and Standardbreds both have their supporters. A number of Russian breeds, including the Akhal-Teke, Tersk and the famously sure-footed Kabardin, are also ideally suited to endurance riding.

Epic Rides

Among the extraordinary feats of non-competitive endurance riding, two stand out as supreme examples of courage, stamina and sheer dogged determination on the part of both horse and rider.

In April 1925 the Swiss-born traveller and writer Aimé Felix Tschiffely (1895–1954) set off from Buenos Aires to ride to Washington DC in the United States. His companions were two Criollo horses, the 16-year-old Mancha and the year-younger Gata. Alternately riding one horse and leading the other as a pack animal, he completed the journey in two and a half years. The two horses were subsequently shipped back to South America where they spent their retirement, Gata living to be 36 and Mancha to 40.

No less impressive, though much less well known was the achievement of the remarkable Baron Carl Gustaf Emil Mannerheim (1867–1951), the Finnish-born soldier and politician, who was educated in the Finnish Cadet Corps and the Officers' Cavalry School in St Petersburg before beginning his military career in the Russian army in 1889. He returned to Finland in 1917 following the Revolution and raised the White Guards, which with German assistance eventually defeated the Red Guards.

A gifted linguist, he had served in Manchuria during 1904–5 and in 1906 set off on horseback across Asia to study remote peoples and their languages, an epic journey which he recorded in his book, Across Asia From West to East in 1906–1908. A good home was found for his trusty steed in the Far East before the Baron embarked on his journey home.

SPINS, STOPS & ROLLBACKS

Although the sport of reining has its roots in other centuries and other continents, its closest links are with the North American cowboy.

The reining horse stops by bringing both hind legs under him and sliding to a halt.

Reining, now officially recognized by the United States Equestrian Team (USET) as an international discipline, alongside such sports as dressage and horse trials, traces its history back to the horsemanship of Spain, Portugal, France and North Africa. Manoeuvres used by riders in battle, and subsequently by the cowhand when herding cattle or evading a charging bull, are replicated in this enthralling and highly skilful event, with its combination of speed, power, control and finesse.

Reining is designed to demonstrate the athletic ability of a ranch-type horse within the confines of a show arena. It is a team effort between a highly educated horse and an extremely skilled rider. Movements performed as an everyday part of ranch work are here brought to a peak of perfection, and reining has been well described as "an a rtful elaboration of mounted cow work", "a counterpart to dressage". One of the fastest-growing disciplines in the equestrian world, it is a fascinating sport for both rider and spectator.

Reining History

As long ago as 1949 reining was approved as a recognized event by the American Quarter Horse Association (AQHA). Incidentally, the AQHA, with some 315,000 members worldwide, is the world's largest breed oranization. Then in 1966 came the formation of the National Reining Horse Association, launched to encourage the showing of reining horses by providing worthwhile purses,

developing standard contest guidelines, and acting as a forum for breeders, trainers and riders.

The NRHA is responsible for the enforcement of the sport's standards of competition and its promotion. Since the introduction, in 1990, of the NRHA's Affiliate Championship Program, designed to encourage reining at grass-roots level, more than 16,000 horses have been licensed with the Association. And it is not just numbers which are impressive. The present-day reining horse can earn prize purses that rival those of offer in Grand Prix jumping: the Open Futurity champion picks up a cool $100,000. In early 1998 reining finally "came of age" when the USET adopted it as its first Western riding discipline.

The Required Movements

WALK-IN

The horse walks from the gate to the centre of the arena to begin his pattern. He should appear relaxed and confident.

STOPS

Stops are the act of slowing the horse from a lope (a short-striding canter) to a stop position by bringing the hind legs under him in a lock position so that he slides on his hind feet. Throughout the stop the horse should continue in a straight line.

SPINS

Spins – the Western version of pirouettes – are a series of 360° turns executed over a stationary

inside hind leg. The location of the hindquarters should be fixed at the start of, and throughout, the spin.

ROLLBACKS

A rollback is a 180° reversal of forward motion, achieved by running to a stop, rolling or turning the shoulders back to the opposite direction, over the hocks, and departing in a canter – all in one continuous movement.

CIRCLES

Circles are performed at a lope, to a designated size and speed, and are designed to demonstrate control, willingness to guide and degree of difficulty in speed and speed changes.

BACKUPS

In the backup, the horse must move in a reverse motion, in a straight line, for a required distance – at least 10 ft (3 m).

HESITATE

To hesitate is the act of demonstrating the horse's ability to stand in a relaxed manner at a designated time in a pattern. The horse should remain motionless and relaxed. All NRHA patterns require a hesitation at the end, to demonstrate to the judges the completion of the pattern.

LEAD CHANGES

Lead changes (flying changes) must be performed with no change of gait or speed and at the exact geographical position in the arena specified in the pattern description.

RUN DOWNS AND RUN-AROUNDS

Runs through the middle of the arena, from the centre of the arena to the end or along the sides and ends of the arena are known as runs downs or run-arounds. They should demonstrate control and a gradual increase in speed before the sliding stop.

THE REINING ARENA

Three markers are used to enable riders to follow pattern proportions: one marker is placed in the centre of the arena and the other two at least 15.25 m (50 ft) from each end wall. The type of footing used in the arena is most important and should ideally have a clay base with a combination of sand and silt as a loose topping. This enables horses to perform at their optimum level and ensures that they stay sound. Moisture control, particle size and compaction are three important considerations in the preparation of suitable ground.

WHAT'S THE SCORE?

Horses are judged individually as they complete one of several specified patterins. One or more judges scores each horse between 0 and infinity (with 70 denoting an average score). Each horse automatically begins the pattern with a 70. The scoring system then gives or takes away up to 1½ points on each manoeuvre. Penalties are accrued for incorrect performance manoeuvres. Scores are then tabulated and announced at the end of each run. In scoring, credit is given for smoothness, finesse, attitude, quickness and authority when performing the manoeuvres. Controlled speed in the pattern raises the level of difficulty and increased level of difficulty is rewarded with higher scores if the manoeuvres are still performed correctly. As the NRHA Handbook states: "To rein a horse is not only to guide him, but also to control his every movement."

Riders wear appropriate Western attire, although in the interests of safety the Western hat may be replaced by a helmet.

Dress Code & Horses

- Appropriate Western attire, including a long-sleeve shirt and Western hat (or safety helmet) is mandatory.
- Reining is open to horses of any breed, sex, colour or size and there is no requirement for a reining horse to be registered with any breed organization.

CENTRES OF EXCELLENCE

Wherever you go in the modern world you will find tributes to man's enduring partnership with the horse. Equestrian statues are ten a penny. Museums of fine art bristle with equestrian paintings featuring the famous and the noble. Every day of the year countless people are paying to be taught, at state-of-the-art equestrian centres, the finer points of horsemanship and someone, somewhere, will be staging an event at which they can demonstrate their skills. In the vast areas of the world which have been mechanized the horse may no longer be a necessity, but he is far from being forgotten.

Because so much of modern horsemanship centres around competitive riding, many of the most famous equestrian meeting places are concerned with sport. Racecourses the world over, from Epsom in England to Longchamp in Franc, from Santa Anita in the USA to Happy Valley in Hong Kong, boast the sort of facilities which only go to confirm that the horse is alive and well and a vital part of present-day life. Tens of thousands of people make annual pilgrimages to venues whose names mean only one thing: equestrian excellence. Cheltenham is synonymous with all that is finest in jump racing; Ascot holds the same cachet for devotees of the Flat; Cowdray and Palm Beach mean polo; Las Vegas and Calgary the rough and tumble of the rodeo. Events whose titles conjure up their own special brand of magic are legion: the Grand National, the Melbourne Cup, the Hamburg and Hickstead Derbies, the Prix d'Amérique, the Kentucky Futurity, the Prix de l'Arc de Triomphe.

Just as previous centuries had their carousels, so our modern world has its smaller scale but no less enjoyable equestrian entertainments, many devised to enthral the public during lulls in competitions. Mounted police displays, dressage pas de deux, and fast and furious Hungarian trick riding all have their place in the modern equestrian world. So, too, do the colourful musical rides of the few extant cavalry regiments. Even the least horsey person can appreciate the skill and daring of these popular attractions.

Among the many centres of equine excellence either preserved from a bygone era or created by twentieth-century man, some naturally stand out head and shoulders above the rest for their quality, their ambience, their style. The Spanish Riding School, Saumur and Jerez are the great centres for the preservation of classical horsemanship, each possessing its own particular national flavour. Names like Aachen, Rome, Dublin and Spruce Meadows conjure up visions of the ultimate in horse shows. Badminton, Burghley and, more recently, Lexington have become synonymous with all that is finest in three-day eventing. What better way to appreciate the art of great horsemanship than to watch the very best riders in the world, whatever their speciality, in action with the very best horses.

THE DANCING WHITE HORSES

The Spanish Riding School of Vienna is the oldest riding academy in the world where classical horsemanship is still cultivated in its purest form. The spectacular displays by its exquisite pure white stallions enjoy worldwide renown.

The art of training horses to execute difficult exercises in perfect balance and with seeming effortlessness was known in ancient times – the Parthenon frieze of the Acropolis in Athens, which dates from 450 BC, depicts horses performing what today we would call the *passage*, *piaffe* and *levade*. But this art was doomed to oblivion following the decline of ancient Greek civilization.

Re-discovered by the Italians at the turn of the 15th century, this ancient equestrian skill soon spread to France, Spain, Germany and, in the fullness of time, to England – thanks largely to William Cavendish, Duke of Newcastle. The Duke, an ardent Royalist, fled to the Continent when Oliver Cromwell came to power and while in exile established a renowned riding school in Antwerp. His *Méthode et Invention Nouvelle de Dresser les Chevaux*, published in French in 1658, is still considered one of the classic works on equitation.

Horses in Vienna

There are references to an exercise ground for horses in Vienna, on a site which is now the Josefsplatz, as early as the 1560s, though this was an open-air *manége*. Dedicated horsemen soon found that they needed shelter from the rigours of the

winter weather, and the existence of a covered "Spanish Riding Hall" was first recorded in 1572.

When Austria was at the peak of her power, the splendour of the monarchy was reflected in the construction of a series of buildings, among them the grandiose *Winterreitschule* (winter riding school), built by the renowned architect Joseph Emanuel Fischer von Erlach from 1729 to 1735. Until 1894 this building was in frequent use for balls and concerts – Beethoven conducted a mammoth concert there in 1814, featuring more than a thousand musicians – as well as for equestrian training, but since then it has been devoted exclusively to *haute école*.

Why Spanish?

Older than the winter riding school itself is the institution which it houses. The word Spanish in its title derives from the breed of horse native to the Iberian peninsula which proved especially suited to classical horsemanship.

Archduke Maximilian was responsible for introducing Spanish horses into Austria in the early 16th century, founding the royal stud at Kladrub. In time this stud began to concentrate on the production of coach horses for ceremonial use, and it was the stud at Lipizza, founded in 1580 by Archduke

Charles and situated in present-day Slovenia, which was to have the most decisive influence on the history of the school.

Johann Weichard Freiherr von Valvasor, writing in 1689, commented that the Archduke had a royal stable and stud established in Lipizza, where the best horses were bred and supplied to the Imperial Court. These were hand-picked animals, "'very hardy and full of stamina because they are accustomed to moving on hard and rocky ground, and on pastures with hardly any grass." The breed of Lipizzaner horses which resulted from the Archduke's policy is to this day noted for its hardiness, stamina and longevity.

Surviving the Centuries

The School's 400-year history has not been without its troubles and it is only thanks to the tireless efforts of successive heads of the school, including the emperors, that the Spanish Riding School – and the stud which serves it – managed to preserve its great traditions.

During the Napoleonic wars the whole stud (300 horses) was evacuated to Hungary, a journey which took 14 days. When the horses were returned home it was discovered that the stud buildings, together with its equipment and archives, had been destroyed by the French. Early attempts at rebuilding were foiled by, of all things, an earthquake.

After the First World War and the fall of the monarchy, Austria lost Lipizza to Italy and the horses were divided between the two countries. Not knowing what to do with the 97 horses it had inherited, the new Austria planned to sell them at auction. They were saved from dispersal only at the eleventh hour. Eventually accepted by the

Republic of Austria on November 5, 1920, they were sent to their new home at Piber, in Styria.

Justifying the existence of the school, with all its aristocratic connotations, in the difficult post-war years proved a problem even to its most ardent supporters. But thanks to the devotion of Count Rudolf van der Straten, the last Master of the Horses under the old monarchy, and of his colleagues, the school eventually resumed its activities in the charge of the Federal Ministry of Agriculture and Forestry, which it represents to this day.

The world has to thank two more men of vision – Colonel Alois Podhajsky, the then director of the school, and General Patton, of the United States Army – for securing the future of the school after the ravages of the Second World War. Having been under the high command of the

German armed forces during hostilities, the stallions were placed in the care of the American Army and the stud stock, which had been transferred to Czechoslovakia and whose future was precarious, was taken back to Austria under military escort.

On October 11, 1955, after the conclusion of the State Treaty, the horses of the Spanish Riding School finally returned to their home in Vienna's Hofburg and to the stud at Piber which, thanks to its similar climate, soil and vegetation, has proved such an excellent substitute for Lipizza.

The Horses

Say "Lipizzaner" and most people immediately think of a white-coated horse. The pale colouring is certainly dominant in adult horses, but all

Lipizzaners are born dark or black brown and some retain their dark coats. It is a tradition at the Spanish Riding School to keep and train one such dark-coloured horse. The majority who turn white do so gradually between the ages of four and ten.

Lipizzaners are medium-sized horses, standing between 15.1hh and 16.2hh. They are strikingly attractive, with small, elegant heads and large, expressive eyes. The powerful hindquarters enable them to perform the most strenuous of high-school movements with apparent effortlessness.

On average, it takes eight years' training for a horse to reach the required level for participation in the school quadrille.

A Lipizzaner at liberty, showing the power and grace that make him the perfect high-school horse.

Identification Brands

All the School's horses are marked with brands, which make identification a simple task. On the left side of the hindquarters is the Stud brand: the letter P with the Austrian Crown above it.

Also on the left side, under where the saddle flap lies, is the ancestral brand, representing the horse's parents. The letter (the initial letter of the name of one of the six stallion lines) indicates the sire, the symbol beneath it the sire of the dam. Beside the letter is the breed number.

On the opposite side to the ancestral brand is a number indicating where to find the horse in the foal register.

The school quadrille, regarded by horsemen the world over as the epitome of haute ecole.

The Stallion Lines

All the horses in the stud at Piber and at the Spanish Riding School are descended from six stallion lines:

PLUTO

A white horse of pure Spanish descent, Pluto was born in 1765 at the Royal Danish Court Stud in Frederiksborg.

CONVERSANO

A black horse with Neapolitan origins, born in 1767. Neapolitan horses were of direct Spanish descent.

FAVORY

A dun, born in 1779, from the imperial stud of Kladrub.

NEAPOLITANO

A brown horse from the Po region, born in 1790.

SIGLAVY

This white Arabian horse from Syria arrived at the stud in Lipizza in 1810.

MAESTOSO

Although he was sired by a Neapolitan stallion out of a Spanish mare, the white Maestoso was foaled at Mezohegyes, in Hungary, in 1819.

The Performance

The beginning of each public performance features the young stallions with the student riders. The main part of the programme features the Riders, Chief Riders and First Chief Rider of the School

with the mature horses, who perform all the steps and movements of the classical school, a pas de deux, work on the short hand rein, work on the long rein, schools above the ground and, to finish, the beautiful eight-horse school quadrille, a relic of the times when carousels were a popular form of entertainment and widely regarded as the highlight of the School's performances.

ABOVE: *The dramatic capriole, a remnant of war-time training.*
RIGHT: *A perfectly balanced levade.*

SCHOOLS ON AND ABOVE THE GROUND

The schools on the ground comprise the piaffe, the passage and the pirouette. The spectacular schools above the ground may look like "circus tricks" but they are, as with all dressage movements, based on the horse's natural movements – albeit in a much more stylized form. They date from a time when the horse was used in warfare, when the ability to leap into the air on request from the rider could mean the difference between life and death for both rider and horse.

THE LEVADE

The horse rises on his haunches to an angle of 30°–45°. The rider is vertical to the ground.

THE COURBETTE

The horse balances his weight on his hindquarters, raises his forehand and propels himself forward on his hindfeet.

THE CAPRIOLE

The horse leaps from the ground with all four legs at once, and when his body is horizontal to the ground, kicks out with his hindlegs.

AACHEN: THE EQUESTRIAN FESTIVAL PAR EXCELLENCE

When it comes to international horse shows, one name stands head and shoulders above the rest in terms of size, scope, prestige, atmosphere, and popularity with both riders and the public: Aachen.

Midsummer sees the cream of the world's horses and riders from three separate disciplines assembling at the splendid Soers showground on the outskirts of Aachen, situated on Germany's western border with the Netherlands, for six exhilarating days of sporting endeavour. Show jumping, dressage and carriage driving at the very highest level all feature at what is widely regarded as the world's greatest horse show.

The quality of the entries and competition is matched only by the enthusiasm of the knowledge-able spectators who flock to the Soers showground in their tens of thousands. Aachen is, quite simply, a horse show on a scale that cannot be surpassed anywhere in the equestrian world.

A History of Aachen

Legend has it that the imperial city of Aachen (pre-viously known to the Romans as *Aquis granum* – "water site") originated around the year 800 AD after Charlemagne's horse had pawed the ground and released a hot spring. Whatever the truth of the matter, the city, which subsequently grew and flourished for 700 years as the coronation site of the German emperors, has certainly seen a lot of horses through the centuries. One particularly notable equestrian festival took place in 1520 to mark the entry of Charles V into the city. Some

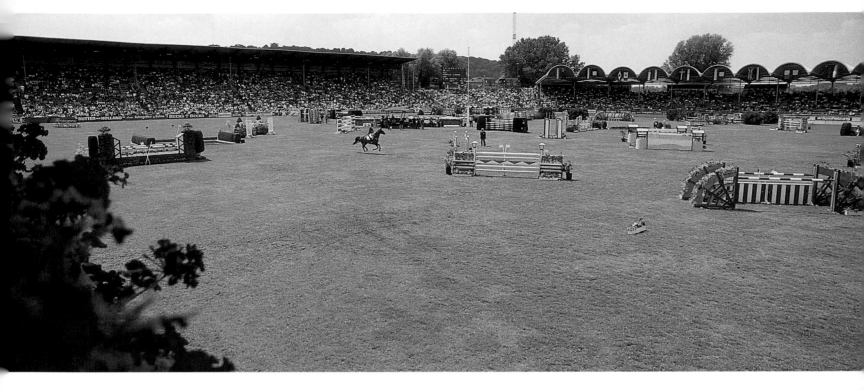

5,000 riders took part in the parade, and other attractions included tournaments and racing.

Indeed, racing has long been a feature of the countryside around Aachen. During the 19th century races were held for Thoroughbreds, part-breds, farmers' working horses – in fact more or less any horse with four sound legs which could either gallop or trot at speed. So enthusiastic were the horse lovers in the area that in 1898, in the nearby village of Laurensberg, they conceived the idea of forming an equestrian club. So began what is today the Aachen-Laurensberger Rennverein, the association which manages the Soers showground, home of the world-renowned Aachen Horse Show.

It was on August 1, 1925 that the first "riding, jumping, and driving tournament with cross country" took place at Aachen. The tournament was staged over four days and attracted in excess of 200 horses. Presaging what was to come, more than 20,000 spectators attended. As well as a covered wooden grandstand, the showground also boasted a restaurant, a judges' tower and long-distance telephones for journalists. The show staged the first show jumping Grand Prix of Aachen – still one of the most sought-after individual prizes in the jumping world – and a few years later, in 1929, the inaugural Aachen Nations Cup.

ABOVE: *The vast Soers showground provides one of the world's most exhilarating experiences for the show jumper.*

RIGHT: *A section of Aachen's crowd facing the water splash, one of the famous permanent obstacles.*

Very early on German riders began to show the supremacy in competitive dressage that they hold to this day. Driving competitions, in the minority in the early years, soon grew in popularity until by the 1930s they constituted 25 per cent of the programme. They included tests for six-in-hands, four-in-hands and pairs, and there was a three-day marathon which attracted huge public interest along its 200-km (125-mile) route and ended with a triumphal entry into the Soers arena.

By 1938 a total of some 120,000 spectators were attending the show, and the equine entry had risen to 600. That year the show jumping Nations Cup alone (won for the one and only time by a team from Rumania) was watched by 30,000 people.

The first post-war Aachen show was organized in September, 1946. Not surprisingly, it was a pale shadow of its former self, with only seven classes, but mankind's unquenchable love of the horse was reflected in the fact that a crowd of 15,000 turned up on the final day.

Although German riders were not allowed to

take part in the 1948 Olympics, the resurrected Aachen show was by then highly enough thought of to be chosen by a number of nations as their final preparatory outing before the Games.

In the years that followed, the show established itself as one of the major events of the equestrian calendar, once again offering top-flight sport in the three disciplines which had made it famous. It has become the "mecca" of the outdoor competitive season for every dressage and jumping rider – the Nations Cup is generally considered the toughest in the calendar – and has hosted a record four show jumping World Championships.

LEXINGTON

The legendary Bluegrass country of Kentucky has long been synonymous with all that is excellent in the world of the horse – in particular the world of that mega-bucks mega-star on four legs, the racehorse.

In the countryside surrounding the city of Lexington – countryside once aptly summed up as "a land of dreams and sunshine" – lie some of the most famous stud farms in the equine universe: Spendthrift, whose leading stallion in the 1970s, Never Bend, sired the great Mill Reef, champion of England and France; Calumet, one of the most beautifully appointed Thoroughbred studs in the area; Castleton, whose owner in the last quarter of the 18th century, Steward M. Ford, bred carriage and show horses – though he was perhaps more famous as the owner of Ford's Theatre in Washington, site of the assassination of President Lincoln – and which by the 20th century was breeding world-beating pacers like Bret Hanover; and Walnut Hall, renowned for its trotters. With such stud farms (a few of which are open to the public), race tracks, museums, horse shows, horse trials, polo and much, much more, the horseman in Lexington is never at a loss for something to do.

TOP: *"The Mostest Hoss": A statue commemorates Lexington's famous Man O' War.*

RIGHT: *Racing the Red Mile at Lexington, an international centre for harness racing.*

Monarch of All He Surveys

One of the most famous of the areas's horses was the mighty Lexington-bred Man o'War, whose statue presides over the Kentucky Horse Park. Affectionately known as "Big Red" because of his fiery chestnut colour, Man o' War was foaled in 1917, and raced in 1919 and 1920, winning 20 of his 21 starts in awesome style. His only defeat was widely attributed – including by the rider of the winning horse who narrowly defeated him – to jockey error. Retired to stud at Lexington, he was to become a powerful influence on the development of the Thoroughbred breed. During the 26 years that he was on view at stud, more than half a million people signed his guest book. Many, many more neglected to add their names, so caught up were they by seeing "Big Red" in his box and hearing his exploits

ABOVE: *Entrance to the Kentucky Horse Park and International Museum of the Horse.*

described by his devoted groom, Will Harbut.

When he died in 1947, only a month after the death of Will, the big horse was laid in a huge oak box and buried in a memorial plot in his old paddock, marked by this imposing bronze statue. As Will Harbut was wont to say, Man o' War was, quite simply, the "mostest hoss".

THE KENTUCKY HORSE PARK AND INTERNATIONAL MUSEUM OF THE HORSE

Appropriately enough Lexington, horse capital of the USA, is home to the ultimate equestrian theme park. Standing on a site covering 1,032 acres, the renowned Kentucky Horse Park is a sort of equine Disneyland though with serious overtones. It boasts the largest equestrian museum in the world, whose comprehensive range of exhibits trace the history of the horse and his five-thousand year relationship with mankind. The 4,800 m^2 (52,000 square ft) Museum is packed with intriguing artifacts, houses a 3,000-volume research library, the William G. Kenton Jr Art Gallery and a Visitor Center Photo Gallery, and also supports an education programme which hosts more than 32,000 school children each year.

In the Visitor Center members of the public are given a fascinating introduction to the world of horses with a spectacular film entitled *Thou Shalt Fly Without Wings*. A visit to the Museum is followed by the Walking Farm Tour. At certain times of the year there is a Parade of Breeds, capturing the excite-

RIGHT: *Harness racing at the Calumet Stud.*

FAR RIGHT: *Thoroughbreds at Lexington.*

ment of the show ring and featuring some of the 40 different equine breeds housed at the Park. This is very much a hands-on experience – after the parade visitors can give their favourite horses a pat and talk with the riders. Legendary horses from Thoroughbred, Standardbred and Quarter Horse racing can be viewed at close quarters in the Hall of Champions, while the Park's extensive and superbly equipped show facilities can be explored by horse-drawn streetcar or carriage – or on horseback.

THE ON-LINE MUSEUM

The on-line version of the International Museum of the Horse is one of the largest internet museum projects ever undertaken. Over 1,000 pages of information, including the complete text from the Museum's exhibits, and hundreds of photographs, are available to school children, scholars and horse lovers throughout the world. In addition, speciality exhibits have been provided by many of the nations' leading horse-related museums.

A Day at the Races

The United States gave the world the Standardbred, the fastest trotting/pacing horse on earth, and Lexington is home to the nation's oldest active harness racing track, the famous Red Mile. Here descendents of the English Thoroughbred Messenger, whose export to Philadelphia in 1788 resulted in the foundation of a world-beating line of harness racehorses, can be seen pounding round the immaculately prepared dirt track at speeds in excess of 48 km/ph (30mph).

The Red Mile, a centre for harness racing since 1875, annually hosts the third race of the trotters' Triple Crown, the supreme achievement for harness racehorses. Known as the Kentucky Futurity, the race was first contested in 1893. It is the oldest of the three legs of the Triple Crown, is run in two heats and is restricted to three-year-olds.

What's On & When
A VISITOR'S CHECKLIST

- **Enjoy the Kentucky Horse Park and International Museum of the Horse experience. Open daily from 10 to 5.30.**
- **Meet your favourites at the Parade of Breeds, presented at the Horse Park twice daily from April through October.**
- **See greatness in the flesh in the Horse Park's Hall of Champions: three daily presentations, April through October.**
- **Don't miss the Thoroughbred Park, with its exquisite life-size bronze statues of horses and jockeys. A unique 2.75-acre downtown park devoted to Lexington's equine heritage.**
- **Go Thoroughbred racing at the historic Keeneland track in April and October. From mid-March through mid-November you can also watch the horses working out from 6 to 10am and soak up the behind-the-scenes atmosphere by taking breakfast at the track kitchen.**
- **Take in top-class harness racing at the Red Mile Harness Track, which meets late April through June and September and early October. The Kentucky Futurity is run in October.**
- **Dreaming of owner a Derby winner? Visit the Keeneland Sales in September where the cream of the young Thoroughbred crop goes under the hammer – often for seven-figure sums.**
- **See the top horse trials riders in action in the annual Lexington Three-Day Event.**

DUBLIN HORSE SHOW

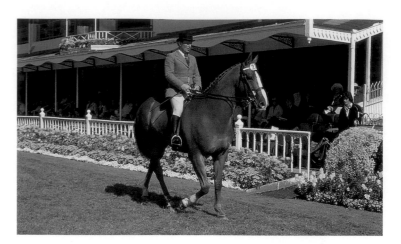

It is billed as Ireland's equestrian and social event of the year. But the Dublin Horse Show, held annually over five days in early August, is far more than that.

In the world of the sports horse the Dublin Horse Show has long been ranked among Europe's prime shop windows. Many a future champion has taken his or her first steps up the ladder to fame in the famous Ballsbridge arena. To win in the show ring there is to reach the very pinnacle of achievement. Add to the excellence of the equine content the unique flavour of Irish hospitality and you have, unquestionably, one of the world's best-loved equestrian gatherings.

The Dublin Horse Show is the feature event organised by the Royal Dublin Society, which was founded in 1731 to promote agriculture, science, the arts and industry in Ireland. The RDS has been responsible for the establishment of many important national institutions, including the National Botanic Gardens and the National Museum. The Veterinary College also owes its foundation to the Society. As part of its commitment to the promotion of agriculture, premiums were granted to horses – specifically imported stallions – as long ago as 1740. They were also granted to an extensive list of products/activities of benefit to the community, including fine arts, brewing and the killing of rats. Today the chief event organized by the Society is the annual horse show. It dates from the 1870s, which makes it one of the oldest events of its kind in the world.

Show Jumping at Dublin

In 1864 the first of two trial horse shows was held on Leinster Lawn in Dublin. The shows included competitions entitled the High Jump and the Wide Leap. Intended primarily to test the qualifications of the hunters, these contests were the forerunners of show jumping as we know it today. One of the features of the jumping course during the early years of the Dublin Show, which has been staged at Ballsbridge since 1881, was the stone wall. This had a solid base topped with loose stones and horses were penalized according to the number of stones they dislodged. Natural obstacles, not coloured poles, were the norm in those early days of show jumping and the Irish banks so popular then remain a celebrated feature of the modern show ring at Ballsbridge. There is nothing to compare with watching a fleet-footed Irish hunter negotiate these daunting looking obstacles at speed, adroitly "changing legs" on the top before dropping down to earth again. As the sport of show jumping gathered momentum in the years following the First World War, Dublin became one of the major fixtures, thanks largely to the introduction in 1926 of Ireland's first Nations Cup. The magnificent Aga Khan Trophy is still competed by the world's leading nations and is one of the plum prizes of the season.

TOP: *A champion ridden hunter. Dublin is renowned for the quality of its hunter classes.*

RIGHT: *Competing for the Aga Khan Trophy, Ireland's coveted Nations Cup.*

VIVE LE CHEVAL!

Housed in the world's most beautiful stables is the largest horse museum of its type anywhere in the world: Le Musée Vivant du Cheval at Chantilly.

In 1959 Yves Bienaimé, at 25 years of age France's youngest riding master of the day, began his career in the equestrian world working at a riding school. Nothing remarkable in that, except that the riding school was housed in the Grandes Ecuries at Chantilly. So impressed was this young man by the splendour of the buildings – not to mention their relative neglect – that he made a vow to return one day and give them a new lease of life.

More than two decades later, following four years of negotiations with the owners of the stables, the Institut de France, he fulfilled his promise when he and his wife, Annabel, opened one of the most remarkable museums in the world, the Musée Vivant du Cheval.

Officially inaugurated in June 1982, the museum received a million visitors in its first seven years of operation. Today it is the most frequently visited equestrian museum in the world, annually attracting more than 200,000 people. Created very much as an educational museum, it welcomes some 60,000 school children and their teachers each year.

Chantilly History

According to legend Louis-Henri de Bourbon, 7th Prince de Condé, was a firm believer in metempsychosis: he was convinced that after his death his

The interior of the impressive Grandes Ecuries, built for the 7th Duke de Condé.

*Colourful displays by Andalusian horses are a feature
of the hugely successful Musee Vivant at Chantilly.*

What's On & When
A VISITOR'S CHECKLIST

- Tour the spectacular buildings, including the stables, the kennel courtyard and the box yard, with their varied exhibits. Open daily from 10.30 (except some Tuesdays) throughout the year (afternoons only on weekdays, November 1 to March 31).

- Watch magnificent Andalusian and Portuguese horses, similar to those ridden by the 18th-century princes, perform fascinating educational equestrian demonstrations, in which the horses perform "airs" such as the Spanish walk and the riders explain their training techniques. Demonstrations take place three times daily in summer (at 11.30, 3.30 and 5.15) and at 3.30 in winter. After each demonstration the riders welcome questions from the audience.

- Enjoy a day at the races. The premier meeting is in June, when two Classics are contested, the Prix du Jockey-Club (the French equivalent of the English Derby) and the Prix de Diane (popularly known in the racing world as the French Oaks, although it is run over a shorter distance than its Epsom equivalent).

- Watch out for special entertainments, such as Cheval et Gospel (a vibrant mix of horses, spirituals and jazz) and Le Cheval en Fêtes. Both last for more than an hour and feature colourful costumes and highly trained ridden and liberty horses.

- During the Christmas holidays spend a family afternoon at the museum, where the guest of honour at a special festive show – Le Cheval et l'Enfant – is, naturally, Santa Claus.

soul would return to earth – in the body of a horse. Evidently having no wish to lead a lifestyle inferior to the one he had enjoyed in human form, in 1719 he commissioned the architect Jean Aubert to design and build a stable block of appropriate grandeur in which he could reside in his reincarnated form.

The stables, or Grandes Ecuries, which Aubert produced are remarkable both for their beauty and their size. Some 186 metres (200 yards) long, they housed 240 horses and up to 500 hounds during the 18th century. Lavish celebrations were staged there and visiting dignitaries, including Joseph II, Emperor of Austria, and the future Tsar Paul I of Russia, were entertained in regal style.

In 1830 the Chantilly estate was bequeathed by the Duc de Bourbon to his nephew, the Duc d'Aumale, fourth son of King Louis-Philippe. Then in 1886 the childless Henri d'Orléans left the entire estate – comprising the Grandes Ecuries, the chateau, the racecourse and around 8,000 hectares of forest – to the Institut de France, to be preserved for posterity. Although the Musée Vivant du Cheval was privately designed by Yves and Annabel Bienaimé at their own expense, the Grandes Ecuries are still the property of the Institut.

In 1989, in celebration of the museum's millionth visitor, Yves and Annabel gave the Institut a replica of the famous La Renomée equestrian statue which had crowned the dome of the stables during the 18th century. Having been bombarded by national guardsmen in 1792 the statue, the work of Louis XIV's favourite sculptor, Antoine Coysevox, was removed to Paris and it took the patronage of the museum's founders to return it, albeit in replica form, to its spiritual home.

The Living Horse Museum

The museum, situated 40 km (25 miles) north of Paris, comprises a grandiose central nave and more than 30 rooms, with exhibits ranging from the Princes de Condé's harness and 19th-century merry-go-round horses, to the horse in naive art. But, in keeping with its title, the museum is home to living horses, too – some 30 or so, representing diverse breeds. Together with daily riding demonstrations and other equestrian entertai ments, they give this museum a uniquely "live" atmosphere.

BADMINTON

In a sport regarded as the greatest all–round test of horsemanship, Badminton Horse Trials reigns supreme.

Every year in early May the sleepy Cotswold village of Badminton, population less than 300, awakes to find itself the bustling centre of the equestrian universe. Badminton Horse Trials, 50 years old in 1999, has long been ranked as the world's premier three-day event, the one every rider yearns to win, the one in which every arm-chair rider dreams of taking part.

During four days of competition – dressage takes two days because of the number of entries – upwards of 200,000 people descend on the beautiful and normally serene park at Badminton House, home of the 11th Duke of Beaufort. Off the motorways they pour, eventing aficionados from all walks of life and all parts of the globe, vehicles piled high with dogs, picnics and wet-weather gear – the seasoned horse trials enthusiast, undeterred by bad weather, always possesses the appropriate survival kit. The narrow country lanes

bulge with a burden of traffic for which they were never designed and, with a military precision born of years of experience, the daunting process begins of feeding thousands and thousands of vehicles into their allotted parking spaces in the shortest possible time.

Badminton's History

It was the 10th Duke of Beaufort, inspired by the three-day event staged at Aldershot as part of the London Olympic Games of 1948, who conceived the idea of holding horse trials at Badminton. Having watched the Olympic contest with keen interest, he offered the loan of his land for a similar event to take place the following year, the aim being to enable British riders to become more proficient in time for the next Games.

Held under the aegis of the British Horse Society,

The British pair Mary King and Star Appeal at the famous Badminton Lake, which always provides its share of drama.

the first "Badminton Three Days Event", for national riders only, duly took place in 1949. It was won by Captain John Shedden on Golden Willow, a British-owned horse foaled in the USA – at the outbreak of the Second World War his owner had wisely shipped all her horses, including Golden Willow's dam, to the USA for safe keeping. There was a mere handful of spectators and it quickly became evident that the event's title was not helping, since many members of the public assumed it referred to the game of badminton not an equestrian gathering. As a result, in 1951 the event became the "Olympic Horse Trials, Badminton". Opened up for the first time to overseas competitors, it was won by the Swiss combination of Captain Hans Schwarzenbach and Vae Victis.

In Britain during the years which followed, the sport of horse trials gradually grew in popularity both with riders and spectators. From the late sixties, in particular, Badminton began to fire the imagination of the public. It did so to such effect that by the early seventies in excess of 100,000 spectators were flocking annually to the event.

Badminton came to be regarded not just as the

What's On & When

A VISITOR'S CHECKLIST

- **On Thursday and Friday watch the world's top riders striving to conjure a smooth, accurate dressage test from their super-fit mounts. The atmosphere in the dressage arena – crowds of 15,000-20,000 are the norm on dressage days at Badminton – is always electric.**
- **Walk the four-and-a-half mile cross-country course and decide how you would approach each of the 32 awesome fences – if you dared! To hear how the experts would do it, hire a personal 'guided tour' tape before you set off.**
- **Make an early start on Saturday and be among the 130,000+ people who will witness the cross-country action live. Remember that there is a two-mile steeplechase to be negotiated before the horses reach the cross-country. The course is within walking distance of the main showground area.**
- **Make time to visit the huge shopping area. The number of stands and exhibitors runs into the hundreds - you can buy anything from a dog lead to a dining table.**
- **Book you ringside seat early for the nail-biting show jumping test – 20,000 people turn up on the final day. This is when fortunes can be lost at the drop of a coloured pole.**

top three-day event in Britain but as the toughest all-round test of horse and rider anywhere in the world, the plum prize in the eventers' calendar. Memorable moments included the debut ride of HRH Princess Anne, who in 1971 finished fifth on Doublet, a horse owned and bred by the Queen (the Princess went on to become European Champion later that season). The winner that year was Lt Mark Phillips, who would subsequently become the first man to win the event four times. The third of his victories, in 1974, was with another of the Queen's horses Columbus.

With six wins on six different horses to her credit between 1973 and 1984, Lucinda Green is far and away the most successful rider. And in 1988 Scotsman Ian Stark wrote another page of history by riding the first two horses home, Sir Wattie and Glenburnie.

Only one rider has won the event on three

The New Zealand partnership of Vicky Latta and Chief tackle one of Badminton's formidable cross-country obstacles in style.

consecutive occasions, Britain's Sheila Willcox in 1957–59, while in the days when riders could enter three horses each (nowadays there are too many entries to permit this) Lorna Sutherland (later Clarke) became the first and only woman actually to complete the event (in 1970) on three horses. The only man to achieve such a feat was the great Australian all-rounder Bill Roycroft in 1965.

Thanks to sponsorship, the event now boasts by far the richest prize in the sport, and the current Duke of Beaufort, who succeeded to the title in 1984, like his predecessor is keenly involved in the event. A former successful rider, in 1959, when he was plain "Mr" David Somerset, he lodged his own personal claim to Badminton Horse Trials fame – by riding into second place

12

AROUND THE WORLD

One of the great pleasures of being able to ride is the freedom it gives you to explore some of the wildest and most beautiful regions on earth. With air travel continuing to push back international frontiers, getting there – or thereabouts at any rate – is no longer the protracted business it used to be; and once in the country of your choice you can travel further in the company of a horse than you could on foot, learning something of the equine culture of other people into the bargain. Realizing the tremendous potential of riding holidays, more and more horse enthusiasts are setting up centres in ever-more fascinating locations. Europe, Africa, Asia, India, Australia, New Zealand, Canada and the Americas: whatever your fancy, the chances are you will find something which can be done on the back of a horse.

Checking out a holiday organizers' credentials before you book is always a good idea, though it is not always as simple as it sounds. Some very good centres have no "approved" status whatsoever, either because no inspection scheme exists in their country, or perhaps because they do not feel the need. Word of mouth is always a good yardstick – if a friend whose opinion you trust gives a centre the thumbs-up then unless it has changed hands in the meantime, there should be no problem. The prime consideration, of course, is that the horses are properly cared for and suitable and fit for the job. While you may well encounter saddles which fall short of your own standards of comfort, provided they fit the horse and are not patently unsafe, you will have to make the best of it. Be prepared, though, to give your seatbones some protection, either by acquiring a saddle with a sheepskin on the seat, by wearing padded clothing, or by applying protective sticking plaster to your rear – make sure you do this while you are in a sitting position. Never be backward in pointing out problems to your hosts or guides, whether they are girth galls on the horse or a worn item of tack which might let you down at a crucial moment.

Follow to the letter the advice offered by the holiday organisers regarding equipment to take with you. Remember that they know the climate and terrain better than you. Many people throw all safety precautions out of the window when they go on holiday – why they imagine they are less likely to fall off a horse while galloping across the Mongolian steppes or fording an Icelandic river than they are in the school at home is anybody's guess. If you value your safety, then wear a hard hat.

If you would prefer to take a holiday with your own horse, then that is possible too, though naturally the logistics of getting your four-legged friend to the area of your choice will be a limiting factor. Planning a trail ride in your own land can be great fun, though. In some countries other people may have already done the spade work – watch out for guides to "bed and breakfast for horses'" to help get you started.

TO THE ENDS OF THE EARTH

Penguin-watching on a riding holiday?
You'd better believe it when you head for Chile!

If you are not deterred by distance, then for a holiday with a difference why not head down to South America? Relatively new to the riding holiday market, this vast continent, with its great tradition of horsemanship, offers some fabulous opportunities for anyone who loves life on the wildside.

Bounded on the north by Peru and on the East by the Andes, Chile stretches for more than 4,000 km (2,500 miles) along South America's Pacific Coast. Stretching as it does through half the southern hemisphere, the country has a considerable range of climate, both from north to south and from mountains to coast. Rainless deserts, 915 m (3,000 ft) high cliffs, impenetrable rain forests, spec-

tacular glaciers, windswept fjords – plus a cultivated heartland which enjoys abundant winter rain and dry summers – make up a landscape of endless fascination. And now visitors can explore some of its wildest splendours on the back of a horse.

Expeditions into the huge Torres del Paine National Park on the edge of the Patagonia icecap in the extreme south of the country afford views of some of the world's most dramatic scenery: great fingers of granite towering upwards to the sky, blue-grey glaciers reaching down into lakes of startling blue. Overhead, one of the greatest sights of the natural world: the soaring Andean condor. This magnificent raptor, the world's largest flying

bird, is upwards of 1.22 m (4 ft) in length and possessed of a 3 m (10 ft) wingspan. Ranging from Venezuela in the north right down to Cape Horn, the condor is the majestic emperor of the skies. On the ground, as you ride against a backdrop of glistening glaciers, watch for another local speciality: herds of guanaco – wild llama. And to complete a truly memorable glimpse into another world, see your first iceberg – and, of course, those penguins.

Riding in the Torres del Paine includes pampas, dense forests and wild mountain passes. Galloping is very much on the agenda, but so too are narrow bridges and vertiginous passes. You will need to be fit and a confident outdoor rider to enjoy this one! Argentina, home of the world's greatest polo players, is another country where exciting holiday opportunities are now opening up for the rider. In the northern part of Argentinian Patagonia you can

LEFT: *Criollo and Criollo-cross horses are well suited to the vast gaucho lands of Argentian Patagonia.*

Dramatic scenery is a feature of trekking holidays in Argentina's Lanin National Park. Only the fit need apply!

stay on a working estancia or cattle ranch, explore the vast gaucho lands in the Andean foothills or trek into the Lanin National Park, dominated by the snow-capped Lanin volcano which stands at a majestic 12,270 ft (3,740 m). You can ride through the only indigenous monkey puzzle forest on earth, or across stark grey lunar landscapes that testify to the region's recent volcanic activity, swim in thermal springs and round off the day by taking supper round the camp fire under the stars. From the saddle, watch guanaco, wild boar, the delightful and improbable armadillo, and exotic birds like ibis and black-necked swans.

Another Patagonia experience, further south this time, is to be had riding the centuries-old Gaucho Trail. Here you will hear tales of the legendary outlaws Butch Cassidy and the Sundance Kid, who drove their cattle through the wilderness from Argentina to Chile. Present-day gauchos use the same mountain pass to this day.

Much further north along the Andes' mighty range lies Ecuador, one of the least discovered of tourist countries. Trail riding into the mountains affords yet more spectacular vistas and also takes in visits to ancient, pre-Inca pyramids. Or, if you fancy travel of a more horizontal kind, there are adventurous rides into the Pantanal marshlands of Western Brazil. The flood plains of the Paraguay River are a wetland paradise for birds and elusive jaguars haunt the jungle.

Because of the rugged terrain, riding in South America is definitely for the fit, more experienced rider. Tack tends to be Western style, and if your saddle is covered with a sheepskin, so much the better: it's sheer bliss for the seatbones.

OVERNIGHT LODGING

Accommodation at the start and end of trail rides is usually in comfortable hotels or guest houses. Once "on the trail" tents or mountain refuges are used.

The Horses

The local Chilean-bred horses used in the Torres del Paine are both forward going and eminently sure-footed, which is a great comfort given the nature of the terrain. In northern Patagonia you will ride Criollo crosses. The sturdy Criollo, which when crossed with the Thoroughbred produces a fine stamp of polo pony, is a descendant of the horses taken to South America by the sixteenth-century Conquistadores. Some of the Spanish horses established feral herds on the pampas, an existence which, with its dry, hot summers and severe winters, produced a tremendously tough type of riding horse. Criollos stand around 14-15hh and have plenty of bone and good, sound feet. They are predominantly dun in colour, the result of nature providing their feral antecedents with protective camouflage. In Ecuador you may find yourself mounted on a beautiful Andalusian or part-Thoroughbred.

TAKE THE HIGH ROAD

Is there another country in the world which evokes such romantic thoughts as Scotland?

The great travel writer H.V. Morton was wont to say that the Highlands of Scotland were discovered centuries after America. As recently as the early 18th century, he noted, the Highlands held about as much interest for travellers as Afghanistan. Even Scotsmen (i.e. Lowlanders) "used to make their wills when forced to go there; and to Lowlanders and Englishman alike the mountains were a wild, alien country …"

There is still a splendid primeval wildness to be found "north of the border", at least as far as the scenery is concerned (a trip to the Highlands, thank heavens, no longer goes hand in hand with the dread of mortality). The intoxicating beauty of this majestic land of mountains, glens and lochs is both

ABOVE: *The attractive Highland pony is Scotland's prized native breed. These ponies are strong, active and sure-footed.*

well preserved and, in places, readily available to the horseman.

For the less adventurous there is no better way to sample the richness of the Scottish landscape than by taking one-day or half-day treks from a conveniently located riding centre. You can choose the length of ride which best suits your skill and degree of fitness and opt for as many, or few, days riding as time permits. Remember always to ensure beforehand that you are going to end up with well-cared for animals (and suitably trained guides) by finding out what, if any, "approvals" the centre has. Organizations such as the British Horse Society and

the Trekking and Riding Society of Scotland can help. Trekking is especially suitable for the beginner or nervous rider, since the pace is usually on the slow side and the horses and ponies are (or should be) steady and reliable.

The more intrepid traveller (and more accomplished rider) will be more drawn to the challenge of trail riding – and nowhere is there better trail-riding country than in Argyll, on the Scottish west coast. Less than two hours' drive from the bustling modern metropolis of Glasgow lies some of the finest, remotest riding trails in Europe. The discerning rider heads for the village of Ardrishaig on the shore of Loch Gilp. To the west lies the inner Hebridean island of Jura; to the south west, Islay, famed for its malt whiskies; due south, stretching finger-like towards Northern Ireland, the peninsula of Kintyre. For scenery alone, it is worth a guinea a minute. Add to that some 240 (150 miles) of riding trails, fit horses and as warm a welcome as you could find anywhere, and it all adds up to the holiday of one's dreams.

The trail rides are restricted to small groups and take in some of the most beautiful scenery in the Argyll Highlands. For the coinoisseur of good food there is even a "gourmet trail", where overnight stops are made at the region's finest hotels and meals taken in the best restaurants. Take care not to over-indulge – there is a lot of riding to do the next day!

EQUIPMENT

Even for low-key trekking safe, comfortable clothing is essential. Close-fitting trousers and smooth-soled shoes with a clearly defined heel are the minimum requirements. Beginners without the right equipment should borrow a hat from the centre. Wherever possible, and certainly for trail riding, breeches, jodhpurs or riding trousers are recommended, worn with comfortable "worn-in" riding or jodhpur boots – brand new clothing is never a good idea when you are going to spend long hours in the saddle. Take a hard hat made to the current safety standard.

Even in Scotland it can be warm in summer, so never wear skimpy suntops if you want to avoid sunburn; instead wear a shirt with a collar and short sleeves and take a scarf in case the back of your neck needs extra protection. Riders are also advised to take waterproof clothing and gloves, and a saddle or bum bag is a good idea, to take all those personal things – such as sun block cream, first-aid items and regular medication – which may not fit happily into pockets.

The Horses

To sample the true taste of trekking in Scotland, seek out the country's native breed, the Highland pony. Strong, sturdily built individuals, Highland ponies are real all-rounders. In their time they have carried men into battle, helped herd sheep, hauled timber and carried the hunter's quarry – shot stags – down from the hills. They are eminently sure-footed, well up to the weight of an adult rider, and have good, active paces. To complete the picture, they also come in a range of beautiful coat colours, including dun and grey and, occasionally, bay and liver chestnut with silver mane and tail. Be sure to take your camera!

Horses and ponies of diverse breeds, sizes and ages are available to cater for the trail-rider's needs. The experienced rider can expect a bold, forward-going horse, the less competent one a good "schoolmaster" type. Since the horses used for Argyll Trail Riding also turn their hand to schooling and competition work, they are true all-rounders, fit enough to enjoy a helter-skelter gallop on a nearby glorious stretch of beach but handy enough to negotiate the bogs, ditches and steep inclines encountered inland. They also have the necessary stamina to cover distances of some 40 km (25 miles) a day.

BELOW: *Riding through Scotland's spectacular and beautiful scenery.*

INTO AFRICA

If you love both riding and wildlife, why not combine the two on an exhilarating horse safari?

Gone are the days when the only way to watch wild animals was from the cocooned safety of a 4 by 4, with someone else's zoom lens propped against your ear. The burgeoning number of riding tours now available in the southern African countries of Namibia, Botswana, South Africa and Zimbabwe, as well as further north in Malawi and Kenya, provides the adventurous visitor with what has been aptly described as the ultimate safari experience.

Remember the film footage of the famous wildebeest crossing of Kenya's Mara river, opportunist crocodiles lying in wait, ever hopeful of an easy meal? Now you can follow in the very tracks of those intrepid wildebeest — evince no alarm: the experienced safari guides are there to ensure that their clients don't end up on the croc's menu. Marvel at the grace, symmetry and sheer unlikeliness of nature as you canter alongside loping giraffe; gallop with herds of highly-strung zebra; spot white and black rhinos, hippos, elephants, big cats, baboons, a bewildering variety of antelope, spectacular birds — South Africa's Waterberg Mountains alone are home to nearly 300 different species — and much, much more. On horseback, the vast, awesome splendour of Africa will unfold before you in all its incredible beauty and variety. What's more, bored though they have become with Land Rovers and minibuses, the animals tend to be keenly inter-

Wild horses roaming the Namib Desert, where horse riding treks are becoming increasingly popular.

Horseback safari trekkers on the lookout for one of the many
species of wildlife that can be spotted in Africa

ested in horses and respond accordingly.

Those who yearn for utter solitude should head for Namibia, home to the world's oldest desert. The Namib Desert trail is one of Africa's more recent riding safari opportunities and because of the demanding nature of the tour – eight or more hours in the saddle on nine consecutive days – only the fittest should apply. Those who do have the stamina will not be disappointed. Starting from the capital, Winhoek, this remarkable 400 km (248-mile) desert trail ride passes through the central highlands, across red sand dunes, into the 50,000-acre Namib-Nauklluft Park and on across the Namib Desert. The ultimate destination is Swakopmund, on the Skeleton Coast. Splendid rides on the dunes bring this spectacular tour to a conclusion.

Neighbouring Botswana has no coastline, but it does have the Okavango Delta, Jewel of the Kalahari. The Okavango River rises in Angola, flows for hundreds of miles, briefly touching Namibia, before arriving triumphantly at the north-west corner of Botswana. There it forms one of the largest inland deltas anywhere on earth, a bewitching area of floodplains, forests, crystal pools and palm-thatched islands. Here live huge herds of buffalo, and fish eagles are as common as sparrows in an English garden: the life-giving Delta, not surprisingly, fairly teems with wildlife. More relaxing than the Namib Desert trail, holidays at the Delta are none the less exciting and include some exhilarating canters through the wetlands.

Different again is Zimbabwe's Mavuradonna Wilderness, a rugged, uninhabited area stretching across hundreds of thousands of acres. Here, an improbably short drive (only two hours) north of the city of Harare, is one of the world's last great wild places, a land of stunning, untouched, forgotten beauty. Only the occasional delicate cave painting acts as a reminder of the bushmen who once hunted these valleys. Inaccessible except to those on foot or horseback, Mavuradonna is a magical place for the equestrian explorer, with its mountains, plunging rivers and thundering waterfalls. True, the rugged terrain dictates a slower pace than on other horse safaris, but the rewards

are just as rich. Follow elephant paths through the bush, emerge on to mountain passes with awe-inspiring views, sleep rough in the heart of the Wilderness, go in search of cave paintings – and watch the evening flight of the giant Egyptian fruit bat, whose population in the Wilderness bat caves is estimated to approach twenty thousand.

To the north west, in Malawi's Nyika National Park, lie the rolling grasslands of the high plateau, alive with herds of zebra, roan antelope, eland and well-camouflaged reedbuck. The visitor may get glimpses, too, of the rarer jackal, bushpig and red forest duiker. And if flowers fill you with joy, then be there in summer, when the grasslands erupt into a magnificent blaze of colour.

As for Kenya, what better way to take one of the great cultural leaps still available to 20th-century Westernized man than to head for Masai country and there experience first-hand something of its inhabitants' lifestyle.

OVERNIGHT LODGING

Accommodation can vary from permanent cottage-type dwellings to a bed-roll on the ground, by way of luxury twin-bedded tents –and they really are luxurious. It all depends on the type of safari.

EQUIPMENT

In warm climates cotton clothing is always de rigeur and sensitive parts of the anatomy (such as the

back of your neck and your upper arms) will need to be covered. As, of course, will your head. Lightweight cotton jodhpurs worn with half-chaps are often the most successful legwear. Team them with dual-purpose leisure/riding boots (with safe soles that cannot become trapped in the stirrup irons) so that both walking and riding can be achieved with equal ease. Remember to take sun glasses, sun screen, insect repellent and antihistamine cream. You will want a camera, but keep it small and light. Remember, too, that it can become quite cold at night, particularly at the higher altitudes, such as in Malawi's Nyika National Park.

The Horses

Horsepower at African safari centres comes in a variety of models, but with stamina and, at times, speed being prime requirements, it is not surprising to find plenty of Thoroughbred blood in evidence. Trakehners and Quarter Horse crosses can also be found and, for the Namib Desert trail rides, sturdy Haflinger ponies – which originate from Austria's southern Tirol. Horses are wisely chosen for their equable temperament, but while they provide a safe, well-mannered means of transport, they are by no means "dozy". Generally speaking, safaris will be best enjoyed by the competent rider who is also physically fit enough to spend long days in the saddle without regretting it next morning.

GO WEST!

The one big problem with choosing a riding holiday in North America is knowing where to start.

Horses give you access to the archetypal Western landscape, complete with cacti.

Say "horse" in the same breath as "America" and what comes to mind? Why, cowboys, cacti and the Rocky Mountains, naturally. So where better to start than at that end of the varied spectrum of delights which North America has to offer the holiday maker on horseback.

Throughout the Rocky Mountain states of Colorado, Idaho, Montana and Wyoming there are riding opportunities for those who like their scenery on the rugged side but still enjoy a bit of cossetting at the end of the day. Dotted throughout the millions of acres of national parkland are ranches which cater for just about everyone from small children to experienced, go-for-it riding types. The scenery, and there is plenty of it, is magnificent, likewise the hospitality, and you can bet your bottom dollar there will be side attractions such as Western dancing or cattle penning if that is where your fancy lies.

What you opt for is very much a question of

individual preference: day rides from the ranch at slow, medium or fast paces, depending on your degree of competence in the saddle; overnight wilderness trips for the more adventurous; all aspects of cattle ranching; perhaps even some carriage driving. For the really hands-on individual, there might be a chance to rope a steer – now what could be more authentically Western than that? As for wildlife of the conservation kind, the Rockies are still home to that too: at the right time of year you could see anything from elk and eagles to grizzly bears and mountain lions. And, of course, in certain areas there are still mustangs.

While climate dictates that Rocky Mountain riding is confined to the summer months, further south in Arizona winter tends to be the prime time, though where the summers are not too bakingly

hot some ranches may stay open virtually all year round. Here are the cacti, the desert sands and the rough-hewn mountains beloved of the movie makers. Here, for a while, you can settle into your Western saddle and dream of life on the High Chaparral.

South of the border, in Mexico, comes the chance to combine a riding holiday with a visit to the world-famous Monarch Butterfly Sanctuary – the large monarch butterfly is remarkable both for its beauty and for its long-distance migrations. A couple of hours drive west from Mexico City excellent riding is to be had in the southern Sierra Madre Occidental, with stunning mountain vistas. Here the countryside varies from pine forests, via sub-tropical farmland to tropical forest, alive with brilliantly coloured birds and flowers.

Alternatively, head for the isolated fishing village of Yelapa, which lies not far from Puerta Vallarta on the Pacific Coast and can only be approached by boat. In this remote spot the traveller can enjoy a Mexico of a bygone age, an area where mechanization has yet to spread its tentacles: no cars, no electricity, just little horses and mules and a natural paradise waiting to be explored.

Northward towards the topmost end of the Rockies, in the Canadian province of Alberta, lies one of the most popular mountain regions in the whole of North America, if not the world: the Banff National Park. There are day rides for the less adventurous, but undoubtedly the best way to enjoy this scenically stupendous area is to embark on a wilderness ride, sleeping overnight in tents or cabins. Because of the mountainous terrain, the pace is necessarily slow.

For something a little different, try Cariboo hill country not far from the town of Clinton, in British Columbia. There the visitor has the chance to combine trail riding over Big Bar Mountain with rafting on the Fraser River. Again the scenery is breathtaking, and the wildlife includes coyote and bears. The huge eastern province of Quebec offers something different again, rolling hills and wilderness areas, numerous rivers and lakes, and a spectacularly colourful fall season.

As for the eastern states of America, Maine, Vermont, New York State, and the Virginias all have their attractions, albeit very different from those of the Rockies. Maine's low-lying mountains, pine forests and lakes offer good trail riding opportunities, while at Lake Placid, in New York State's Adirondack Mountains, you can ride over soft, rolling trails set in countryside that has hosted Olympic cross-country skiing.

Finally, there is the ultimate escapist's holiday: a "posse week" offered by a ranch in Southern New Mexico, only a few hours' drive from Albuquerque. Visitors elect to be good guys or bad guys – camps are provided for the latter to "hang out" at – the riding is fast and furious, the weapons of the laser or paint-gun variety – and if the outlaws successfully lay their hands on the loot, they stand to win another free week's holiday!

OVERNIGHT LODGING

Everything from well-appointed ranch houses, via long cabins and tents to bedrolls under the stars – take your pick.

EQUIPMENT

For Western riding close-fitting jodhpur-jeans are ideal, especially if worn with chaps or half chaps, which give added protection against contact with "foreign objects" such as cactus spikes. Short boots, with a heel, are a must. Remember that in the mountains it may be necessary to do a certain amount of walking up steep slopes, so comfort is paramount. As always, aim for easily removable layers of clothing, wear a hat and take suitable rainwear.

The Horses

North America is home to a huge variety of breeds and types of horse and pony. The powerful and intelligent Quarter horse, for decades the "right-hand man" of the cattle rancher, will be much in evidence, or you might get to ride a Morgan, or an eye-catching Paint or Appaloosa. In addition there is an endless permutation of cross-breds featuring, among others, Thoroughbred, Arab, Spanish, Criollo and Trakehner blood.

The Rocky Mountains of North America and Canada offer
some of the world's most spectacular riding opportunities.

IN THE STEPPES OF CENTRAL ASIA

Nowhere in the world has there been a horse–based culture to equal that of the peoples of Central Asia. Now YOU can discover what it is like to ride in the land of Genghis Khan.

Mongolia provides the ideal "get away from it all" experience.

Remembered principally for the terror his hordes instilled into those who lay in his way, the marauding Genghis Khan (c.1177–1227 AD) formed an empire which stretched from the northern provinces of China, westward to Samarkand, Turkistan and Georgia. Moving south, his armies crossed the Indus to reach Peshawar and Lahore, and were responsible for the sacking of Herat in Afghanistan. And all of this was achieved, as the equestrian writer and historian Elwyn Hartley Edwards so aptly points out, "on the backs of shaggy Mongolian ponies".

The steppes of Mongolia are still, happily, home to quantities of shaggy little horses, though not – as far as we know – to embrionic Genghis Khans which, incidentally, translates as "perfect warrior emperors". In the lives of the present-day peace-loving Steppe dwellers the little horses – there are as many horses as people in Mongolia, around two and a half million of each – play a part in transportation, subsistence, leisure pursuits and, nowadays, tourism.

For the ultimate "get away from it all" riding holiday it would be hard to beat trail riding in Mongolia, with its endless vistas of treeless steppe, bordered to the south by the Gobi desert, to the north by dense forests, while on the extreme western border rise the peaks of the Altai Mountains, a region of great fascination for the horse historian. Underlining the long-time importance of the horse in this entire region, it was in the northern part of this range – in southern Siberia – that nineteenth and twentieth century archeologists unearthed from the permafrost the most extraordinary remains of an ancient people, dating back to the fifth century BC.

Among many remarkable discoveries in the frozen burial mounds at Pazyrik were perfectly preserved articles of leather, felt, wood and textiles – only the intense cold enabled such organic substances to survive the passage of time. Finds included complete saddles and bridles, beautifully decorated saddle-clothes, mummified humans and the bodies – including the skins, not just the skeletons – of their horses. Virtually all the saddles found in the Pazyrik tombs were padded with the hair of reindeer, an animal which together with the horse and the yak still plays an integral part in the life of the modern Mongolian steppe dweller. Herding reindeer, hunting, breeding horses, these are age-old occupations of the nomadic people of this remote and beautiful region.

To take a Mongolian trekking holiday is to do something most people only ever dream about: to get a tantalizing taste of the life of the nomad. No hotels – except in your point of arrival and departure, the Mongolian capital Ulaanbaatar, no motorized back-up vehicles: just you, your horses, your guides, and yaks to carry provisions. Attractions include riding across the steppes which lie to the north east of Ulaanbaatar and on into the Gorkhi-Terelj National Park, an area of mountain and forest which is, in essence, a part of the taiga forest of southern Siberia. Or you can fly 1200 km (745

miles) west from the capital to the Altai region.

And don't be put off by the word "steppe". Yes, there are vast areas of undulating grassland, but Mongolia also encompasses far more: mountains, lakes, rushing rivers and carpets of wild flowers make riding trips in the steppes of Central Asia scenically as breathtaking as anything on offer elsewhere. Add to that the invariably warm, hospitable nature of the local people and a pace of life unlike anything to be found in the "developed" countries of the West, and it all adds up to one of the most memorable experiences to be had on horseback.

EQUIPMENT

As with other trips to remote regions, wear layers and give prime consideration to comfort. Saddles in this part of the world may come as a rude surprise to those more accustomed to the spring-tree variety. Frames may be of tubular metal and sometimes no amount of leather or felt covering disguises the fact. Riding clothes with some form of built-in protection for your seatbones are therefore advisable, especially if you are skinny. Holiday riders can do worse than follow the example of the locals and keep their bottoms well out of the saddle when progressing at anything faster than a walk!

OVERNIGHT LODGING

Tents are the order of the day. If you are lucky (and want to get the true feel of nomadic existence), accommodation may be in a yurt, the large, round, wood framed, felt-covered tent that is the traditional home of the Asian steppe dweller. Cool in summer and warm in winter, the yurt is the perfect place to enjoy another tradition, a bowl of airak or fermented mares' milk

The Horses

Small (12.2-14hh), wiry and functional rather than creatures of eye-catching beauty, Mongolian horses are nevertheless ideal for the job in hand and will carry the traveller efficiently and safely all day – if not in Rolls Royce comfort – every day.

The tough little Mongolian horses know how to for themselves in semi-feral herds.

PICTURE CREDITS

The publishers would like to thank the following sources for their kind permission to reproduce the pictures in this book:

The Bridgeman Art Library, London/Altimira, Spain *Cave painting of a horse, c.15000 BC,* 8/9/The Stapleton Collection/Private Collection/*The Marquis of Newcastle Giving Captian Mazin a Riding Lesson,* plate 15 from '*The Method and New Invention of Dressing Horses*' by William Cavendish Marquis of Newcastle, engraved by Lucas Vorstermans II 1657 by Abraham Jansz. van Diepenbeke, 166

Caldene Clothing Company Ltd., Halifax 28, 29cr

Carlton Books Ltd./Adam Wright 78

Corbis 178, 182bl/Anthony Bannister 215/Dean Conger 218/Peter Johnson 214/Brian Viklander 219

ET Archive 10cl

FLPA/E & D Hosking 208bl/W Wisniewski 208/9t,

Kit Houghton 2/3, 6/7, 11, 12, 13, 14, 15t, 16t, 26 , 29tr, 30, 32, 33, 34/5, 36, 37, 39, 41, 44, 45, 46, 47, 48, 49, 51c, 53, 54, 55, 56, 57, 59, 66/7, 68/9, 72, 73, 76, 77, 79, 81, 82, 83, 84/5, 87, 91, 92/3, 94, 96, 97b, 98, 100, 101, 102, 103l, 104, 106t, 109, 112, 113t, 116, 118, 119bcr, 119bcl, 119br, 120t, 122, 128/9, 130br, 133b, 134, 135b, 139tl, 141, 142, 147cr, bl, 148t, 149, 152, 153, 154, 155, 157, 158bl, 161tl, 165, 169, 171, 172, 176, 177, 180, 181, 182/3, 184, 185, 187, 195t, 197tr, 200, 202, 203, 206/7, 210/1, 212, 213, 224

HorseSource Ltd./Peter Llewellyn 88

Hows Racesafe, Leicestershire 31

Image Bank/Anthony Edwards 119tc/Grant V Faint 119tr/William Lesch 119bl/Steve Satushek 119tl

Bob Langrish 1, 10b, 15c, 16bl, 17br, 18, 20/1, 23, 24/5, 27, 38, 40, 42, 43, 50, 51br, 51t, 51b, 52, 58, 60, 61, 62, 63, 64, 65, 70/1, 74/5, 86, 89, 90, 95, 97t, 99, 103r, 105, 106b, 107, 108, 110/1, 113b, 113c, 114, 115, 117, 120b, 121, 123, 124/5, 126/7, 130/1, 132, 133tr, tl, 135t, c, 136/7, 138, 139tr, 140, 142/3, 143, 144, 145, 146, 147bc, br, 148b, 150/1, 156, 158t, 159, 160, 161tr, tc, 162/3, 164, 167, 168, 170, 173, 174, 175, 179, 186, 191, 192/3, 195cr, 196tr, 196/7b, 198/9, 204, 205, 216, 217

Zoë Mercer 22

Ride-Away, York 29c

Royal Dublin Society 201

Special thanks are due to Kit Houghton and Debbie Cook, Bob Langrish, Nicola Coombs and Sally Waters, and Maria Wynne at Charles Owen and Company for their help.

Every effort has been made to acknowledge correctly and contact the source and/copyright holder of each picture, and Carlton Books Limited apologises for any unintentional errors or omissions which will be corrected in future editions of this book.